A MIDDLE EAST STUDIES HANDBOOK

A MIDDLE EAST STUDIES HANDBOOK

JERE L. BACHARACH

UNIVERSITY OF WASHINGTON PRESS
Seattle • London

Printed in the United States of America

A Middle East Studies Handbook is a revised and expanded version of *A Near East Studies Handbook* (copyright © 1974, 1976 by the University of Washington Press).

Library of Congress Cataloging in Publication Data

Bacharach, Jere L., 1938-
A Middle East studies handbook.

Rev. Ed. of: A Near East studies handbook. Rev. ed. c1976.
Includes bibliographical references and index.
1. Islamic Empire--History--Handbooks, manuals, etc.
2. Near East--History--1517- --Handbooks, manuals, etc. I. Bacharach, Jere L., 1938- . Near East studies handbook. II. Title.
DS61.B3 1984 956 84-2225
ISBN 0-295-96138-4
ISBN 0-295-96144-9 (pbk.)

TO

Ruth • *Debby* • *Julie*

Contents

Preface

Increasing interest in the Middle East, particularly over the last decade, necessitated a major revision and updating of the volume, originally published in 1974 entitled *A Near East Studies Handbook: 570-1974*. The new title reflects the growing use of the term "Middle East." The geographical area covered includes Iran, Turkey, Egypt, the Fertile Crescent (modern Iraq, Syria, Lebanon, Jordan and Israel), and the Arabian Peninsula. Occasionally material touching on Libya, the Sudan, the Ottomans in Europe, the Muslims in Spain or Afghanistan has been added. A more accurate (though less popular) geographic description of this area would be, simply, Southwest Asia and Egypt. And this is used on most of the historical maps in Chapter VIII. The work spans the centuries from the birth of Muḥammad the Prophet — traditionally 570 A.D. to the events of autumn, 1983.

As there is no single, accepted transliteration system from the Arabic script to the Latin alphabet, the first chapter identifies some of the common Latin variations for Arabic consonant and vowel sounds. A complete transliteration table, as used by the Middle East Studies Association, is provided. A new addition to this chapter is a section on Islamic names.

The second chapter is a list of the abbreviations for 89 periodicals and reference works, which represents a 20-percent increase over previous editions. The third chapter includes a brief discussion on the problems of converting dates from the Muslim to the Western calendar (and vice versa), a new section on Muslim holidays, and a date conversion table from 622 A.D. to 2000 A.D.

The fourth chapter involves the combining of three chapters from the earlier editions. All of the material related to lists of dynasties, rulers, administrators and, when appropriate, a genealogy table, has been consolidated in this chapter. The material is now easier to locate, but has the added advantage of placing related data together. Chapter V is comprised of six supplementary charts illustrating language families, tribal ties and *ṣūfī isnād*s.

The Chronology is now Chapter VI and covers events into December, 1983. In addition to including the post-1976 material, the data in the earlier editions have been strengthened. The result has been a 25-percent increase in the number of items. Chapter VII lists 80 twentieth-century social, political and economic organizations by their acronyms — an increase of almost 20 percent.

There are now 51 maps in Chapter VIII, the Historical Atlas. This atlas now includes city maps of Jerusalem, Istanbul, Beirut, and major developments in the Middle East since 1976. As an aid to those interested in contemporary affairs, six maps with only the major cities indicated have been added to this section. The atlas is thoroughly indexed with its own index. Chapter IX, a Gazetteer, is an entirely new feature of this edition. It lists alphabetically approximately 125 cities with alternate spellings, population figures, and longitudes and latitudes. Chapter X is a Glossary of 300 items, an increase of almost 25 percent over earlier editions.

Besides my debt to scholarly works which I acknowledge in almost every chapter, a number of individuals have aided me and I wish to thank them, recognizing that others could have been added to this list:

Barb Shurin typed this entire manuscript and designed it. George Shurin patiently persevered through all the hours Barb and I spent working on this book. Alice Alden, as always, demonstrated her professional skills in preparing the maps and genealogy tables. April Richardson did additional design work. Felicia J. Hecker offered valuable, last-minute suggestions. The University of Washington Press suggested the idea for a revision and was very supportive during the long process of preparing the manuscript. Additional financial support from Exxon Corporation was greatly appreciated.

Many scholars provided information and ideas to improve this edition of the handbook. In particular, I wish to thank the contributions and comments of Michael Bates, Jacob Goldberg, Arthur Goldschmidt, Jacob Landau, Christopher Murphy, Tamara Sonn, Charles Woods, Khalid Yahya, and Mohsen Zakari. The names of those who helped in the previous editions — Calvin Allen, Andrew S.

Ehrenkreutz, Nicholas Heer, Judith S. Heide, Michael M. Pixley, Stephanie Sayers, Walid Shahouk, and Farhat J. Ziadeh — should not be forgotten. Professor Janet Abu Lughod generously gave me permission to adapt her map of al-Fusṭāṭ (Cairo), and I wish to thank her.

Finally, Ruth, Debby and Julie were very patient and supportive as I reworked the manuscript while trying to juggle a dozen other activities, and I am very pleased to dedicate this work to them. Obviously, any errors remain my responsibility.

A number of the maps were adapted from previously produced works:

- From *An Atlas of Middle Eastern Affairs,* by Robert C. Kingsbury and Norman J.G. Pounds (New York: Frederick A. Praeger, Inc., 1963). Excerpted and adapted by permission.
- From *History of the Arabs*, by Philip Hitti (New York: St. Martin's Press, 1965). Excerpted and adapted by permission.
- From *The Historical Atlas of the Muslim Peoples*, by R. Roolvink (Amsterdam: Djambatan, Inc., 1957). Excerpted and adapted by permission.
- From *South West Asia*, by William C. Brice (London: University of London Press, Ltd., 1967). Excerpted and adapted by permission.
- From "La Répartition Confessionelle au Liban et l'Équilibre de l'État Libanais," by Etienne de Vaumas, *Revue de Géographie Alpine* 43 (1965). Excerpted and adapted by permission.
- From *The Historical Atlas of Jerusalem: A Brief Illustrated Survey*, by Dan Bahat (New York: Charles Scribner's Sons, 1973). Excerpted and adapted by permission.

A MIDDLE EAST STUDIES HANDBOOK

I. Transliteration Systems and Islamic Names

Transliteration Systems

Because there is no single, universally accepted system of transliteration from the Arabic script to the Latin alphabet, one often finds variant spellings of words that can confuse the unwary. As an example, for the Holy Book of the Muslims (or Moslems), one will see "Qur'ān" or "Koran."

The following remarks indicate some of the problems one may face when coming across Arabic, Persian and Ottoman words written in a Western script. The section includes the transliteration system used by the Middle East Studies Association, as well as a number of other important variants. A very good discussion of many of the problems is in Marshall G.S. Hodgson, *The Venture of Islam*, 3 vols. (Chicago: University of Chicago Press, 1974), 1:8-20.

For words transliterated from Arabic, the major variants are q or k, j or dj, u or o, i or y, or e. In the preceding example, there was "Qur'ān" or "Koran," illustrating two variants. The *Encyclopedia of Islam*, in the manner of the old European system, used "k" and "dj" for "q" and "j," respectively. Therefore, the modern Muslim reformist, Jamāl al-Dīn al-Afghānī, is found in the *Encyclopedia of Islam* under "dj." Another problem is the use of the definite article "al." It can be transliterated according to its spelling, which always includes the "l," or according to its pronunciation. In the latter case, the "l" is assimilated when followed by certain letters — t, th, d, dh, r, z, s, sh, ṣ, ḍ, ṭ, ẓ and n — e.g.: *al-dīn* or *ad-dīn*.

The transliteration system used for Persian has been heavily influenced by the forms used for Arabic. As a whole, this has not caused serious problems, except in the transliteration of vowels and a few consonants (e.g.: i or e, u or o, w or v, and various forms for diphthongs). One may, therefore, find Isfahan or Esfahan, Mulk or Molk, Firdawsi or Ferdosi, and Qazwin or Qazvin.

Ottoman Turkish is the most troublesome, and even the Library of Congress has not adopted an official transliteration system. The fullest discussion can be found in an article by Eleazar Birnbaum, "The Transliteration of Ottoman Turkish for Library and General Purposes," *Journal of the American Oriental Society*, (1967) 87:122-156, where he suggests his own system. The modern Turks, having adopted a Latin script in 1928, have their own system of transliterating Ottoman. Therefore, if one were to take the Ottoman word for "member of the old Turkish dynasty": عثمانلی, it could be transliterated as ʿUthmānlī, ʿOsmānlī or Osmanlı, using an Arabic-based system, MESA rules and modern Turkish forms, respectively.

Finally, a graphic but special example of transliteration: the Persian word for "teacher" or "educated person" is خواجه ; and it can be found as *hoca* in modern Turkish, but it will be found in the *Encyclopedia of Islam* under *k͟hwādja*!

		MESA System (1983)			Selected Variations		
Arabic		Persian	Ottoman Turkish	Modern Turkish	*Encyclopedia of Islam*	*Geschichte des arabischen Schrifttums*	*Encyclopaedia Iranica*
ا	'	'	'	--			
ب	b	b	b	b or p			
پ	--	p	p	p			
ت	t	t	t	t			
ث	th	s	s	s	t͟h	ṯ	ṯ, s̱
ج	j	j	c	c	d͟j	ǧ	ǰ
چ	--	ch	ç	ç	č		č
ح	ḥ	ḥ	ḥ	h			
خ	kh	kh	h	h	k͟h	ẖ	
د	d	d	d	d			
ذ	dh	z	z	z	d͟h	ḏ	d, z
ر	r	r	r	r			
ز	z	z	z	z			
ژ	--	zh	j	j	z͟h		z͟h
س	s	s	s	s			
ش	sh	sh	ş	ş	s͟h	š	š
ص	ṣ	ṣ	ṣ	s			
ض	ḍ	ż	ż	z			
ط	ṭ	ṭ	ṭ	t			
ظ	ẓ	ẓ	ẓ	z			
ع	c	c	c	--	c		
غ	gh	gh	g or ğ	g or ğ	g͟h	ġ	ḡ
ف	f	f	f	f			
ق	q	q	ḳ	k	ḳ		
ك	k	k or g	k,ñ,y,ğ	k,n,y,ğ	g		
گ	--	g	g	g			
ل	l	l	l	l			
م	m	m	m	m			
ن	n	n	n	n			
ه	h	h	h*	h*			
و	w	v or u	v	v	ou		v, w

[continued]

Arabic	MESA System (1983) Persian	Ottoman Turkish	Modern Turkish	Selected Variations *Encyclopedia of Islam*	*Geschichte des arabischen Schrifttums*	*Encyclopaedia Iranica*
ی y	y	y	y			
ة -a**						
ال al-***						
'l-***						

* When not final.
** -at when in construct state.
*** The "l" in the article may change to t, th, d, dh, r, z, s, sh, ṣ, ḍ, ṭ, ẓ or n if the word to which it is attached begins with that letter; e.g., *al-dīn* or *ad-dīn*.

V O W E L S

Arabic and Persian	Ottoman Turkish	Modern Turkish
Long: ا or â ىٰ	â words of Arabic	â
û و	û and Persian	û
î ي	î origin only	î
Doubled: iyy (final form î) يّ	iy (final form: î)	iy (final form: î)
uww (final form û), etc. وّ	uvv	uvv
Diphthongs: au or aw وَ	ev or av+	ev or av+
ai or ay ىَ	ey or ay+	ey or ay+
Short: a َ	a or e	a or e
u ُ	u or ü	u or ü
	o or ö	o or ö
i ِ	ı or i	ı or i

+ Not MESA system.

Islamic Names

Not only does the problem of transliterating Islamic names pose difficulties; e.g., ᶜAbd al-Nāṣir vs. Nasser and al-Qadhdhāfī vs. Qaddafi, but identifying which part of the name to use — particularly a pre-19th-century one — is not always clear. Traditional Middle Eastern names are composed of a number of elements, beginning with the name given at birth (*ism*) and the name of the father (*nasab*). The individual may become a parent or acquire an epithet or honorific sense of parentage (*kunya*). It is also very common for a person in power to acquire an honorific title (*laqab*); while everyone would acquire titles reflecting their occupations, places of origins, etc. (*nisbah*).

In medieval dictionaries and in the British Museum, most Muslims are listed by their *ism* or proper name. An *ism* can be:

- a Qur'ānic form of a Biblical name; e.g., Sulaymān (Solomon) or Hārūn (Aaron);
- a purely Arabic name; e.g., Aḥmad, ᶜAlī, Ḥusayn or Muḥammad;
- a compound name associated with God, implying "servant" of God; e.g., ᶜAbd Allāh or Abdullah, ᶜAbd al-Malik. The "ᶜAbd" may not be dropped as it is part of the name; or
- a non-Arabic name; e.g., Rustam, Hulagu or Timur.

The *nasab* refers to one's pedigree or ancestors and is *ibn* (son of) or *bint* (daughter of) plus an *ism*. Sometimes the *nasab* becomes the common name for a family and does not reflect an actual parent/child relationship. The famous 14th-century historian-thinker, Ibn Khaldūn, is not the son of Khaldūn, who was a more distant relative. In Persian an "i" is added to indicate the *nasab* in names, or "zāde" is used as a suffix to the father's name or title. Turkish uses "oghlu" or "zāde" as a suffix to indicate the *nasab*. The *kunya* is the term *abū* (father) and, occasionally, *umm* (mother), followed by the real name of a child or an attribute; e.g., Abū al-Faḍl is either "the father of al-Faḍl" or "the father of merit."

The *laqab* is an honorific title or descriptive epithet which can be earned or acquired as an attribute or nickname. Many *laqab*s are compound names which end in *al-dīn* (religion), *al-dawla* (state) and *al-mulk* (kingdom), and were originally held by powerful political and military figures, but then became more common. Some examples are:

- Jalāl al-Dīn [Majesty of the Faith],
- Nāṣir al-Dawla [Defender of the State], and
- Niẓām al-Mulk [Order of the Kingdom].

Other *laqab*s could be nicknames; e.g., al-Aṭrash (the Deaf); or honorific titles for ᶜAbbāsid caliphs; e.g., al-Rashīd (the Rightly Guided).

The *nisbah* constitutes the broadest category and can include profession, place or origin, birth or residence. Individuals can have more than one *nisbah*, and they usually begin with the article "al-" and end with a long "i." Thus, an individual can have *nisbah*s, such as:

- al-Qudsī [from Jerusalem],
- al-Juhaynī [of the Juhayn tribe],
- al-Ṣayrafī [the money-changer].

The full name of the famous 15th-century scholar, known as al-Suyūṭī (or Jalāl al-Dīn al-Suyūṭī), was ᶜAbd al-Raḥmān b. [Ibn] Abī Bakr b. Muḥammad b. Khiḍr b. Ayyūb b. Muḥammad b. al-Humān al-Khuḍayrī al-Suyūṭī. Looking up the full name in a source could pose many problems. The easiest way to locate information on pre-Modern figures is to check the *Encyclopedia of Islam* (*EI*), either edition, under the name by which the individual is best known; e.g.: al-Suyūṭī.

For a more detailed discussion of Muslim names, see:

- C.H. Phillips, ed., *Handbook of Oriental History* (London: Royal Historical Society, 1951), pp. 7-9;
- Marshall G.S. Hodgson, *The Venture of Islam*, 3 vols. (Chicago: University of Chicago Press, 1974), 1:16-20.

II. Periodicals and Reference Works

An extensive list of periodical abbreviations can be found in James D. Pearson, *Index Islamicus, 1906-1955* (Cambridge: Hevver, 1953), and the succeeding supplements. Another excellent source, particularly for journals concerned with the contemporary Middle East, is the last annual issue (No. 4) of each year of the *Middle East Journal*, where an extensive list of sources with abbreviations is cited.

Annotated bibliographies for Middle East studies are limited. For the Medieval period — that is, until the rise and success of the Ottomans — the best annotated bibliography is Jean Sauvaget, *Introduction to the History of the Muslim East: A Bibliographical Guide*, edited/revised by Claude Cahen (Berkeley: University of California Press, 1965). Another valuable tool, but with fewer annotations, is Derek Hopwood and Diana Grimwood-Jones, *Middle East and Islam: A Bibliographical Introduction* (Zurich: Inter-Documentation Company, 1972). A work which is very useful for many libraries for the Medieval and Modern Eras is David W. Littlefield, *The Islamic Near East and North Africa: An Annotated Guide for Public and College Libraries and Readers* (Littleton Co., Libraries Unlimited, 1977).

For the more Modern Era, there are a number of references which one may use:

- *The Arab Culture and Society in Change: A Partially Annotated Bibliography* (Beirut: St. Joseph's University, 1973) has almost 5,000 items.
- George Atiyeh, *The Contemporary Middle East, 1948-1973: A Selective Annotated Bibliography* (Boston: G.K. Hall, 1975), is also very useful.
- Another source is Henry Field, *Bibliography of Southwestern Asia* (Coral Gables, FL: University of Miami Press, 1953-), vol. 1-.

For those seeking periodical material on topics related to the Middle East, there are two major sources for material published in the West. *Index Islamicus*, cited above, has extensive lists of articles on pre-Modern topics. It is now published quarterly and, every five years, gathered into a single volume. The fifth supplementary volume has just been published in two segments: one for articles and one for books. *Mideast File* (Medford, NJ: Learned Information) is a quarterly begun in March 1982 by the Shiloah Center for Middle Eastern and African Studies, Tel Aviv, Israel. It has annotations on books and articles published in Arabic, English, French, German, Hebrew, Persian and Turkish. It emphasizes the contemporary world and the social sciences. Each issue of *MEJ* has an extensive list of recent articles arranged by topic. These periodical lists were gathered together in Peter M. Rossie and Wayne E. White, *Articles on the Middle East, 1947-1971: A Cumulation of the Bibliographies from the MIDDLE EAST JOURNAL* (Ann Arbor: Pierian Press, 1980). For publications in Arabic, there is *Al-Fihrist: Kashaf al-Dawriyyāt al-ᶜArabiyyah* (Beirut: Watwat al-Zarif, 1982), which appears quarterly and has subject headings and cross-listings.

For those seeking book reviews of works related to Middle East topics, the following tools may be helpful: Wolfgang H. Behn, *Islamic Book Review Index* (Berlin: Behn, 1982), has an extensive coverage of European language reviews. Volume I lists approximately 2,600 titles. At the end of each issue of *MEJ* there is a list of the books reviewed in the journals which are surveyed by *MEJ*. There is no cumulative index of all of these references.

Standard references for most book reviews are:

- *The Combined Retrospective Index to Book Reviews in Scholarly Journals: 1886-1974* (New York: Research Publications, Inc., 1982).
- *The Book Review Index: 1969-1979, 1980-*, which is published bi-monthly, and then consolidated annually.
- *An Index to Book Reviews, 1960-*.
- *Current Book Review Citations, 1976-*, which is published monthly, except February and August, and is then consolidated annually.

List of Abbreviations

AARP *Art and Archeology Research Papers*

AAS *Asian and African Studies*

AHR *American Historical Review*

AHS *African Historical Studies*

AI *Ars Islamica*

AIYS News. *American Institute for Yemen Studies Newsletter*

And. *al-Andalus*

AO *Acta orientalia*

ARCE News. *American Research Center in Egypt Newsletter*

ArO *Archiv orientâlnî*

ArOtt *Archivum Ottomanicum*

BEO *Bulletin d'études orientales*

BGA *Bibliotheca geographorum Arabicorum*

BIE *Bulletin de l'Institut d'Égypte*

BIFAO *Bulletin de l'Institut Français d'Archéologie Orientale*

BRISMES Bull. *British Society for Middle East Studies Bulletin*

BSOAS *Bulletin of the School of Oriental & African Studies* (London University)

BZ *Byzantinische Zeitschrift*

CH *Current History*

CIA *Corpus Inscriptionum Arabicorum*

CSSH *Comparative Studies in Society and History*

DI *Der Islam*

EHR *English Historical Review/Economic Historical Review*

EI[1] *The Encyclopaedia of Islam.* 4 Vols., Supp. (Leiden, 1913-1942)

EI[2] *The Encyclopaedia of Islam.* 2nd ed. (Leiden, 1954-)

EIr *Encyclopaedia Iranica*

GAL Brockelmann, C. *Geschichte der arabischen Litteratur.* 2nd ed., 2 Vols. (Leiden, 1943-1949)

GALS Brockelmann, C. *Geschichte der arabischen Litteratur Supplement.* 3 Vols. (Leiden, 1937-1942)

GAS Sezgin, F. *Geschichte des arabischen Schrifttums* (Leiden, 1967-)

GMS *Gibb Memorial Series*

HO Spuler, B. (Ed.). *Handbuch der Orientalistik* (Leiden, 1952-)

IA *Islam Ansiklopedisi*

IC *Islamic Culture*

IEJ *Israel Exploration Journal*

IJAHS *International Journal of African Historical Studies*

IJMES *International Journal of Middle East Studies*

IJTS *International Journal of Turkish Studies*

IQ *Islamic Quarterly*

IrS *Iranian Studies*

IS *Islamic Studies*

JA *Journal asiatique*

JAH *Journal of African History*

JAL *Journal of Arab Literature*

JAOS *Journal of the American Oriental Society*

JCH *Journal of Contemporary History*

JESHO *Journal of the Economic and Social History of the Orient*

JJS *Journal of Jewish Studies*

JMAS *Journal of Modern African Studies*

JMH *Journal of Modern History*

JNES *Journal of Near Eastern Studies*

JPS *Journal of Palestine Studies*

JQ *The Jerusalem Quarterly*

JRAS *Journal of the Royal Asiatic Society of Great Britain and Ireland*

JSAI *Jerusalem Studies in Arabic and Islam*

JSS *Journal of Semitic Studies*

JWH *Journal of World History*

MEED *Middle East Economic Digest*

MEF *Middle East Forum*

MEJ *Middle East Journal*

MELA Notes *Middle East Librarians' Association Notes*

MEOC News. *Middle East Outreach Coordinators' Newsletter*

MERIP Reports *Middle East Research and Information Project Reports*

MES	*Middle Eastern Studies*
MESA Bull.	*Middle East Studies Association Bulletin*
MIDEO	*Mélanges des l'Institut Dominicain d'Études Orientales du Caire*
MIFAO	*Mémoires de l'Institut Français d'Archéologie Orientale*
MSG News.	*Maghrib Studies Group Newsletter*
MW	*Muslim World* [formerly *Moslem World*]
NAHIA News.	*National Association of Historians of Islamic Art Newsletter*
OM	*Oriente moderno*
Ors	*Oriens*
PO	*Patrologia Orientalis*
RAAD	*Revue de l'Académie Arabe de Damas*
REI	*Revue des études islamiques*
REJ	*Revue des études juives*
RH	*Revue historique*
RHC	*Recueil des historiens des croisades*
RIMA	*Revue de l'Institut des Manuscripts Arabes*
RMM	*Revue de monde musulman*
ROC	*Revue de l'Orient chrétien*
RSO	*Rivista degli studi orientali*
SEI	*Shorter Encyclopaedia of Islam*
SI	*Studia Islamica*
SIS News.	*Society for Iranian Studies Newsletter*
Spec.	*Speculum*
TSA Bull.	*Turkish Studies Association Bulletin*
WI	*Die Welt des Islams*
WO	*Die Welt des Orients*
ZDMG	*Zeitschrift der Deutschen Morgenländischen Gesellschaft*

III. Islamic Calendar and Conversion Table

Caliph ᶜUmār established the first year of the Muslim calendar as the year in which Muḥammad left Mecca for Medina. This departure or *hijra* became the name for the Islamic calendar (A.H. = *Anno Hejirae*) and 1/1/1 *hijra* was calculated as 16 July 622. The Islamic calendar, like many other calendars, is based on a lunar year of approximately 354 days, or about 11 days less than a solar year. In order to keep the lunar months in alignment with the major seasons, most users of a lunar calendar interpolate an extra or 13th month.

The Muslim calendar has no extra month, as a Qur'ānic revelation (Sūra IX, Verse 30) fixed the calendar year at 12 lunar months. The net result is that knowing the Muslim month and year in which an event took place does not indicate the corresponding season or specific month in the Gregorian (Western) solar calendar. One relatively easy way to calculate the Muslim equivalent for a Western date, and vice versa, is to use the formulae which follow:

$$H = 1.013\ [W - 622]$$
$$W = H - H/31 + 622$$

Another procedure is to use the accompanying Conversion Table where Muslim dates are listed and the equivalent Western date can be found to the right of them.

A few words of caution are necessary before using any table to calculate the exact Western date for a given Islamic-era date (or vice versa). The Islamic calendar is based upon observation of the moon, not a fixed number of days. Therefore, although the tables and officially printed calendars say a new Islamic-era month begins on a particular Western day, unless the *ᶜulamā'* see the new moon, the month has not begun. This tradition persists today when the *ᶜulamā'*, and not the government calendar, determine when the Muslim month of fasting (Ramaḍān) begins and ends. The net result is that a local calendar can be up to two days different from the calculated tables.

A second problem is that an Islamic calendar month does not have to start on the same Western calendar day in two different cities. For example, the first day of Ramaḍān 500 A.H. in Cairo may or may not be the same day of the week in Baghdad, or any other city.

Finally, the Muslim day begins at sunset. Therefore, when calculating the corresponding Western date for an event held in the evening on the Islamic calendar, it is necessary to subtract one day from the calculated Western date. All of the preceding is a warning not to push an argument on the relationship between two very close pre-1800 events if it is based primarily on their respective Islamic (or corresponding Western) dates — unless those dates have been very carefully checked.

If you have a Muslim date with a month and wish to calculate the approximate Western date using the accompanying table, the following procedure should be used: first, locate on the table the Western date for the first day of that particular Muslim year. Then add the appropriate number of months of the Muslim date to the Western date, and that will create a ballpark estimate. The Muslim months are as follows:

Muḥarram	Jumādā l-ūlā	Ramaḍān
Ṣafar	Jumādā l-ākhira	Shawwāl
Rabīᶜ al-awwal	Rajab	Dhū-l-Qaᶜda
Rabīᶜ al-thānī	Shaᶜbān	Dhū-l-Ḥijja

Marshall G.S. Hodgson, *The Venture of Islam*, 3 vols. (Chicago: University of Chicago Press, 1974), 1:22, lists the most common month names of the solar calendar. They are repeated here in both their Arabic and Persian forms:

Arabic		Persian	
Kānūn al-thānī	Jan.	Bahman	Jan./Feb.
Shubāṭ	Feb.	Isfand	Feb./March
Adhār	March	Farvardīn	Mar./April
Nīsān	April	Urdī-bihisht	April/May
Ayyār	May	Khurdād	May/June
Ḥazīrān	June	Tīr	June/July
Tamūz	July	Murdād	July/Aug.
Āb	Aug.	Shahrīvar	
Aylūl	Sept.	[Shahrīr]	Aug./Sept.
Tishrīn al-awwal	Oct.	Mihr	Sept./Oct.
Tishrīn al-thānī	Nov.	Ābān	Oct./Nov.
Kānūn al-awwal	Dec.	Āzar	Nov./Dec.
		Day	Dec./Jan.

In order to calculate the exact Western day

for a Muslim day, more elaborate tables than the one in this handbook must be used. The work by G.S.P. Freeman-Grenville, *The Muslim and Christian Calendars* (London: Oxford University Press, 1963), has clear instructions and can be used for such purposes. A more detailed work which includes other calendars, including the special Ottoman financial calendar, is E. Mahler, *Wustenfeld-Mahlersche Vergleichungs-Tabellen der mohammedanischen und christlichen Zeitrechnung* (Leipzig, 1926; 3rd ed., Wiesbaden, 1961).

The best source for transforming the various calendars used by the Ottomans into Gregorian dates is Faik Resit Unat, *Hicri Tarihleri Milade Tarihe Cevirme Kilavuzu*, 3rd ed. (Ankara, Turkey: Turk Tarih kurumu basimlvi, 1959).

A general survey of the types of calendars found in the Islamic world is H. Taqizadeh, "Various Eras and Calendars Used in the Countries of Islam," *BSOAS*, vol. 9 (1937-1939):902-999; and vol. 10 (1940-1942):107-132. The most comprehensive list of tables of the numerous pre-Ottoman medieval calendars is found in V. Grummel, *La chronologie (Traite d'études byzantines)*, vol. 1, ed. P. Lemerle (Paris, 1958). Among the calendars found in this work are Julian, Armenian, Coptic, Sassanian, Mongolian and Muslim calendars, plus data on comets, eclipses, earthquakes, etc. to 1453.

Selected Muslim Holidays

• Muḥarram 1 [*Rās al-Sana*: The New Year] is the first day of the first month and, while it is not a particularly religious holiday, it now is celebrated throughout the Islamic world.

• Muḥarram 10 [*ᶜAshūrā'*: The Tenth] is the day on which many pious Muslims fast from dawn to sunset. For Shīᶜī Muslims this day is of particular importance, as it commemorates the assassination of ᶜAlī's son, Ḥusayn.

• Rabīᶜ al-awwal 12 [*Mawlid al-Nabī*; The Prophet's Birthday] is a holiday associated with festivities and exchanging of gifts. Often passages eulogizing Muḥammad are read.

• Rajab 27 [*Lailat al-Isrā' wa'l-miᶜrāj*: The Night of Journey and Ascent] commemorates Muḥammad's night journey from Mecca to the Ḥaram al-Sharīf area in Jerusalem and his ascent to Heaven and return to Jerusalem, and then Mecca — all in one night. This night is traditionally celebrated by prayers.

• Shaᶜbān 14 [*Lailat al-Barā'a*: Night of Remembrance] is, according to Muslim tradition, the night God approaches earth to grant forgiveness for an individual's sins.

• Ramaḍān [ninth month of the Muslim year] is devoted to spiritual purification through the abstinence from food, drink and physical pleasure from dawn until dusk.

• Ramaḍān 27 [*Lailat al-Qadar*: Night of Power and Greatness] is considered a particularly holy time, as it is the night, by tradition, on which Muḥammad received the first revelation.

• Shawwal 1 [*ᶜīd al-Fiṭr*: The Lesser Feast] is the most joyous festival in the Islamic calendar and marks the end of abstinence during Ramaḍān.

• Dhū-l-Ḥijja 1-10: The period in which Muslims are to undertake a pilgrimage to Mecca and its environs in imitation of Muḥammad's last pilgrimage.

• Dhū-l-Ḥijja 10 [*ᶜīd al-Aḍḥā*: The Greater Feast] is the high point of the pilgrimage and is celebrated by Muslims throughout the world, even if not actually participating in the pilgrimage. It is most often marked by the slaughtering of lambs and the distribution of meat to the needy.

Hebrew Calendar

Jews, for religious purposes and within their own communities, use a lunar calendar composed of 12 lunar months. In order to keep fall and spring holidays in the appropriate season, a 13th month — called the Second Adar — is added after the sixth Jewish month [Adar] in the following 19-year cycle: 3rd year, 6th, 8th, 11th, 14th, 17th and 19th year. Thus, a particular holiday may vary by 28 days between years, but it will always be in the same season.

The Jewish New Year is in the fall, usually in September. In order to calculate the Western year since the rise of Islam in which most of the Jewish year falls, add 240 to the Hebrew date, and then subtract 4,000.

Calendar Conversion Table

Hijra Year	Western Date of Muḥarram 1	Hijra Year	Western Date of Muḥarram 1	Hijra Year	Western Date of Muḥarram 1	Hijra Year	Western Date of Muḥarram 1
1	16 July 622	65	18 Aug 684	128	3 Oct 745	191	17 Nov 806
2	5 July 623	66	8 Aug 685	129	22 Sept 746	192	6 Nov 807
3	24 June 624	67	28 July 686	130	11 Sept 747	193	25 Oct 808
4	13 June 625	68	18 July 687	131	31 Aug 748	194	15 Oct 809
5	2 June 626	69	6 July 688	132	20 Aug 749	195	4 Oct 810
6	23 May 627	70	25 June 689	133	9 Aug 750	196	23 Sept 811
7	11 May 628	71	15 June 690	134	30 July 751	197	12 Sept 812
8	1 May 629	72	4 June 691	135	18 July 752	198	1 Sept 813
9	20 Apr 630	73	23 May 692	136	7 July 753	199	22 Aug 814
10	9 Apr 631	74	13 May 693	137	27 June 754	200	11 Aug 815
11	29 Mar 632	75	2 May 694	138	16 June 755	201	30 July 816
12	18 Mar 633	76	21 Apr 695	139	5 June 756	202	20 July 817
13	7 Mar 634	77	10 Apr 696	140	25 May 757	203	9 July 818
14	25 Feb 635	78	30 Mar 697	141	14 May 758	204	28 June 819
15	14 Feb 636	79	20 Mar 698	142	4 May 759	205	17 June 820
16	2 Feb 637	80	9 Mar 699	143	22 Apr 760	206	6 June 821
17	23 Jan 638			144	11 Apr 761	207	27 May 822
18	12 Jan 639	81	26 Feb 700	145	1 Apr 762	208	16 May 823
19	2 Jan 640	82	15 Feb 701	146	21 Mar 763	209	4 May 824
20	21 Dec 640	83	4 Feb 702	147	10 Mar 764	210	24 Apr 825
21	10 Dec 641	84	24 Jan 703	148	27 Feb 765	211	13 Apr 826
22	30 Nov 642	85	14 Jan 704	149	16 Feb 766	212	2 Apr 827
23	19 Nov 643	86	2 Jan 705	150	6 Feb 767	213	22 Mar 828
24	7 Nov 644	87	23 Dec 705	151	26 Jan 768	214	11 Mar 829
25	28 Oct 645	88	12 Dec 706	152	14 Jan 769	215	25 Feb 830
26	17 Oct 646	89	1 Dec 707	153	4 Jan 770	216	18 Feb 831
27	7 Oct 647	90	20 Nov 708	154	24 Dec 770	217	7 Feb 832
28	25 Sept 648	91	9 Nov 709	155	13 Dec 771	218	27 Jan 833
29	14 Sept 649	92	29 Oct 710	156	2 Dec 772	219	16 Jan 834
30	4 Sept 650	93	19 Oct 711	157	21 Nov 773	220	5 Jan 835
31	24 Aug 651	94	7 Oct 712	158	11 Nov 774	221	26 Dec 835
32	12 Aug 652	95	26 Sept 713	159	31 Oct 775	222	14 Dec 836
33	2 Aug 653	96	16 Sept 714	160	19 Oct 776	223	3 Dec 837
34	22 July 654	97	5 Sept 715	161	9 Oct 777	224	23 Nov 838
35	11 July 655	98	25 Aug 716	162	28 Sept 778	225	12 Nov 839
36	30 June 656	99	14 Aug 717	163	17 Sept 779	226	31 Oct 840
37	19 June 657	100	3 Aug 718	164	6 Sept 780	227	21 Oct 841
38	9 June 658	101	24 July 719	165	26 Aug 781	228	10 Oct 842
39	29 May 659	102	12 July 720	166	15 Aug 782	229	20 Sept 843
40	17 May 660	103	1 July 721	167	5 Aug 783	230	18 Sept 844
41	7 May 661	104	21 June 722	168	24 July 784	231	7 Sept 845
42	26 Apr 662	105	10 June 723	169	14 July 785	232	28 Aug 846
43	15 Apr 663	106	29 May 724	170	3 July 786	233	17 Aug 847
44	4 Apr 664	107	19 May 725	171	22 June 787	234	5 Aug 848
45	24 Mar 665	108	8 May 726	172	11 June 788	235	26 July 849
46	13 Mar 666	109	28 Apr 727	173	31 May 789	236	15 July 850
47	3 Mar 667	110	16 Apr 728	174	20 May 790	237	5 July 851
48	20 Feb 668	111	5 Apr 729	175	10 May 791	238	23 June 852
49	9 Feb 669	112	26 Mar 730	176	28 Apr 792	239	12 June 853
50	29 Jan 670	113	15 Mar 731	177	18 Apr 793	240	2 June 854
51	18 Jan 671	114	3 Mar 732	178	7 Apr 794	241	22 May 855
52	8 Jan 672	115	21 Feb 733	179	27 Mar 795	242	10 May 856
53	27 Dec 672	116	10 Feb 734	180	16 Mar 796	243	30 Apr 857
54	16 Dec 673	117	31 Jan 735	181	5 Mar 797	244	19 Apr 858
55	6 Dec 674	118	20 Jan 736	182	22 Feb 798	245	8 Apr 859
56	25 Nov 675	119	8 Jan 737	183	12 Feb 799	246	28 Mar 860
57	14 Nov 676	120	29 Dec 737			247	17 Mar 861
58	3 Nov 677	121	18 Dec 738	184	1 Feb 800	248	7 Mar 862
59	23 Oct 678	122	7 Dec 739	185	20 Jan 801	249	24 Feb 863
60	13 Oct 679	123	26 Nov 740	186	10 Jan 802	250	13 Feb 864
61	1 Oct 680	124	15 Nov 741	187	30 Dec 802	251	2 Feb 865
62	20 Sept 681	125	4 Nov 742	188	20 Dec 803	252	22 Jan 866
63	10 Sept 682	126	25 Oct 743	189	8 Dec 804	253	11 Jan 867
64	30 Aug 683	127	13 Oct 744	190	27 Nov 805	254	1 Jan 868

Calendar Conversion Table

Hijra Year	Western Date of Muḥarram 1
255	20 Dec 868
256	9 Dec 869
257	29 Nov. 870
258	18 Nov 871
259	7 Nov 872
260	27 Oct 873
261	16 Oct 874
262	6 Oct 875
263	24 Sept 876
264	13 Sept 877
265	3 Sept 878
266	23 Aug 879
267	12 Aug 880
268	1 Aug 881
269	21 July 882
270	11 July 883
271	29 June 884
272	18 June 885
273	8 June 886
274	28 May 887
275	16 May 888
276	6 May 889
277	25 Apr 890
278	15 Apr 891
279	3 Apr 892
280	23 Mar 893
281	13 Mar 894
282	2 Mar 895
283	19 Feb 896
284	8 Feb 897
285	28 Jan 898
286	17 Jan 899
287	7 Jan 900
288	26 Dec 900
289	16 Dec 901
290	5 Dec 902
291	24 Nov 903
292	13 Nov 904
293	2 Nov 905
294	22 Oct 906
295	12 Oct 907
296	30 Sept 908
297	20 Sept 909
298	9 Sept 910
299	29 Aug 911
300	18 Aug 912
301	7 Aug 913
302	27 July 914
303	17 July 915
304	5 July 916
305	24 June 917
306	14 June 918
307	3 June 919
308	23 May 920
309	12 May 921
310	1 May 922
311	21 Apr 923
312	9 Apr 924
313	29 Mar 925
314	19 Mar 926
315	8 Mar 927
316	25 Feb 928
317	14 Feb 929
318	3 Feb 930
319	24 Jan 931
320	13 Jan 932
321	1 Jan 933
322	22 Dec 933
323	11 Dec 934
324	30 Nov 935
325	19 Nov 936
326	8 Nov 937
327	29 Oct 938
328	18 Oct 939
329	6 Oct 940
330	26 Sept 941
331	15 Sept 942
332	4 Sept 943
333	24 Aug 944
334	13 Aug 945
335	2 Aug 946
336	23 July 947
337	11 July 948
338	1 July 949
339	20 June 950
340	9 June 951
341	29 May 952
342	18 May 953
343	7 May 954
344	27 Apr 955
345	15 Apr 956
346	4 Apr 957
347	25 Mar 958
348	14 Mar 959
349	3 Mar 960
350	20 Feb 961
351	9 Feb 962
352	30 Jan 963
353	19 Jan 964
354	7 Jan 965
355	28 Dec 965
356	17 Dec 966
357	7 Dec 967
358	25 Nov 968
359	14 Nov 969
360	4 Nov 970
361	24 Oct 971
362	12 Oct 972
363	2 Oct 973
364	21 Sept 974
365	10 Sept 975
366	30 Aug 976
367	19 Aug 977
368	9 Aug 978
369	29 July 979
370	17 July 980
371	7 July 981
372	26 June 982
373	15 June 983
374	4 June 984
375	24 May 985
376	13 May 986
377	3 May 987
378	21 Apr 988
379	11 Apr 989
380	31 Mar 990
381	20 Mar 991
382	9 Mar 992
383	26 Feb 993
384	15 Feb 994
385	5 Feb 995
386	25 Jan 996
387	14 Jan 997
388	3 Jan 998
389	23 Dec 998
390	13 Dec 999
391	1 Dec 1000
392	20 Nov 1001
393	10 Nov 1002
394	30 Oct 1003
395	18 Oct 1004
396	8 Oct 1005
397	27 Sept 1006
398	17 Sept 1007
399	5 Sept 1008
400	25 Aug 1009
401	15 Aug 1010
402	4 Aug 1011
403	23 July 1012
404	13 July 1013
405	3 July 1014
406	21 June 1015
407	10 June 1016
408	30 May 1017
409	20 May 1018
410	9 May 1019
411	27 Apr 1020
412	17 Apr 1021
413	6 Apr 1022
414	26 Mar 1023
415	15 Mar 1024
416	4 Mar 1025
417	22 Feb 1026
418	11 Feb 1027
419	31 Jan 1028
420	20 Jan 1029
421	9 Jan 1030
422	29 Dec 1030
423	19 Dec 1031
424	7 Dec 1032
425	26 Nov 1033
426	16 Nov 1034
427	5 Nov 1035
428	25 Oct 1036
429	14 Oct 1037
430	3 Oct 1038
431	23 Sept 1039
432	11 Sept 1040
433	31 Aug 1041
434	21 Aug 1042
435	10 Aug 1043
436	29 July 1044
437	19 July 1045
438	8 July 1046
439	28 June 1047
440	16 June 1048
441	5 June 1049
442	26 May 1050
443	15 May 1051
444	3 May 1052
445	23 Apr 1053
446	12 Apr 1054
447	2 Apr 1055
448	21 Mar 1056
449	10 Mar 1057
450	28 Feb 1058
451	17 Feb 1059
452	6 Feb 1060
453	26 Jan 1061
454	15 Jan 1062
455	4 Jan 1063
456	25 Dec 1063
457	13 Dec 1064
458	3 Dec 1065
459	22 Nov 1066
460	11 Nov 1067
461	31 Oct 1068
462	20 Oct 1069
463	9 Oct 1070
464	29 Sept 1071
465	17 Sept 1072
466	6 Sept 1073
467	27 Aug 1074
468	16 Aug 1075
469	5 Aug 1076
470	25 July 1077
471	14 July 1078
472	4 July 1079
473	22 June 1080
474	11 June 1081
475	1 June 1082
476	21 May 1083
477	10 May 1084
478	29 Apr 1085
479	18 Apr 1086
480	8 Apr 1087
481	27 Mar 1088
482	16 Mar 1089
483	6 Mar 1090
484	23 Feb 1091
485	12 Feb 1092
486	1 Feb 1093
487	21 Jan 1094
488	11 Jan 1095
489	31 Dec 1095
490	19 Dec 1096
491	9 Dec 1097
492	28 Nov 1098
493	17 Nov 1099
494	6 Nov 1100
495	26 Oct 1101
496	15 Oct 1102
497	5 Oct 1103
498	23 Sept 1104
499	13 Sept 1105
500	2 Sept 1106
501	22 Aug 1107
502	11 Aug 1108
503	31 July 1109
504	20 July 1110
505	10 July 1111
506	28 June 1112
507	18 June 1113

Calendar Conversion Table

Hijra Year	Western Date of Muḥarram 1	Hijra Year	Western Date of Muḥarram 1	Hijra Year	Western Date of Muḥarram 1	Hijra Year	Western Date of Muḥarram 1
508	7 June 1114	572	10 July 1176	635	24 Aug 1237	699	28 Sept 1299
509	27 May 1115	573	30 June 1177	636	14 Aug 1238		
510	16 May 1116	574	19 June 1178	637	3 Aug 1239	700	16 Sept 1300
511	5 May 1117	575	8 June 1179	638	23 July 1240	701	5 Sept 1301
512	24 Apr 1118	576	28 May 1180	639	12 July 1241	702	26 Aug 1302
513	14 Apr 1119	577	17 May 1181	640	1 July 1242	703	15 Aug 1303
514	2 Apr 1120	578	7 May 1182	641	21 June 1243	704	4 Aug 1304
515	22 Mar 1121	579	26 Apr 1183	642	9 June 1244	705	24 July 1305
516	12 Mar 1122	580	14 Apr 1184	643	29 May 1245	706	13 July 1306
517	1 Mar 1123	581	4 Apr 1185	644	19 May 1246	707	3 July 1307
518	19 Feb 1124	582	24 Mar 1186	645	8 May 1247	708	21 June 1308
519	7 Feb 1125	583	13 Mar 1187	646	26 Apr 1248	709	11 June 1309
520	27 Jan 1126	584	2 Mar 1188	647	16 Apr 1249	710	31 May 1310
521	17 Jan 1127	585	19 Feb 1189	648	5 Apr 1250	711	20 May 1311
522	6 Jan 1128	586	8 Feb 1190	649	26 Mar 1251	712	9 May 1312
523	25 Dec 1128	587	29 Jan 1191	650	14 Mar 1252	713	28 Apr 1313
524	15 Dec 1129	588	18 Jan 1192	651	3 Mar 1253	714	17 Apr 1314
525	4 Dec 1130	589	7 Jan 1193	652	21 Feb 1254	715	7 Apr 1315
526	23 Nov 1131	590	27 Dec 1193	653	10 Feb 1255	716	26 Mar 1316
527	12 Nov 1132	591	16 Dec 1194	654	30 Jan 1256	717	16 Mar 1317
528	1 Nov 1133	592	6 Dec 1195	655	19 Jan 1257	718	5 Mar 1318
529	22 Oct 1134	593	24 Nov 1196	656	8 Jan 1258	719	22 Feb 1319
530	11 Oct 1135	594	13 Nov 1197	657	29 Dec 1258	720	12 Feb 1320
531	29 Sept 1136	595	3 Nov 1198	658	18 Dec 1259	721	31 Jan 1321
532	19 Sept 1137	596	23 Oct 1199	659	6 Dec 1260	722	20 Jan 1322
533	8 Sept 1138			660	26 Nov 1261	723	10 Jan 1323
534	28 Aug 1139	597	12 Oct 1200	661	15 Nov 1262	724	30 Dec 1323
535	17 Aug 1140	598	1 Oct 1201	662	4 Nov 1263	725	18 Dec 1324
536	6 Aug 1141	599	20 Sept 1202	663	24 Oct 1264	726	8 Dec 1325
537	27 July 1142	600	10 Sept 1203	664	13 Oct 1265	727	27 Nov 1326
538	16 July 1143	601	29 Aug 1204	665	2 Oct 1266	728	17 Nov 1327
539	4 July 1144	602	18 Aug 1205	666	22 Sept 1267	729	5 Nov 1328
540	24 June 1145	603	8 Aug 1206	667	10 Sept 1268	730	25 Oct 1329
541	13 June 1146	604	28 July 1207	668	31 Aug 1269	731	15 Oct 1330
542	2 June 1147	605	16 July 1208	669	20 Aug 1270	732	4 Oct 1331
543	22 May 1148	606	6 July 1209	670	9 Aug 1271	733	22 Sept 1332
544	11 May 1149	607	25 June 1210	671	29 July 1272	734	12 Sept 1333
545	30 Apr 1150	608	15 June 1211	672	18 July 1273	735	1 Sept 1334
546	20 Apr 1151	609	3 June 1212	673	7 July 1274	736	21 Aug 1335
547	8 Apr 1152	610	23 May 1213	674	27 June 1275	737	10 Aug 1336
548	27 Mar 1153	611	13 May 1214	675	15 June 1276	738	30 July 1337
549	18 Mar 1154	612	2 May 1215	676	4 June 1277	739	20 July 1338
550	7 Mar 1155	613	20 Apr 1216	677	25 May 1278	740	9 July 1339
551	25 Feb 1156	614	10 Apr 1217	678	14 May 1279	741	27 June 1340
552	13 Feb 1157	615	30 Mar 1218	679	3 May 1280	742	17 June 1341
553	2 Feb 1158	616	19 Mar 1219	680	22 Apr 1281	743	6 June 1342
554	23 Jan 1159	617	8 Mar 1220	681	11 Apr 1282	744	26 May 1343
555	12 Jan 1160	618	25 Feb 1221	682	1 Apr 1823	745	15 May 1344
556	31 Dec 1160	619	15 Feb 1222	683	20 Mar 1284	746	4 May 1345
557	21 Dec 1161	620	4 Feb 1223	684	9 Mar 1285	747	24 Apr 1346
558	10 Dec 1162	621	24 Jan 1224	685	27 Feb 1286	748	13 Apr 1347
559	30 Nov 1163	622	13 Jan 1225	686	16 Feb 1287	749	1 Apr 1348
560	18 Nov 1164	623	2 Jan 1226	687	6 Feb 1288	750	22 Mar 1349
561	7 Nov 1165	624	22 Dec 1226	688	25 Jan 1289	751	11 Mar 1350
562	28 Oct 1166	625	12 Dec 1227	689	14 Jan 1290	752	28 Feb 1351
563	17 Oct 1167	626	30 Nov 1228	690	4 Jan 1291	753	18 Feb 1352
564	5 Oct 1168	627	20 Nov 1229	691	24 Dec 1921	754	6 Feb 1353
565	25 Sept 1169	628	9 Nov 1230	692	12 Dec 1292	755	26 Jan 1354
566	14 Sept 1170	629	29 Oct 1231	693	2 Dec 1293	756	16 Jan 1355
567	4 Sept 1171	630	18 Oct 1232	694	21 Nov 1294	757	5 Jan 1356
568	23 Aug 1172	631	7 Oct 1233	695	10 Nov 1295	758	25 Dec 1356
569	12 Aug 1173	632	26 Sept 1234	696	30 Oct 1296	759	15 Dec 1357
570	2 Aug 1174	633	16 Sept 1235	697	19 Oct 1297	760	3 Dec 1358
571	22 July 1175	634	4 Sept 1236	698	9 Oct 1298	761	23 Nov 1359

Calendar Conversion Table

Hijra Year	Western Date of Muḥarram 1
762	11 Nov 1360
763	31 Oct 1361
764	21 Oct 1362
765	10 Oct 1363
766	28 Sept 1364
767	18 Sept 1365
768	7 Sept 1366
769	28 Aug 1367
770	16 Aug 1368
771	5 Aug 1369
772	26 July 1370
773	15 July 1371
774	3 July 1372
775	23 June 1373
776	12 June 1374
777	2 June 1375
778	21 May 1376
779	10 May 1377
780	30 Apr 1378
781	19 Apr 1379
782	7 Apr 1380
783	28 Mar 1381
784	17 Mar 1382
785	6 Mar 1383
786	24 Feb 1384
787	12 Feb 1385
788	2 Feb 1386
789	22 Jan 1387
790	11 Jan 1388
791	31 Dec 1388
792	20 Dec 1389
793	9 Dec 1390
794	29 Nov 1391
795	17 Nov 1392
796	6 Nov 1393
797	27 Oct 1394
798	16 Oct 1395
799	5 Oct 1396
800	24 Sept 1397
801	13 Sept 1398
802	3 Sept 1399
803	22 Aug 1400
804	11 Aug 1401
805	1 Aug 1402
806	21 July 1403
807	10 July 1404
808	29 June 1405
809	18 June 1406
810	8 June 1407
811	27 May 1408
812	16 May 1409
813	6 May 1410
814	25 Apr 1411
815	13 Apr 1412
816	3 Apr 1413
817	23 Mar 1414
818	13 Mar 1415
819	1 Mar 1416
820	18 Feb 1417
821	8 Feb 1418
822	28 Jan 1419
823	17 Jan 1420
824	6 Jan 1421
825	26 Dec 1421
826	15 Dec 1422
827	5 Dec 1423
828	23 Nov 1424
829	13 Nov 1425
830	2 Nov 1426
831	22 Oct 1427
832	11 Oct 1428
833	30 Sept 1429
834	19 Sept 1430
835	9 Sept 1431
836	28 Aug 1432
837	18 Aug 1433
838	7 Aug 1434
839	27 July 1435
840	16 July 1436
841	5 July 1437
842	24 June 1438
843	14 June 1439
844	2 June 1440
845	22 May 1441
846	12 May 1442
847	1 May 1443
848	20 Apr 1444
849	9 Apr 1445
850	29 Mar 1446
851	19 Mar 1447
852	7 Mar 1448
853	24 Feb 1449
854	14 Feb 1450
855	3 Feb 1451
856	23 Jan 1452
857	12 Jan 1453
858	1 Jan 1454
859	22 Dec 1454
860	11 Dec 1455
861	29 Nov 1456
862	19 Nov 1457
863	8 Nov 1458
864	28 Oct 1459
865	17 Oct 1460
866	6 Oct 1461
867	26 Sept 1462
868	15 Sept 1463
869	3 Sept 1464
870	23 Aug 1465
871	13 Aug 1466
872	2 Aug 1467
873	22 July 1468
874	11 July 1469
875	30 June 1470
876	20 June 1471
877	8 June 1472
878	29 May 1473
879	18 May 1474
880	7 May 1475
881	26 Apr 1476
882	15 Apr 1477
883	4 Apr 1478
884	25 Mar 1479
885	13 Mar 1480
886	2 Mar 1481
887	20 Feb 1482
888	9 Feb 1483
889	30 Jan 1484
890	18 Jan 1485
891	7 Jan 1486
892	28 Dec 1486
893	17 Dec 1487
894	5 Dec 1488
895	25 Nov 1489
896	14 Nov 1490
897	4 Nov 1491
898	23 Oct 1492
899	12 Oct 1493
900	2 Oct 1494
901	21 Sept 1495
902	9 Sept 1496
903	30 Aug 1497
904	19 Aug 1498
905	8 Aug 1499
906	28 July 1500
907	17 July 1501
908	7 July 1502
909	26 June 1503
910	14 June 1504
911	4 June 1505
912	24 May 1506
913	13 May 1507
914	2 May 1508
915	21 Apr 1509
916	10 Apr 1510
917	31 Mar 1511
918	19 Mar 1512
919	9 Mar 1513
920	26 Feb 1514
921	15 Feb 1515
922	5 Feb 1516
923	24 Jan 1517
924	13 Jan 1518
925	3 Jan 1519
926	23 Dec 1519
927	12 Dec 1520
928	1 Dec 1521
929	20 Nov 1522
930	10 Nov 1523
931	29 Oct 1524
932	18 Oct 1525
933	8 Oct 1526
934	27 Oct 1527
935	15 Sept 1528
936	5 Sept 1529
937	25 Aug 1530
938	15 Aug 1531
939	3 Aug 1532
940	23 July 1533
941	13 July 1534
942	2 July 1535
943	20 June 1536
944	10 June 1537
945	30 May 1538
946	19 May 1539
947	8 May 1540
948	27 Apr 1541
949	17 Apr 1542
950	6 Apr 1543
951	25 Mar 1544
952	15 Mar 1545
953	4 Mar 1546
954	21 Feb 1547
955	11 Feb 1548
956	30 Jan 1549
957	20 Jan 1550
958	9 Jan 1551
959	29 Dec 1551
960	18 Dec 1552
961	7 Dec 1553
962	26 Nov 1554
963	16 Nov 1555
964	4 Nov 1556
965	24 Oct 1557
966	14 Oct 1558
967	3 Oct 1559
968	22 Sept 1560
969	11 Sept 1561
970	31 Aug 1562
971	21 Aug 1563
972	9 Aug 1564
973	29 July 1565
974	19 July 1566
975	8 July 1567
976	26 June 1568
977	16 June 1569
978	5 June 1570
979	26 May 1571
980	14 May 1572
981	3 May 1573
982	23 Apr 1574
983	12 Apr 1575
984	31 Mar 1576
985	21 Mar 1577
986	10 Mar 1578
987	28 Feb 1579
988	17 Feb 1580
989	5 Feb 1581
990	26 Jan 1582
991	25 Jan 1583
992	14 Jan 1584
993	3 Jan 1585
994	23 Dec 1585
995	12 Dec 1586
996	2 Dec 1587
997	20 Nov 1588
998	10 Nov 1589
999	30 Oct 1590
1000	19 Oct 1591
1001	8 Oct 1592
1002	27 Sept 1593
1003	16 Sept 1594
1004	6 Sept 1595
1005	28 Aug 1596
1006	14 Aug 1597
1007	4 Aug 1598
1008	24 July 1599
1009	13 July 1600
1010	2 July 1601
1011	21 June 1602
1012	11 June 1603
1013	30 May 1604

Calendar Conversion Table

Hijra Year	Western Date of Muḥarram 1	Hijra Year	Western Date of Muḥarram 1	Hijra Year	Western Date od Muḥarram 1	Hijra Year	Western Date of Muḥarram 1
1014	19 May 1605	1078	23 June 1667	1141	7 Aug 1728	1205	10 Sept 1790
1015	9 May 1606	1079	11 June 1668	1142	27 July 1729	1206	31 Aug 1791
1016	28 Apr 1607	1080	1 June 1669	1143	17 July 1730	1207	19 Aug 1792
1017	17 Apr 1608	1081	21 May 1670	1144	6 July 1731	1208	9 Aug 1793
1018	6 Apr 1609	1082	10 May 1671	1145	24 June 1732	1209	29 July 1794
1019	26 Mar 1610	1083	29 Apr 1672	1146	14 June 1733	1210	18 July 1795
1020	16 Mar 1611	1084	18 Apr 1673	1147	3 June 1734	1211	7 July 1796
1021	4 Mar 1612	1085	7 Apr 1674	1148	24 May 1735	1212	26 June 1797
1022	21 Feb 1613	1086	28 Mar 1675	1149	12 May 1736	1213	15 June 1798
1023	11 Feb 1614	1087	16 Mar 1676	1150	1 May 1737	1214	5 June 1799
1024	31 Jan 1615	1088	6 Mar 1677	1151	21 Apr 1738		
1025	20 Jan 1616	1089	23 Feb 1678	1152	10 Apr 1739	1215	25 May 1800
1026	9 Jan 1617	1090	12 Feb 1679	1153	29 Mar 1740	1216	14 May 1801
1027	29 Dec 1617	1091	2 Feb 1680	1154	19 Mar 1741	1217	4 May 1802
1028	19 Dec 1618	1092	21 Jan 1681	1155	8 Mar 1742	1218	23 Apr 1803
1029	8 Dec 1619	1093	10 Jan 1682	1156	25 Feb 1743	1219	12 Apr 1804
1030	26 Nov 1620	1094	31 Dec 1682	1157	15 Feb 1744	1220	1 Apr 1805
1031	16 Nov 1621	1095	20 Dec 1683	1158	3 Feb 1745	1221	21 Mar 1806
1032	5 Nov 1622	1096	8 Dec 1684	1159	24 Jan 1746	1222	11 Mar 1807
1033	25 Oct 1623	1097	28 Nov 1685	1160	13 Jan 1747	1223	28 Feb 1808
1034	14 Oct 1624	1098	17 Nov 1686	1161	2 Jan 1748	1224	16 Feb 1809
1035	3 Oct 1625	1099	7 Nov 1687	1162	22 Dec 1748	1225	6 Feb 1810
1036	22 Sept 1626	1100	26 Oct 1688	1163	11 Dec 1749	1226	26 Jan 1811
1037	12 Sept 1627	1101	15 Oct 1689	1164	30 Nov 1750	1227	16 Jan 1812
1038	31 Aug 1638	1102	5 Oct 1690	1165	20 Nov 1751	1228	4 Jan 1813
1039	21 Aug 1629	1103	24 Sept 1691	1166	8 Nov 1752	1229	24 Dec 1813
1040	10 Aug 1630	1104	12 Sept 1692	1167	29 Oct 1753	1230	14 Dec 1814
1041	30 July 1631	1105	2 Sept 1693	1168	18 Oct 1754	1231	3 Dec 1815
1042	19 July 1632	1106	22 Aug 1694	1169	7 Oct 1755	1232	21 Nov 1816
1043	8 July 1633	1107	12 Aug 1695	1170	26 Sept 1756	1233	11 Nov 1817
1044	27 June 1634	1108	31 July 1696	1171	15 Sept 1757	1234	31 Oct 1818
1045	17 June 1635	1109	20 July 1697	1172	4 Sept 1758	1235	20 Oct 1819
1046	5 June 1636	1110	10 July 1698	1173	25 Aug 1759	1236	9 Oct 1820
1047	26 May 1637	1111	29 June 1699	1174	13 Aug 1760	1237	28 Sept 1821
1048	15 May 1638			1175	2 Aug 1761	1238	18 Sept 1822
1049	4 May 1639	1112	18 June 1700	1176	23 July 1762	1239	7 Sept 1823
1050	23 Apr 1640	1113	8 June 1701	1177	12 July 1763	1240	26 Aug 1824
1051	12 Apr 1641	1114	28 May 1702	1178	1 July 1764	1241	16 Aug 1825
1052	1 Apr 1642	1115	17 May 1703	1179	20 June 1765	1242	5 Aug 1826
1053	22 Mar 1643	1116	6 May 1704	1180	9 June 1766	1243	25 July 1827
1054	10 Mar 1644	1117	25 Apr 1705	1181	30 May 1767	1244	14 July 1828
1055	27 Feb 1645	1118	15 Apr 1706	1182	18 May 1768	1245	3 July 1829
1056	17 Feb 1646	1119	4 Apr 1707	1183	7 May 1769	1246	22 June 1830
1057	6 Feb 1647	1120	23 Mar 1708	1184	27 Apr 1770	1247	12 June 1831
1058	27 Jan 1648	1121	13 Mar 1709	1185	16 Apr 1771	1248	31 May 1832
1059	15 Jan 1649	1122	2 Mar 1710	1186	4 Apr 1772	1249	21 May 1833
1060	4 Jan 1650	1123	19 Feb 1711	1187	25 Mar 1773	1250	10 May 1834
1061	25 Dec 1650	1124	9 Feb 1712	1188	14 Mar 1774	1251	29 Apr 1835
1062	14 Dec 1651	1125	28 Jan 1713	1189	4 Mar 1775	1252	18 Apr 1836
1063	2 Dec 1652	1126	17 Jan 1714	1190	21 Feb 1776	1253	7 Apr 1837
1064	22 Nov 1653	1127	7 Jan 1715	1191	19 Feb 1777	1254	27 Mar 1838
1065	11 Nov 1654	1128	27 Dec 1715	1192	30 Jan 1778	1255	17 Mar 1839
1066	31 Oct 1655	1129	16 Dec 1716	1193	19 Jan 1779	1256	5 Mar 1840
1067	20 Oct 1656	1130	5 Dec 1717	1194	8 Jan 1780	1257	23 Feb 1841
1068	9 Oct 1657	1131	24 Nov 1718	1195	28 Dec 1780	1258	12 Feb 1842
1069	29 Sept 1658	1132	14 Nov 1719	1196	17 Dec 1781	1259	1 Feb 1843
1070	18 Sept 1659	1133	2 Nov 1720	1197	7 Dec 1782	1260	22 Jan 1844
1071	6 Sept 1660	1134	22 Oct 1721	1198	26 Nov 1783	1261	10 Jan 1845
1072	27 Aug 1661	1135	12 Oct 1722	1199	14 Nov 1784	1262	30 Dec 1845
1073	16 Aug 1662	1136	1 Oct 1723	1200	4 Nov 1785	1263	20 Dec 1846
1074	5 Aug 1663	1137	20 Sept 1724	1201	24 Oct 1786	1264	9 Dec 1847
1075	25 July 1664	1138	9 Sept 1725	1202	13 Oct 1787	1265	27 Nov 1848
1076	14 July 1665	1139	29 Aug 1726	1203	2 Oct 1788	1266	17 Nov 1849
1077	4 July 1666	1140	19 Aug 1727	1204	21 Sept 1789	1267	6 Nov 1850

Calendar Conversion Table

Hijra Year	Western Date of Muḥarram 1
1268	27 Oct 1851
1269	15 Oct 1852
1270	4 Oct 1853
1271	24 Sept 1854
1272	13 Sept 1855
1273	1 Sept 1856
1274	22 Aug 1857
1275	11 Aug 1858
1276	31 July 1859
1277	20 July 1860
1278	9 July 1861
1279	29 June 1862
1280	18 June 1863
1281	6 June 1864
1282	27 May 1865
1283	16 May 1866
1284	5 May 1867
1285	24 Apr 1868
1286	13 Apr 1869
1287	3 Apr 1870
1288	23 Mar 1871
1289	11 Mar 1872
1290	1 Mar 1873
1291	18 Feb 1874
1292	7 Feb 1875
1293	28 Jan 1876
1294	16 Jan 1877
1295	5 Jan 1878
1296	26 Dec 1878
1297	15 Dec 1879
1298	4 Dec 1880
1299	23 Nov 1881
1300	12 Nov 1882
1301	2 Nov 1882
1302	21 Oct 1884
1303	10 Oct 1885
1304	30 Sept 1886
1305	19 Sept 1887
1306	7 Sept 1888
1307	28 Aug 1889
1308	17 Aug 1890
1309	7 Aug 1891
1310	26 July 1892
1311	15 July 1893
1312	5 July 1894
1313	24 June 1895
1314	12 June 1896
1315	2 June 1897
1316	22 May 1898
1317	12 May 1899
1318	1 May 1900
1319	20 May 1901
1320	10 Apr 1902
1321	30 Mar 1903
1322	18 Mar 1904
1323	8 Mar 1905
1324	25 Feb 1906
1325	14 Feb 1907
1326	4 Feb 1908
1327	23 Jan 1909
1328	13 Jan 1910
1329	2 Jan 1911
1330	22 Dec 1911
1331	11 Dec 1912
1332	30 Nov 1913
1333	19 Nov 1914
1334	9 Nov 1915
1335	28 Oct 1916
1336	17 Oct 1917
1337	7 Oct 1918
1338	26 Sept 1919
1339	15 Sept 1920
1340	4 Sept 1921
1341	24 Aug 1922
1342	14 Aug 1923
1343	2 Aug 1924
1344	22 July 1925
1345	12 July 1926
1346	1 July 1927
1347	20 June 1928
1348	9 June 1929
1349	29 May 1930
1350	19 May 1931
1351	7 May 1932
1352	26 Apr 1933
1353	16 Apr 1934
1354	5 Apr 1935
1355	24 Mar 1936
1356	14 Mar 1937
1357	3 Mar 1938
1358	21 Feb 1939
1359	10 Feb 1940
1360	29 Jan 1941
1361	19 Jan 1942
1362	8 Jan 1943
1363	28 Dec 1943
1364	17 Dec 1944
1365	6 Dec 1945
1366	25 Nov 1946
1367	15 Nov 1947
1368	3 Nov 1948
1369	24 Oct 1949
1370	13 Oct 1950
1371	2 Oct 1951
1372	21 Sept 1952
1373	10 Sept 1953
1374	30 Aug 1954
1375	20 Aug 1955
1376	8 Aug 1956
1377	29 July 1957
1378	18 July 1958
1379	7 July 1959
1380	25 June 1960
1381	14 June 1961
1382	4 June 1962
1383	25 May 1963
1384	13 May 1964
1385	2 May 1965
1386	22 Apr 1966
1387	11 Apr 1967
1388	31 May 1968
1389	20 Mar 1969
1390	9 Mar 1970
1391	27 Feb 1971
1392	16 Feb 1972
1393	4 Feb 1973
1394	25 Jan 1974
1395	14 Jan 1975
1396	3 Jan 1976
1397	23 Dec 1976
1398	12 Dec 1977
1399	2 Dec 1978
1400	21 Nov 1979
1401	9 Nov 1980
1402	30 Oct 1981
1403	19 Oct 1982
1404	8 Oct 1983
1405	27 Sept 1984
1406	16 Sept 1985
1407	6 Sept 1986
1408	26 Aug 1987
1409	14 Aug 1988
1410	4 Aug 1989
1411	24 July 1990
1412	13 July 1991
1413	2 July 1992
1414	21 June 1993
1415	10 June 1994
1416	31 May 1995
1417	19 May 1996
1418	9 May 1997
1419	28 Apr 1998
1420	17 Apr 1999
1421	6 Apr 2000

IV. Dynasties, Rulers, Administrators

A critical tool for any analysis of political developments is the list of caliphs, sultans, governors, presidents, prime ministers, etc. who ruled over Southwest Asia and Egypt. Students of pre-20th-century Islamic history are very fortunate to have the excellent work by C.E. Bosworth, *The Islamic Dynasties* (Edinburgh: Edinburgh University Press, 1967; 2nd ed., 1980), University of Edinburgh Islamic Surveys, No. 5. In 82 tables, Professor Bosworth lists every major and many minor dynasties from Spain through India. Each section lists the rulers, their regnal dates (in Muslim and Western years), and then presents a brief historical sketch, followed by a few pertinent references. The only weakness of this well-written and fully indexed work is its lack of any genealogical tables.

If one wishes more extensive tables of rulers and genealogical tables for medieval Islamic history — including numerous lists of *wazīr*s and governors, full Muslim dates for the beginning of a rule and, when possible, Muslim dates of death — the best source is Edward von Zambaur, *Manuel de Généalogie et de Chronologie pour l'Histoire de l'Islam* (Hanover, 1927 [reprinted in Berlin, 1955]. There is also an Arabic translation of Zambaur by Zakī M. Ḥasan Bey, Ḥasan Aḥmad Maḥmūd and others, *Muᶜjam al-Ansāb wa'l-Usarāt al-Ḥakīma fī'l-Ta'rīkh al-Islāmī* (Cairo: Arab League, 1370/1951). However, unlike Bosworth, neither Zambaur nor the translation of his work includes Western dates, historical summaries or a bibliography.

One other important source of information on medieval dynasties, *wazīr*s, etc. is *EI*[1] and *EI*[2]. Stanley Lane-Poole's pioneer work, *The Mohammaden Dynasties* (London, 1893 [reprinted New York: Frederick Ungar Publishing Co., 1965]), includes dynasties not in Bosworth and genealogical tables. A.D. Alderson, *The Structure of the Ottoman Dynasty* (Oxford: Clarendon Press, 1956), is the best Western source for data related to the Ottoman family.

A recent reference work in Arabic is by Dr. Aḥmad al-Saᶜīd Sulaymān, entitled *Ta'rīkh al-Duwal al-Islāmiyya wa Muᶜjam al-Usar al-Ḥakīma* (Cairo: Dār al-Maᶜārif [n.d.]). His book includes 115 dynasties with a brief historical introduction, the names and dates of the rulers and, whenever possible, a genealogy table. His dates for Iranian dynasties often differ from those found in Western sources.

The material which follows has been arranged in the following manner: general divisions with a list of the dates of the dynasties (and a few other groups) which ruled in that area for the period covered. Those dynasties, ministers, officials marked by "*" are broken down into a list of the individuals with the dates they were in power, and those categories marked with a "+" are presented in the form of a genealogical table. The choice of those groups given in greater detail or in a genealogical table reflect my teaching experience and are not meant to be comprehensive.

CALIPHS AND WAZĪRS

			Muslim Dates	Christian Dates
*+	A.	Rāshidūn	11 - 40 A.H.	632 - 661 A.D.
*+	B.	Umayyads	41 - 132	661 - 750
*+	C.1.	^{c}Abbāsids in Iraq	132 - 656	750 - 1258
*+	2.	Barmakids	ca. 165 - 221	ca. 781 - 835
*	3.	^{c}Abbāsids in Egypt	659 - 923	1261 - 1517
*+	D.	Selected Early Shī^{c}ites	35 - c.264	656 - ca. 878

A. Rāshidūn

11/632	Abū Bakr	23/644	^{c}Uthmān b. ^{c}Affān
13/634	^{c}Umar b. al-Khaṭṭāb	35-40/656-661	^{c}Alī b. Abī-Ṭālib

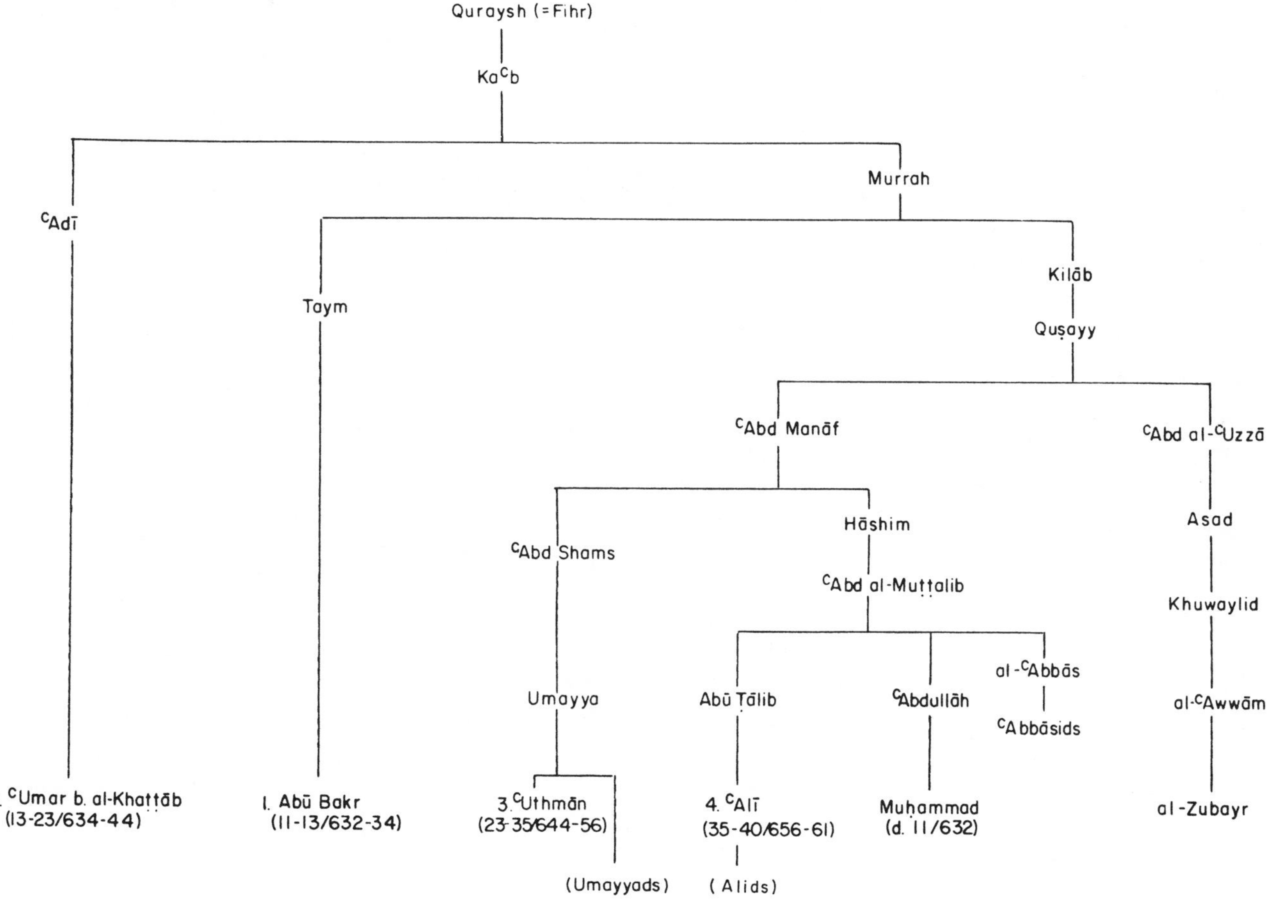

* = Lists of individuals.
+ = Genealogy table.

B. Umayyad Caliphs

41/661	Mu^{c}āwiya I	86/705	al-Walīd I	125/743	al-Walīd II
60/680	Yazīd I	96/715	Sulaymān	126/744	Yazīd III
64/683	Mu^{c}āwiya II	99/717	^{c}Umar II	126/744	Ibrāhīm
64/684	Marwān I	101/720	Yazīd II	127-132/744-750	Marwān II
65/685	^{c}Abd al-Malik	105/724	Hishām		

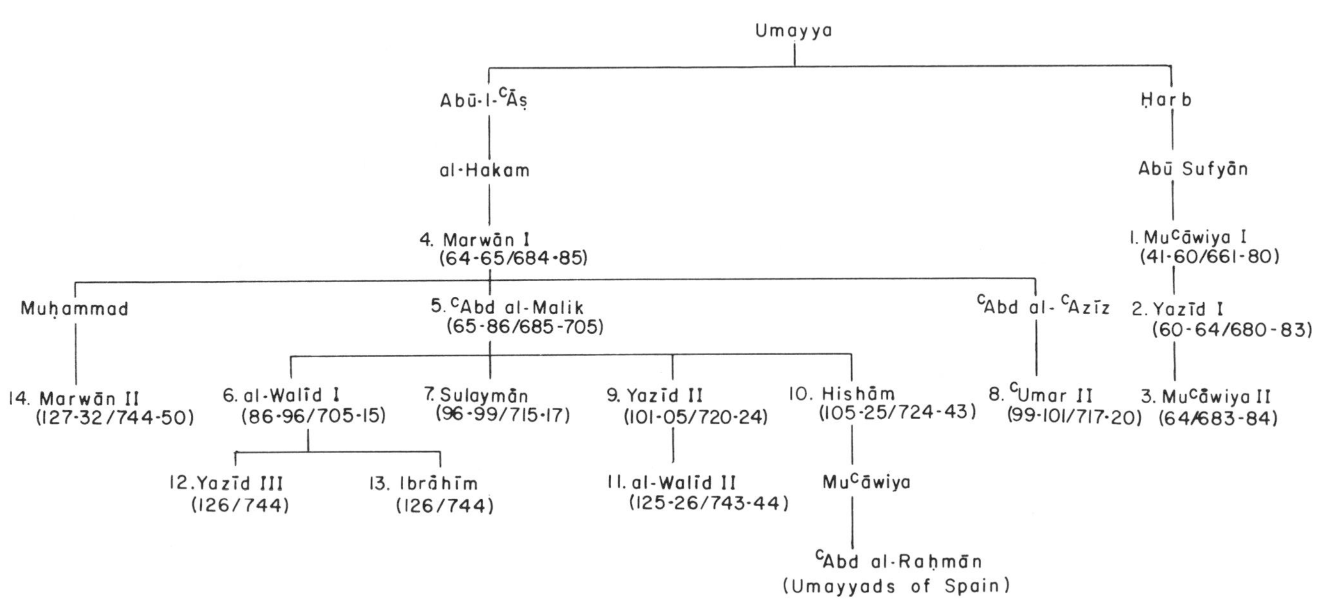

C.1. ^{c}Abbāsids in Iraq

132/749	al-Saffāḥ	255/869	al-Muhtadī	422/1031	al-Qā'im
136/754	al-Manṣūr	256/870	al-Mu^{c}tamid	467/1075	al-Muqtadī
158/775	al-Mahdī	279/892	al-Mu^{c}taḍid	487/1094	al-Mustaẓhir
169/785	al-Hādī	289/902	al-Muktafī	512/1118	al-Mustarshid
170/786	Hārūn al-Rashīd	295/908	al-Muqtadir	529/1135	al-Rāshid
193/809	al-Amīn	320/932	al-Qāhir	530/1136	al-Muqtafī
198/813	al-Ma'mūn	322/934	al-Rāḍī	555/1160	al-Mustanjid
218/833	al-Mu^{c}taṣim	329/940	al-Muttaqī	566/1170	al-Mustaḍī'
227/842	al-Wāthiq	333/944	al-Mustakfī	575/1180	al-Nāṣir
232/847	al-Mutawakkil	334/946	al-Muṭī^{c}	622/1225	al-Ẓāhir
247/861	al-Muntaṣir	363/974	al-Ṭā'i^{c}	623/1226	al-Mustanṣir
248/862	al-Musta^{c}īn	381/991	al-Qādir	640-656/1242-1258	al-Musta^{c}ṣim
252/866	al-Mu^{c}tazz				

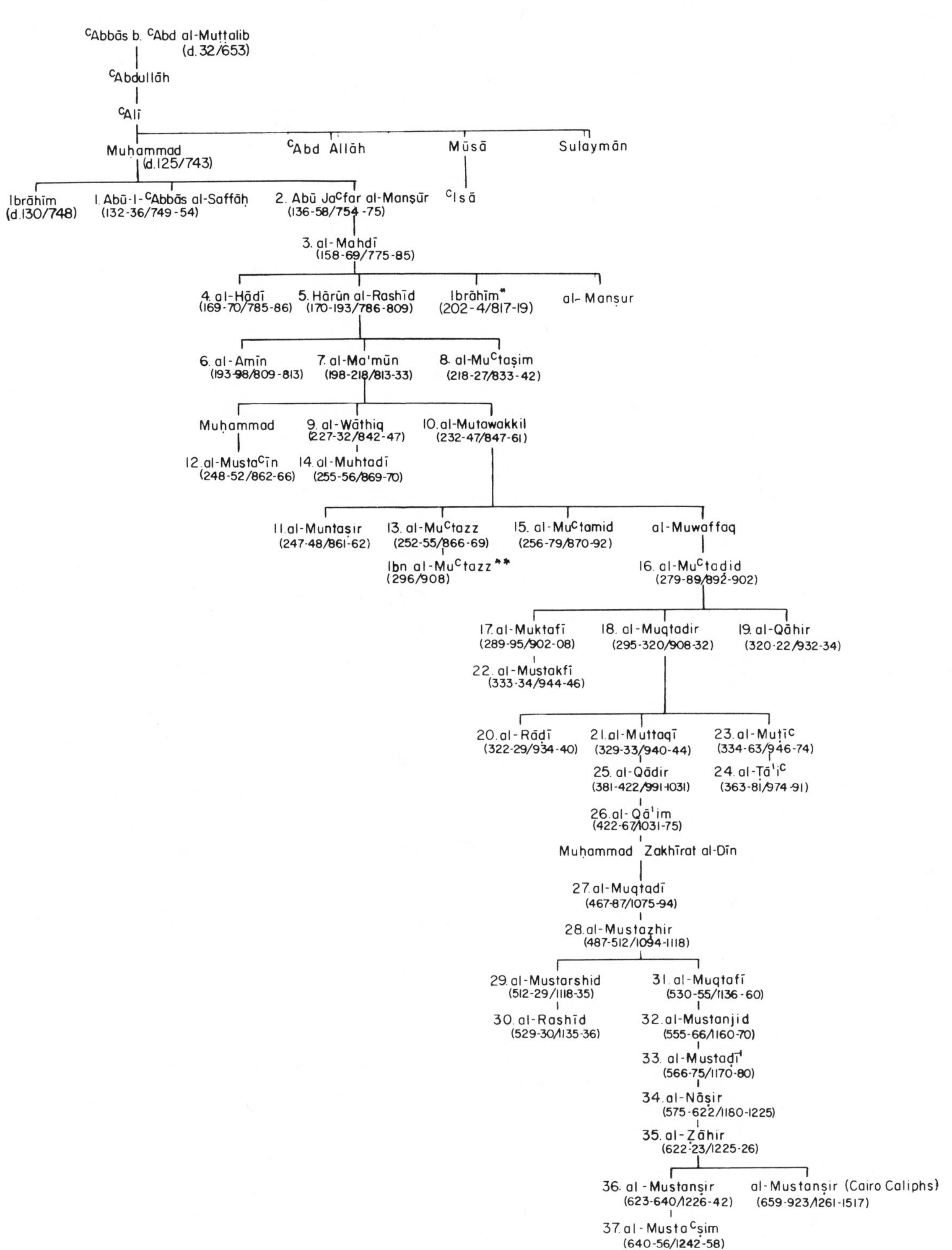

IV ʿABBĀSIDS
(132-650/749-1258)

* In Baghdad

** Caliph for part of a day

C.2. Barmakids

	Barmak	d. 187/803	Ja^{c}far
d. 165/781	Khālid	d. 193/808	al-Faḍl
d. 190/805	Yaḥyā	d. 221/835	Mūsā

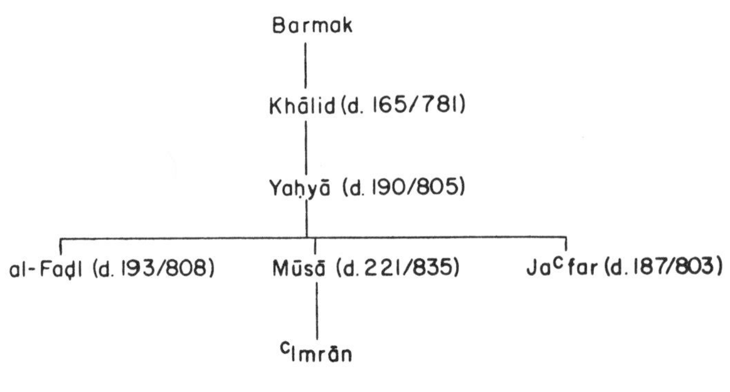

C.3. ^{c}Abbāsids in Egypt

659/1261	al-Mustanṣir	791/1389	al-Mutawakkil I [3rd reign]
660/1261	al-Ḥākim I	808/1406	al-Musta^{c}īn
701/1302	al-Mustakfī I	816/1414	al-Mu^{c}taḍid II
740/1340	al-Wāthiq I	845/1441	al-Mustakfī II
741/1341	al-Ḥākim II	855/1451	al-Qā'im
753/1352	al-Mu^{c}taḍid I	859/1455	al-Mustanjid
763/1362	al-Mutawakkil I [1st reign]	884/1479	al-Mutawakkil II
779/1377	al-Mu^{c}taṣim [1st reign]	903/1497	al-Mustamsik [1st reign]
779/1377	al-Mutawakkil I [2nd reign]	914/1508	al-Mutawakkil III [1st reign]
785/1383	al-Wāthiq II	922/1516	al-Mustamsik [2nd reign]
788/1385	al-Mu^{c}taṣim [2nd reign]	923/1517	al-Mutawakkil III [2nd reign]

D. Selected Early Shī^{c}ites

d. 40/661	^{c}Alī	d. 183/799	Mūsā al-Kāẓim
d.c. 49/669	Ḥasan	d. 203/818	^{c}Alī al-Riḍā
d. 61/680	Ḥusayn	d. 220/835	Muḥammad al-Jawād
d. 94/712	^{c}Alī Zayn al-^{c}Ābidīn	d. 254/868	^{c}Alī al-Hādī
d. 113/731	Muḥammad al-Bāqir	d. 260/874	Ḥasan al-^{c}Askarī
d. 148/765	Ja^{c}far al-Ṣādiq	d.c. 264/878	Muḥammad al-Mantaẓar [al-Mahdī]

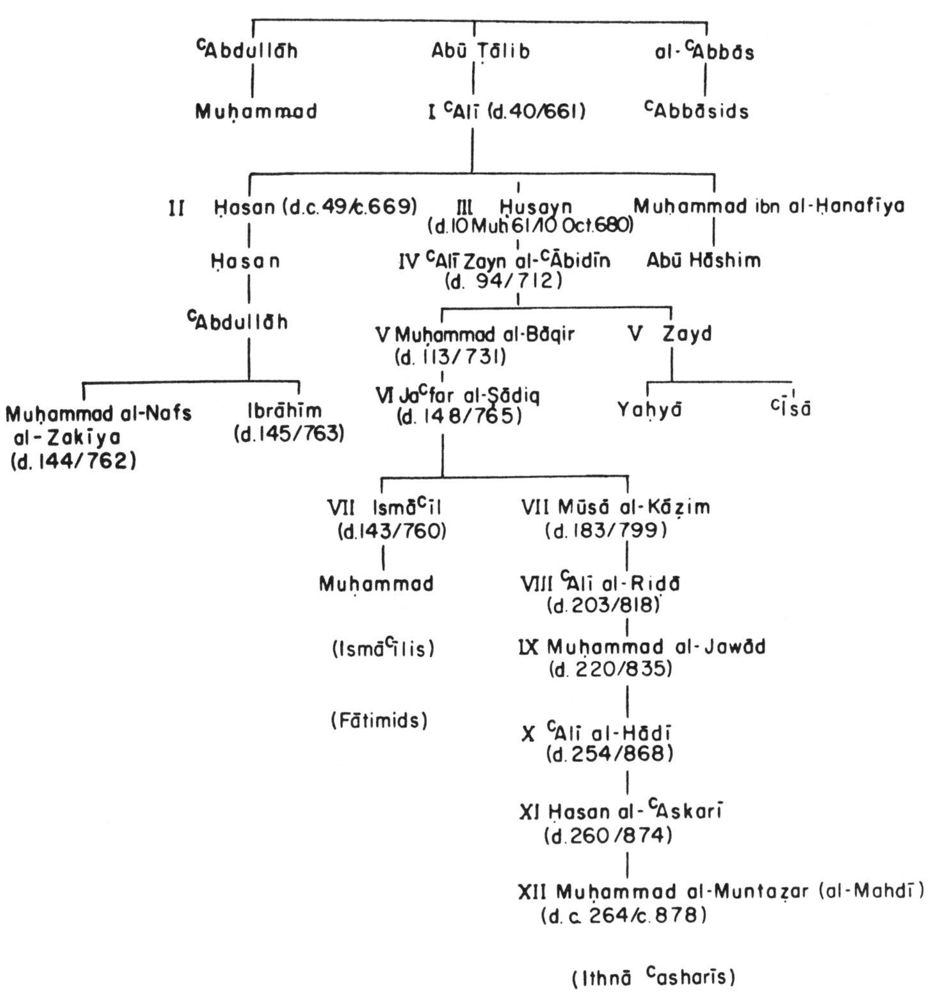

E G Y P T

		Muslim Dates	Christian Dates
*+	A. Ṭūlūnids	254 - 292 A.H.	868 - 905 A.D.
*+	B. Ikhshīdids	323 - 358	935 - 969
*+	C. Fāṭimids	297 - 567	909 - 1171
	D. Ayyūbids, including Syria, Iraq and Yemen:	564 - 9th C.	1169 - 15th C.
*+	1. Egypt	564 - 650	1169 - 1252
*	2. Damascus	582 - 658	1186 - 1260
*	3. Aleppo	579 - 658	1183 - 1260
	4. Mayyāfāriqīn, Sinjār	581 - 658	1185 - 1260
	5. Baᶜlbakk	568 - 658	1172 - 1260
	6. Hama	574 - 732	1178 - 1332
	7. Ḥimṣ	574 - 661	1178 - 1262
*	8. Yemen	569 - 626	1174 - 1229
	9. Ḥisn Kayfā and Āmid	629 - 9th C.	1232 - 15th C.

[continued]

		Muslim Dates	Christian Dates
	E. Mamlūks:	648 - 922 A.H.	1250 - 1517 A.D.
	* 1. Baḥrī	648 - 792	1250 - 1390
	* 2. Circassian (Burji)	784 - 922	1382 - 1517
*+	F. Muḥammad ᶜAlī's Family	1220 - 1372	1805 - 1953
*	G. British Consul Generals, High Commissioners	-- --	1879 - 1936
*	H. Presidents of Egypt	-- --	1953 -

A. Ṭūlūnids

254/868	Aḥmad b. Ṭūlūn	283/896	Hārūn
270/884	Khumārawayh	292/905	Shaybān
282/896	Jaysh		

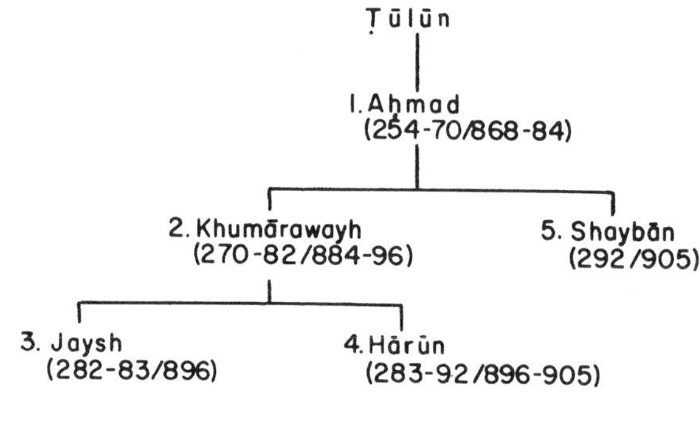

B. Ikhshīdids

323/935	Muḥammad b. Ṭughj al-Ikhshīd	355/966	Kāfūr
334/946	Ūnūjūr	357-358/968-969	Aḥmad
349/960	ᶜAlī		

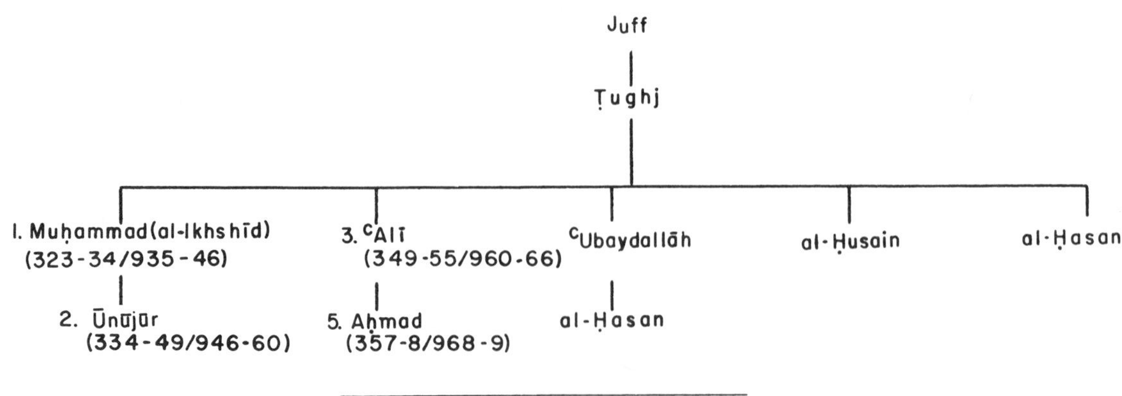

C. Fāṭimids

297/909	^{c}Ubaydullāh al-Mahdī	386/996	al-Ḥākim	524/1130	Interregnum
322/934	al-Qā'im	411/1021	al-Ẓāhir	525/1131	al-Ḥāfiẓ
334/946	al-Manṣūr	427/1036	al-Mustanṣir	544/1149	al-Ẓāfir
341/953	al-Mu^{c}izz	487/1094	al-Musta^{c}lī	549/1154	al-Fā'iz
365/975	al-^{c}Azīz	495/1101	al-Āmir	555-567/1160-1171	al-^{c}Āḍid

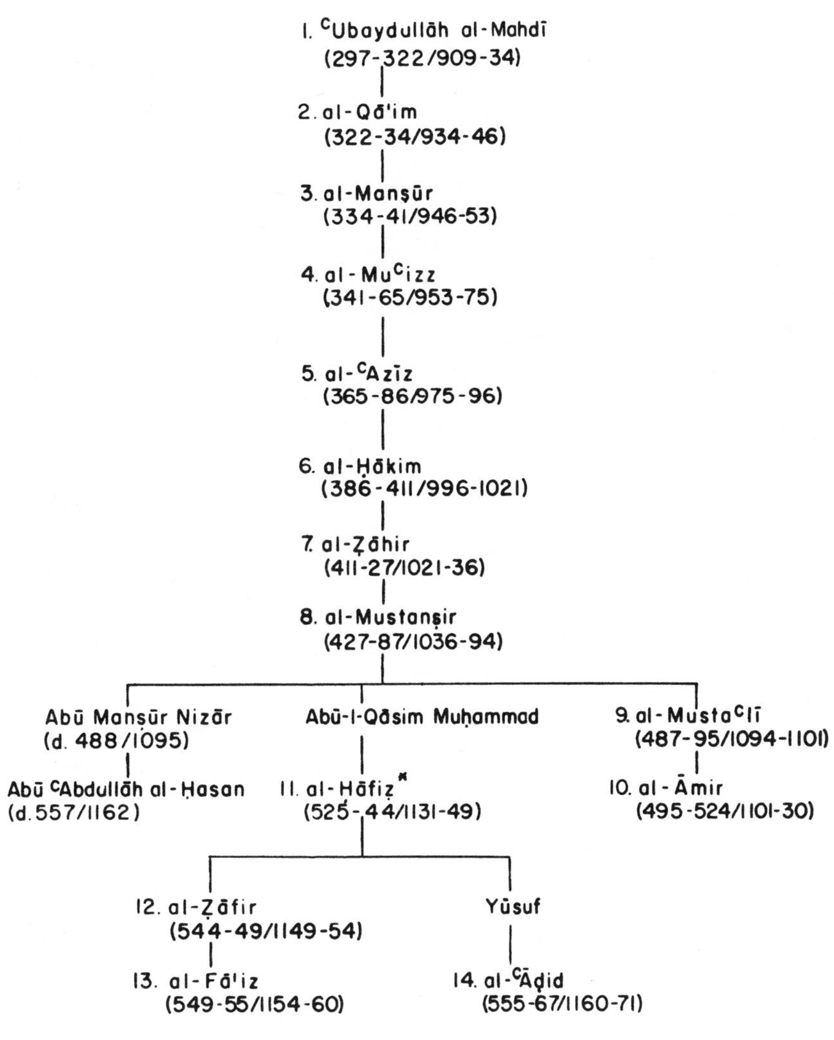

D.1 Ayyūbids in Egypt

564/1169	al-Malik al-Nāṣir Ṣalāḥ al-Dīn [Saladin]	635/1238	al-Malik al-^{c}Ādil II
589/1193	al-Malik al-^{c}Azīz	637/1240	al-Malik al-Ṣāliḥ Najm al-Dīn Ayyūb
595/1198	al-Malik al-Manṣūr	647/1249	al-Malik al-Mu^{c}aẓẓam Tūrān Shāh
596/1200	al-Malik al-^{c}Ādil I	648-50/1250-52	al-Malik al-Ashraf II
615/1218	al-Malik al-Kāmil		

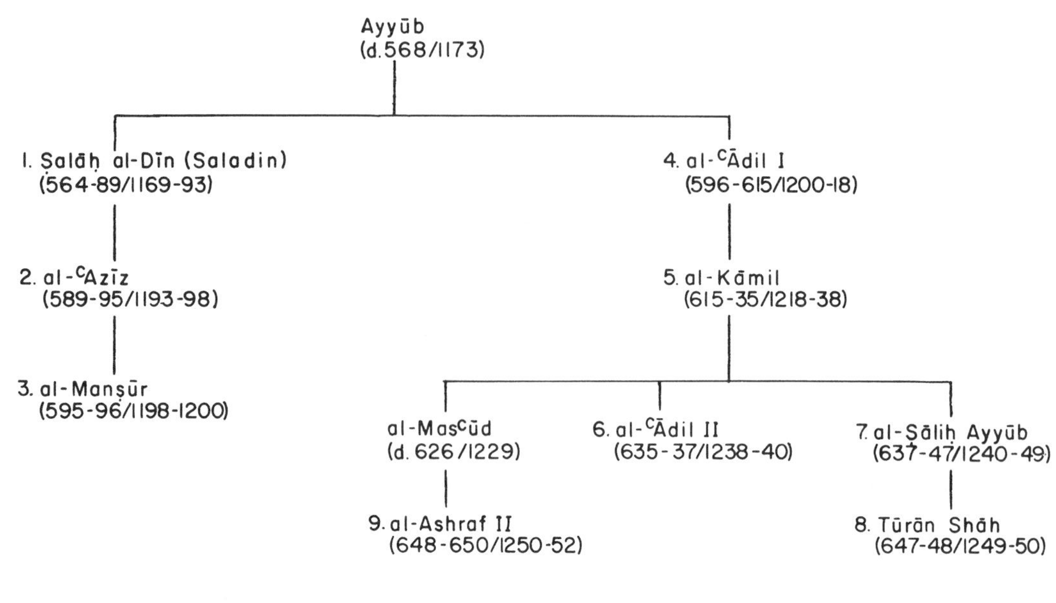

D.2. Ayyūbids in Damascus

582/1186	al-Malik al-Afḍal
592/1196	al-Malik al-ᶜĀdil I
615/1218	al-Malik al-Muᶜaẓẓam
624/1227	al-Malik al-Nāṣir Ṣalāḥ al-Dīn Dā'ūd
626/1229	al-Malik al-Ashraf
634/1237	al-Malik al-Ṣāliḥ Ismāᶜīl [1st reign]
635/1238	al-Malik al-Kāmil
635/1238	al-Malik al-ᶜĀdil II
636/1239	al-Malik al-Ṣāliḥ Najm al-Dīn Ayyūb [1st reign]
637/1239	al-Malik al-Ṣāliḥ Ismāᶜīl [2nd reign]
643/1245	al-Malik al-Ṣāliḥ Najm al-Dīn Ayyūb [2nd reign]
647/1249	al-Malik al-Muᶜaẓẓam Tūrān Shāh
648-58/1250-60	al-Malik al-Nāṣir Ṣalāḥ al-Dīn II

D.3. Ayyūbids in Aleppo

579/1183	al-Malik al-ᶜĀdil I
582/1186	al-Malik al-Ẓāhir Ghiyāth al-Dīn
613/1216	al-Malik al-ᶜAzīz Ghiyāth al-Dīn
634-58/1237-60	al-Malik al-Nāṣir Ṣalāḥ al-Dīn II

D.8. Ayyūbids in Yemen

569/1174	al-Malik al-Muᶜaẓẓam Shams al-Dīn Tūrān Shāh
577/1181	al-Malik al-ᶜAzīz Ẓāhir al-Dīn Tughtigīn
593/1197	Muᶜizz al-Dīn Ismāᶜīl
598/1202	al-Malik al-Nāṣir Ayyūb
611/1214	al-Malik al-Muẓaffar Sulaymān
612-26/1215-29	al-Malik al-Masᶜūd Ṣalāḥ al-Dīn

Note: On other branches, see Bosworth and Zambaur.

E.1. Mamlūks - Baḥrī

Date	Ruler
648/1250	Shajar al-Durr
648/1250	Aybak
655/1257	^{c}Alī
657/1259	Quṭuz
658/1260	Baybars I
676/1277	Baraka Khān
678/1280	Salāmish
678/1280	Qalā'ūn
689/1290	Khalīl
693/1294	al-Nāsir Muḥammad [1st reign]
694/1295	Kitbughā
696/1297	Lājīn
698/1299	al-Nāṣir Muḥammad [2nd reign]
708/1309	Baybars II
709/1309	al-Nāṣir Muḥammad [3rd reign]
741/1340	Abū Bakr
742/1341	Kūjūk
743/1342	Aḥmad
743/1342	Ismā^{c}īl
746/1345	Sha^{c}bān I
747/1346	Ḥājjī I
748/1347	al-Nāṣir al-Ḥasan [1st reign]
752/1351	Ṣāliḥ
755/1354	al-Nāṣir al-Ḥasan [2nd reign]
762/1361	al-Manṣūr Muḥammad
764/1363	Sha^{c}bān II
778/1376	al-Manṣūr ^{c}Alī
783/1382	al-Ṣāliḥ Ḥājjī II
[784/1382	Barqūq]
791/1389	Ḥājjī II [2nd reign]

E.2. Mamlūks - Circassian (Burji)

Date	Ruler
784/1382	Barqūq [1st reign]
[791/1389	Ḥājjī II]
792/1390	Barqūq [2nd reign]
801/1399	Faraj [1st reign]
808/1405	al-Manṣūr ^{c}Abd al-^{c}Azīz
808/1405	Faraj [2nd reign]
815/1412	al-^{c}Ādil al-Musta^{c}īn
815/1412	al-Mu'ayyad Shaykh
824/1421	al-Muẓaffar Aḥmad
824/1421	Ṭaṭār
824/1421	al-Ṣāliḥ Muḥammad
825/1422	Barsbay
841/1437	Yūsuf
842/1438	al-Ẓāhir Jaqmaq
857/1453	^{c}Uthmān
857/1453	Ināl
865/1461	al-Mu'ayyad Aḥmad
865/1461	Khūshqadam
872/1467	Bilbay
872/1468	Timurbughā
872/1468	al-Ashraf Qāyitbāy
901/1496	al-Nāṣir Muḥammad
903/1498	Qānṣūh
905/1500	Jānbalāt
906/1501	al-^{c}Ādil Tūmān Bay
906/1501	Qānṣūh al-Ghawrī
922/1517	al-Ashraf Tūmān Bay

F. Muḥammad ^{c}Alī's Family

Date	Ruler
1220/1805	Muḥammad ^{c}Alī Pāshā
1264/1848	Ibrāhīm Pāshā
1264/1848	^{c}Abbās Pāshā
1270/1854	Sa^{c}īd Pāshā
1280/1863	Ismā^{c}īl [Khedive from 1284/1867]
1296/1879	Tawfīq
1309/1892	^{c}Abbās II Hilmī
1333/1914	Ḥusayn Kāmil [Sulṭān]
1335/1917	Aḥmad Fu'ād I [King from 1340/1922]
1355/1936	Fārūq
1371-72/1952-53	Fu'ād II

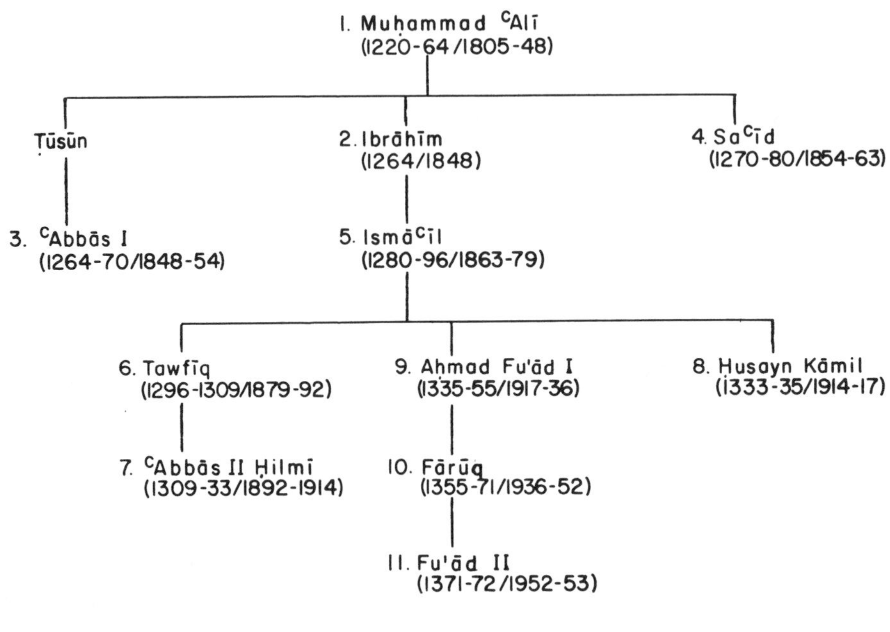

G. British Consul Generals, High Commissioners for Egypt, 1879-1936

1. Consul Generals

1879 Sir Edward Malet
1883 Evelyn Baring [Lord Cromer]
1907 Sir Eldon Gorst
1911 Sir Herbert Kitchener

2. High Commissioners

1914 Sir Henry MacMahon
1916 Sir Reginald Wingate
1919 Sir Edmund Allenby
1925 Lord George Lloyd
1929 Sir Percy Loraine
1933-36 Sir Miles Lampson [Lord Killearn]

H. Presidents of Egypt, 1953-

1953 Muḥammad Nagīb
1954 Gamal ^{c}Abd al-Nāṣir
1971 Anwar al-Sādāt
1981 Ḥusnī Mubārak

III. ARABIAN PENINSULA

		Muslim Dates	Christian Dates
	A. Ziyādids	204 - 409 A.H.	819 - 1018 A.D.
	B. Ya^c^furids	247 - 387	861 - 997
	C. Qarāmiṭa	281 - 5th C.	894 - 11th C.
	D. Zuray'ids	476 - 569	1083 - 1173
	E. Najāḥids	412 - 551	1021 - 1156
	F. Mahdids	554 - 569	1159 - 1173
*	G. Ṣulayḥids [Yemen]	439 - 532	1047 - 1138
	H. Hamdānids of Ṣan^c^ā'	492 - 569	1098 - 1173
	I. Ayyūbids	[See II, Egypt]	-- --
*	J. Rasūlids [Yemen]	626 - 858	1229 - 1454
	K. Ṭāhirids [Yemen]	850 - 923	1446 - 1517
	L. Rassid Zaydī Imāms	246 - 680	860 - 1281
*	M. Qāsimid Zaydī Imāms [Modern Period]	1000 - 1382	1592 - 1962
	N. Āl Bū Sa^c^īd	1154 -	1741 -
	O. Rashīdids	1248 - 1342	1832 - 1923
*+	P. Sa^c^ūdī Family	1159 -	1746 -

G. Ṣulayḥids [Yemen]

439/1047	^c^Alī b. Muḥammad	484/1091	al-Manṣūr Sabā'
459/1067	al-Mukarram Aḥmad	492-532/1099-1138	al-Sayyida Arwā
477/1084	al-Mukarram ^c^Alī		

J. Rasūlids [Yemen]

626/1229	al-Malik al-Manṣūr ^c^Umar I	803/1400	al-Malik al-Nāṣir Aḥmad
647/1250	al-Malik al-Muẓaffar Yūsuf I	827/1424	al-Malik al-Manṣūr ^c^Abdullāh
694/1295	al-Malik al-Ashraf ^c^Umar II	830/1427	al-Malik al-Ashraf Ismā^c^īl II
696/1296	al-Malik al-Mu'ayyad Dā'ūd	831/1428	al-Malik al-Ẓāhir Yaḥyā
721/1322	al-Malik al-Mujāhid ^c^Alī	842/1439	al-Malik al-Ashraf Ismā^c^īl III
764/1363	al-Malik al-Afḍal al-^c^Abbās	845/1442	al-Malik al-Muẓaffar Yūsuf II
778/1377	al-Malik al-Ashraf Ismā^c^īl I		

RIVALS

846/1442	al-Malik al-Mufaḍḍal Muḥammad
846/1442	al-Malik al-Nāṣir ^c^Abdullāh
854/1450	al-Malik al-Mas^c^ūd
855/1451	al-Malik al-Mu'ayyad

M. Qāsimid Zaydī Imāms [Modern Period]

Date	Ruler
1000/1592	al-Qāsim al-Manṣūr
1029/1620	Muḥammad al-Mu'ayyad I
1054/1644	Ismā^{c}īl al-Mutawakkil
1087/1676	Muḥammad al-Mu'ayyad II
1092/1681	Muḥammad al-Hādī
1097/1686	Muḥammad al-Mahdī
1128/1716	al-Qāsim al-Mutawakkil
1139/1726	al-Ḥusayn al-Manṣūr [1st reign]
1139/1726	Muḥammad al-Hādī al-Majīd
1140/1728	al-Ḥusayn al-Manṣūr [2nd reign]
1160/1747	al-^{c}Abbās al-Mahdī
1190/1776	^{c}Alī al-Manṣūr
1221/1806	Aḥmad al-Mahdī
? ?	^{c}Alī al-Manṣūr [2nd reign]
1257/1841	al-Qāsim al-Mahdī
1261/1845	Muḥammad Yaḥyā
1289/1872	Ottoman Occupation
1308/1890	Ḥamīd al-Dīn Yaḥyā
1322/1904	Yaḥyā Maḥmūd al-Mutawakkil
1367/1948	Sayf al-Islām Aḥmad
1382/1962	Muḥammad Badr

P. Sa^{c}ūdī Family

Date	Ruler
1159/1746	Muḥammad b. Sa^{c}ūd
1179/1765	^{c}Abd al-^{c}Azīz I
1218/1803	Sa^{c}ūd b. ^{c}Abd al-^{c}Azīz
1229/1814	^{c}Abdullāh I b. Sa^{c}ūd
1233-38/1818-22	Ottoman Occupation
1238/1823	Turkī
1249/1834	Fayṣal I [1st reign]
1253/1837	Khālid b. Sa^{c}ūd
1257/1841	^{c}Abdullāh II b. Thunayyān
1259/1843	Fayṣal I [2nd reign]
1282/1865	^{c}Abdullāh III b. Fayṣal [1st reign]
1287/1871	Sa^{c}ūd b. Fayṣal
1291/1874	^{c}Abdullāh III [2nd reign]
1305/1887	^{c}Abd al-Raḥmān b. Fayṣal [Governor for Rashīdī]
1308/1891	Rashīdī occupation of Riyādh
1319/1902	^{c}Abd al-^{c}Azīz II
1373/1953	Sa^{c}ūd
1384/1964	Fayṣal II
1395/1975	Khālid
1402/1982	Fahd

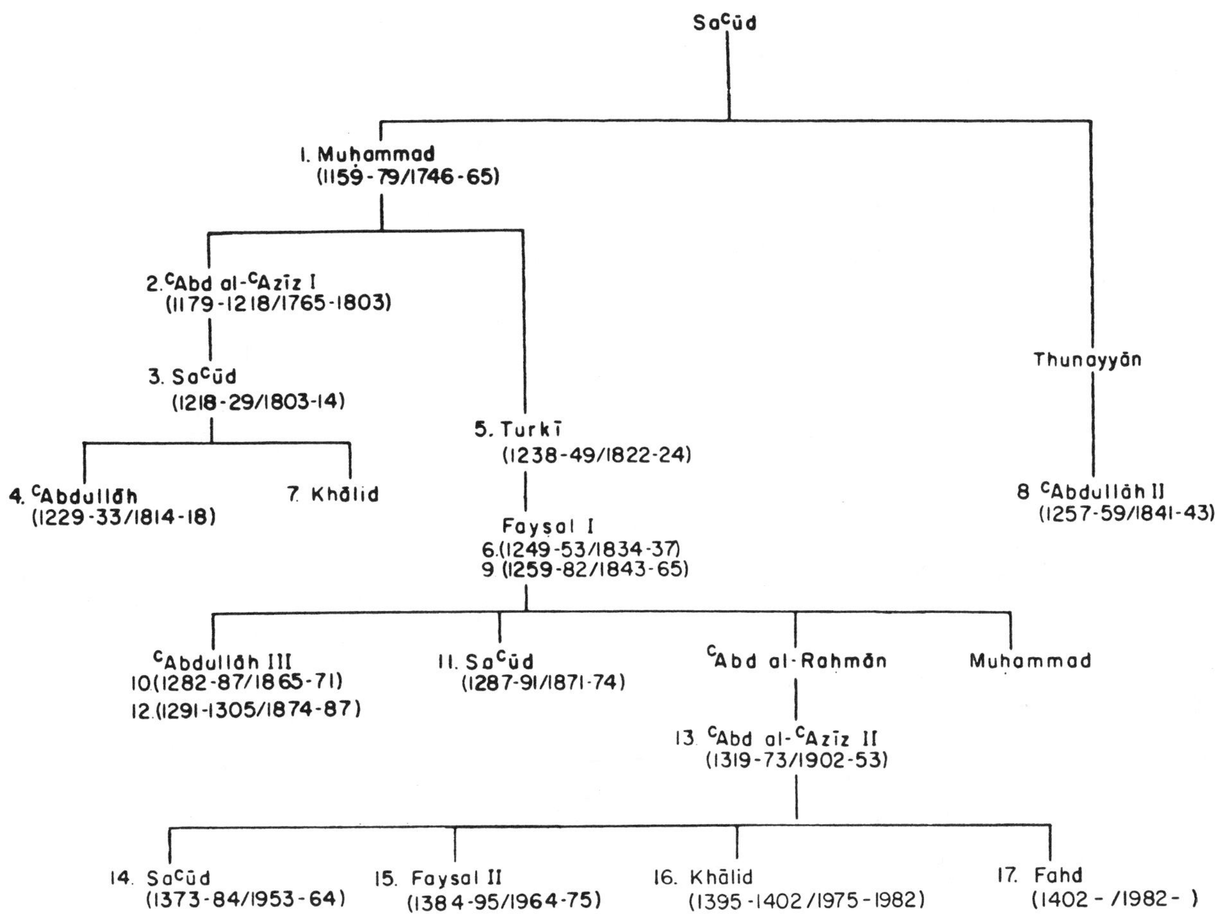

IV. IRAQ AND SYRIA [Before the Seljuks]

		Muslim Dates	Christian Dates
*+	A. Ḥamdānids:	317 - 394 A.H.	927 - 1004 A.D.
	1. Mosul Branch	317 - 391	927 - 1000
	2. Aleppo Branch	333 - 394	945 - 1004
	B. Mirdāsids	414 - 472	1023 - 1079
	C. ^{c}Uqaylids	380 - 489	990 - 1096
	D. Marwānids	372 - 478	983 - 1085
	E. Mazyadids	350 - 545	961 - 1150
	F. Inālids	490 - 579	1096 - 1183

A.1. Hamdānids - Mosul Branch

317/929	Nāṣir al-Dawla al-Ḥasan	379/401	Ibrāhīm]	Joint Rulers
358/969	cUddat al-Dawla Abū Taghlib	989/1010	al-Ḥusayn]	

A.2. Hamdānids - Aleppo Branch

333/945	Sayf al-Dawla cAlī I	392/1002	cAlī II
356/967	Sacd al-Dawla Sharīf I	394/1004	Sharīf II
381/991	Sacīd al-Dawla Sacīd		

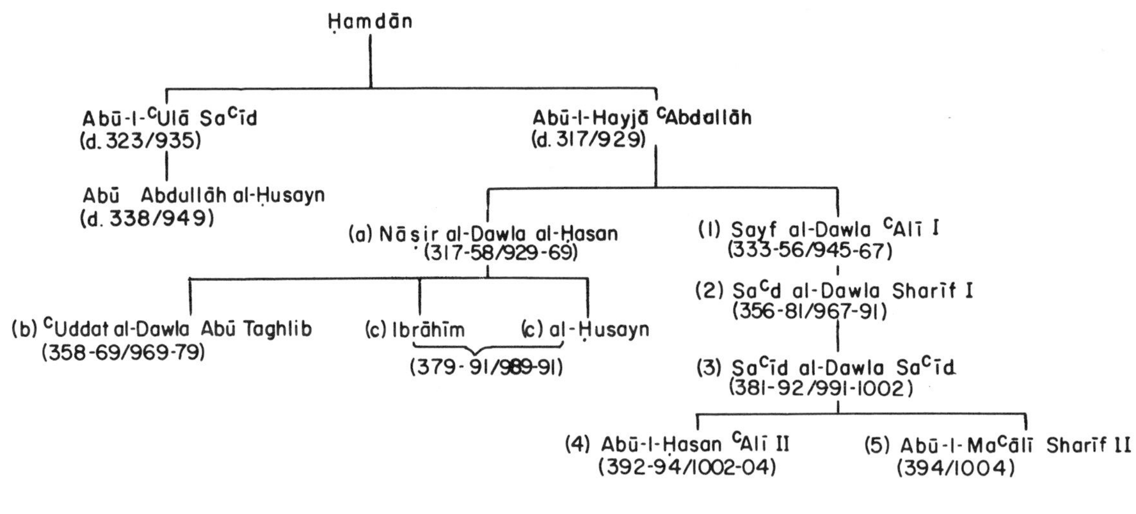

CAUCASUS [Before the Seljuks]

	Muslim Dates	Christian Dates
A. Sājids	266 - 318 A.H.	879 - 930 A.D.
B. Musāfirids [or Sallarids or Kangarids]	304 - 483	916 - 1090
C. Rawwādids	4th C. - 463	10th C. - 1071
D. Sharwān Shāhs:		
1. First Dynasty	183 - 381	799 - 991
2. Second Dynasty	418 - 455	1027 - 1063
3. Fourth Dynasty	1180 - 1236	1766 - 1821
E. Shaddādids	340 - 571	951 - 1174
F. Dābūyids	40 - 142	660 - 760
G. Bāwandids:	45 - 750	665 - 1349
1. Kā'ūsīya Line	45 - 466	665 - 1074
2. Ispahbadīya Line	466 - 606	1074 - 1210
3. Kinkhwārīya Line	635 - 750	1238 - 1349
H. Bādūspānids	40 - 1006	665 - 1599
I. Zaydī cAlīds of Tabaristan	250 - 316	864 - 928

IRAN [Before the Seljuks]

		Muslim Dates	Christian Dates
*+	A. Ṭāhirids	205 - 259 A.H.	821 - 873
*	B. Sāmānids	204 - 395	819 - 1005
*	C. Ṣaffārids	253 - ca. 900	867 - ca. 1495
	D. Būyids [Buwayhids]:	320 - 447	932 - 1055
*+	1. Iraq	334 - 447	945 - 1055
*+	2. Fārs and Khūzistān	322 - 454	934 - 1062
*+	3. Kirmān	324 - 440	936 - 1048
*+	4. Jibāl	320 - 366	932 - 977
*+	5. Hamadān and Iṣfahān	366 - 419	977 - 1028
*+	6. Rayy	366 - 420	977 - 1029
	7. ᶜUmān	363 - 388	974 - 998
	E. Dulafids	210 - 284	825 - 898
	F. Banijurids	233 - 337	848 - 948
	G. Qarakhānids [Īlek Khāns]	382 - 607	992 - 1211
	H. Khwārazm Shāhs:		
	1. Afrīghids	? - 385	? - 995
	2. Ma'mūnids	385 - 408	995 - 1017
	3. Governors	408 - 425	1017 - 1034
*	4. Anūshtigin Line	470 - 624	1077 - 1231
	I. Ziyārids	315 - 483	927 - 1090
	J. Ḥasanwayhids	348 - 405	959 - 1014
	K. Ilyāsids	320 - 357	932 - 968
	L. Kākūyids [Kākwayhids]	398 - 443	1008 - 1051

A. Ṭāhirids

205/821	Ṭāhir I b. al-Ḥusayn	230/845	Ṭāhir II
207/822	Talḥa	248-59/862-73	Muḥammad
213/828	ᶜAbdullāh		

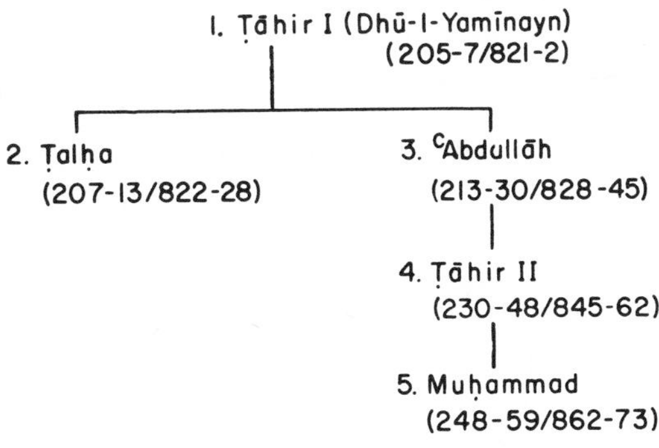

B. Sāmānids

204/819	Aḥmad I b. Asad b. Sāmān	343/954	al-Amīr al-Mu'ayyad ʿAbd al-Malik I
250/864	Naṣr I b. Aḥmad	350/961	al-Amīr al-Sadīd Manṣūr I
279/892	Ismāʿīl I b. Aḥmad	365/976	al-Amīr al-Riḍā Nūḥ II
295/907	Aḥmad II b. Ismāʿīl	387/997	Manṣūr II
301/914	al-Amīr al-Saʿīd Naṣr II	389/999	ʿAbd al-Malik II
331/943	al-Amīr al-Hamīd Nūḥ I	390-95/1000-05	Ismāʿīl II al-Muntaṣir

---

C. Ṣaffārids

253/867	Yaʿqūb b. Layth al-Ṣaffār	296/908	Layth b. ʿAlī
265/879	ʿAmr b. Layth	298/910	Muḥammad b. ʿAlī
288/901	Ṭāhir b. Muḥammad b. ʿAmr		

Note: A full list can be found in Bosworth, p. 103.

D.1. Būyids [Buwayhids] in Iraq

334/945	Muʿizz al-Dawla Aḥmad	403/1012	Sulṭān al-Dawla
356/967	ʿIzz al-Dawla Bakhtiyār	412/1021	Musharrif al-Dawla Ḥasan
367/978	ʿAḍud al-Dawla Fanā-Khusraw	416/1025	Jalāl al-Dawla Shīrzīl
372/983	Ṣamṣām al-Dawla Marzubān	435/1044	ʿImād al-Dīn al-Marzubān
376/987	Sharāf al-Dawla Shīrzīl	440-47/1048-55	al-Malik al-Raḥīm Khusraw-Fīrūz
379/989	Bahā' al-Dawla Fīrūz		

D.2. Būyids in Fārs and Khūzistān

322/932	ʿImād al-Dawla ʿAlī	403/1012	Sulṭān al-Dawla
338/949	ʿAḍud al-Dawla Fanā-Khusraw	412/1021	Musharrif al-Dawla Ḥasan
372/983	Sharāf al-Dawla Shīrzīl	415/1024	ʿImād al-Dīn Marzubān
380/990	Ṣamṣām al-Dawla Marzubān	440/1048	al-Malik al-Raḥīm Khusraw-Fīrūz
388/998	Bahā' al-Dawla Fīrūz	447-54/1055-62	Fūlād-Sutūn [Fārs only]

D.3. Būyids in Kirmān

324/936	Muʿizz al-Dawla Aḥmad	388/998	Bahā' al-Dawla Fīrūz
338/949	ʿAḍud al-Dawla Fanā-Khusraw	403/1012	Qawām al-Dawla
372/983	Ṣamṣām al-Dawla Marzubān	419-40/1028-48	ʿImād al-Dīn Marzubān

---

D.4. Būyids in Jibāl

320/932	ʿImād al-Dawla ʿAlī	335-366/947-977	Rukn al-Dawla Ḥasan

---

D.5. Būyids in Hamadān and Isfahān

366/977	Mu'ayyid al-Dawla Būya	387/997	Shams al-Dawla
373/983	Fakhr al-Dawla ᶜAlī	412-c.419/1021-c.28	Samā' al-Dawla

D.6. Būyids in Rayy

366/977	Fakhr al-Dawla ᶜAlī	387-420/997-1029	Majd al-Dawla Rustam

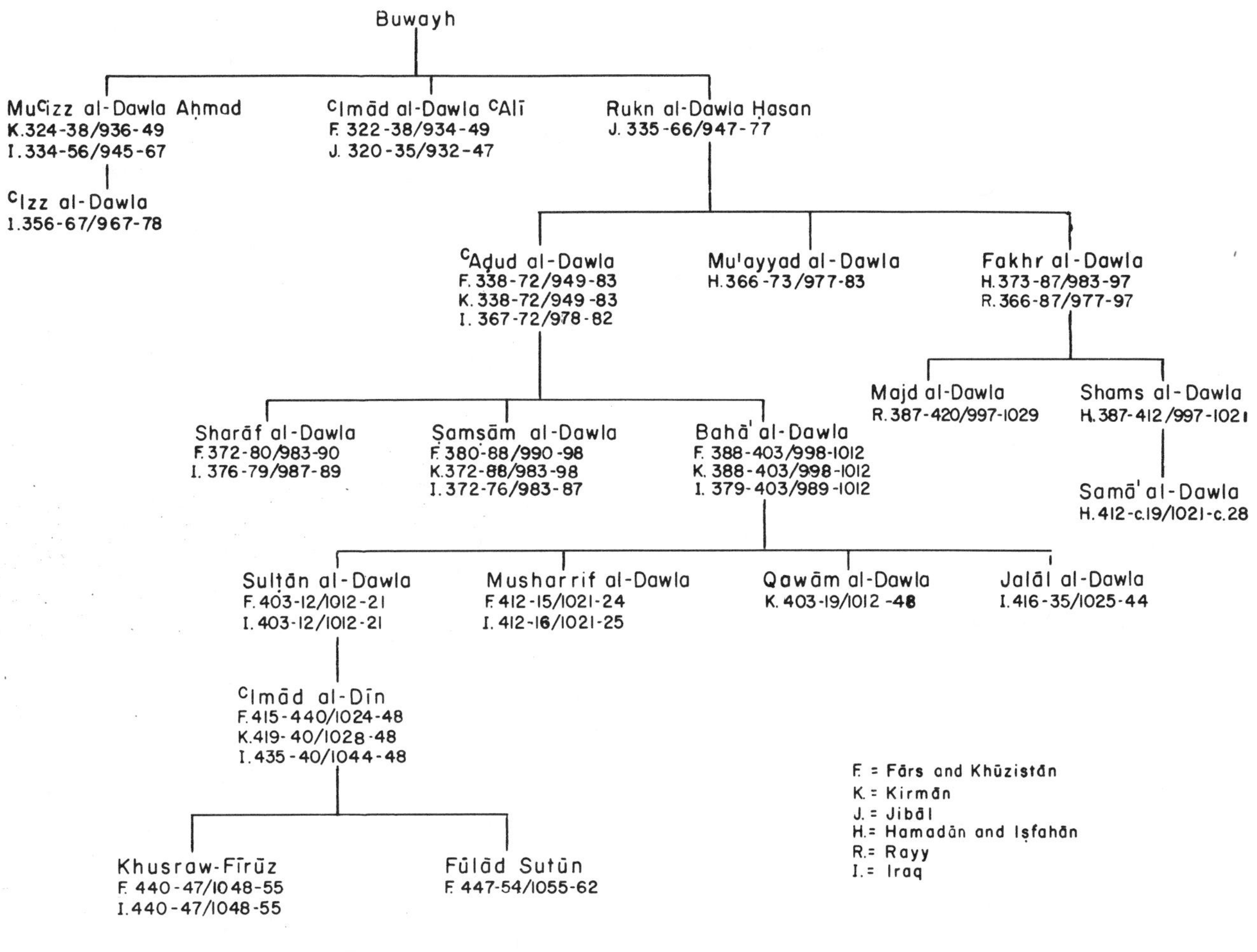

H.4. Khwārazm Shāhs - Anūshtigin Line

ca.470/ca.1077	Anūshtigin Gharcha'ī	567/1172	ᶜAlā' al-Dīn Tekish
490/1097	Turkish Governor	567-89/1172-93	Rival Ruler
490/1097	Quṭb al-Dīn Muḥammad	596/1200	ᶜAlā' al-Dīn Muḥammad
521/1127	ᶜAlā' al-Dīn Atsīz	617-28/1220-31	Jalāl al-Dīn
551/1156	Īl-Arslān		

SELJUKS AND ATABEǦS

		Muslim Dates	Christian Dates
	A. Seljuks:	429 - 700 A.H.	1037 - 1300 A.D.
*+	1. Great Seljuks	429 - 552	1037 - 1157
	2. Seljuks of Iraq	511 - 590	1117 - 1194
	3. Seljuks of Syria	471 - 511	1078 - 1117
	4. Seljuks of Kirmān	433 - 583	1041 - 1187
	5. Seljuks of Rūm	[See VIII, Asia Minor]	-- --
	B. Būrids	497 - 549	1104 - 1154
	C. Zangids:		
*+	1. Mosul	521 - 619	1127 - 1222
*+	2. Aleppo	541 - 577	1146 - 1181
	3. Sinjār	566 - 617	1170 - 1220
	4. Jazīra	576 - 648	1180 - 1250
	D. Begteginids	539 - 630	1145 - 1233
	E. Artugids:	491 - 811	1098 - 1408
	1. Ḥisn Kayfā Line	491 - 629	1098 - 1232
	2. Mārdin Line	497 - 811	1104 - 1408
	F. Suqman Shāhs	493 - 604	1100 - 1207
	G. Eldeguzids [or Ildenizids]	531 - 622	1136 - 1225
	H. Salghurids	543 - 668	1148 - 1270
	I. Faḍlawayhids	448 - 718	1056 - 1318
	J. Hazarāspids	550 - 827	1155 - 1424
	K. Qutlugh Khāns	619 - 706	1222 - 1306

A.1. Great Seljuks

429/1038	Rukn al-Dunyā wa-l-Dīn Toghril I [Tughril]	487/1094	Rukn al-Dīn Berk-yāruq [Barkiyāruq]
455/1063	ᶜAḍud al-Dawla Alp-Arslān	498/1105	Muᶜizz al-Dīn Malik-Shāh II
465/1072	Jalāl al-Dawla Malik Shāh I	498/1105	Ghiyāth al-Dīn Muḥammad I
485/1092	Nāṣir al-Dīn Maḥmūd I	511-52/1118-57	Muᶜizz al-Dīn Sanjar

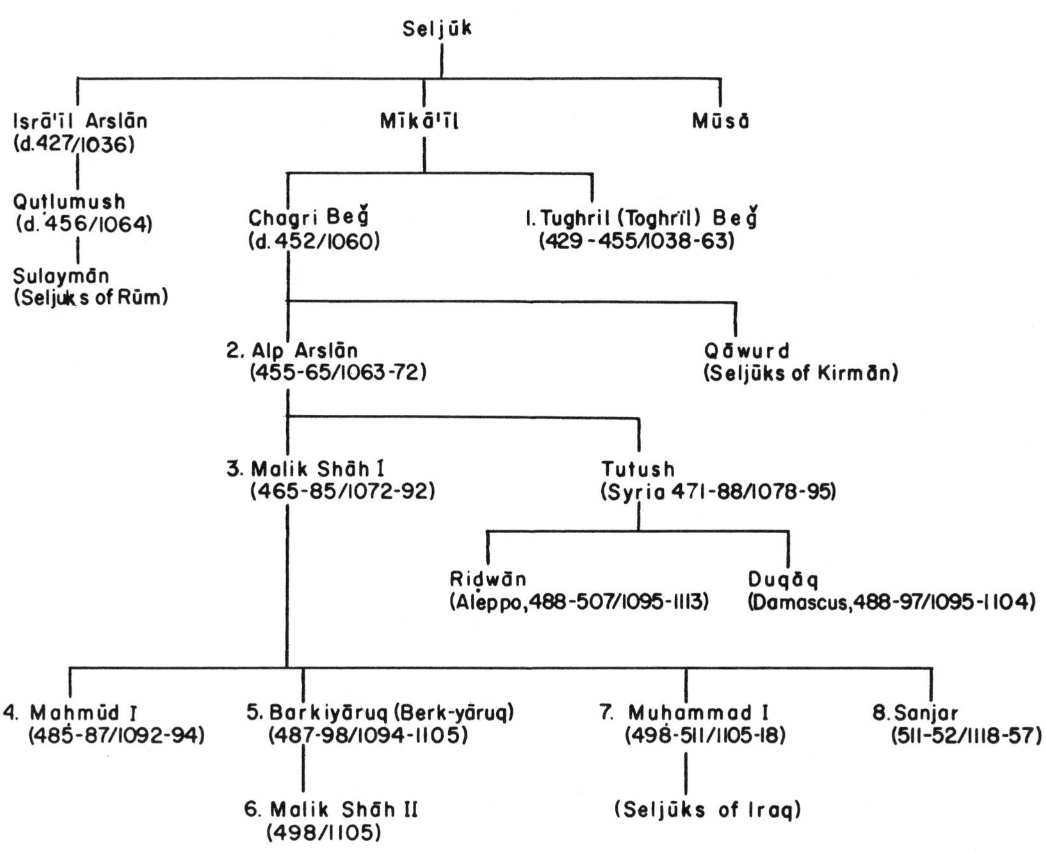

C.1. <u>Zangids - Mosul</u>

521/1127	ʿImād al-Dīn Zangī b. Aq Sonqur
541/1146	Sayf al-Dīn Ghāzī I
544/1149	Quṭb al-Dīn Mawdūd
564/1169	Sayf al-Dīn Ghāzī II
572/1176	ʿIzz al-Dīn Masʿūd I
589/1193	Nūr al-Dīn Arslān Shāh I
607/1211	ʿIzz al-Dīn Masʿūd II
615/1218	Nūr al-Dīn Arslān Shāh II
616-19/1219-22	Nāṣir al-Dīn Maḥmūd

C.2. <u>Zangids - Aleppo</u>

541/1146	Nūr al-Dīn Maḥmūd b. Zangī
569-77/1174-81	Nūr al-Dīn Ismāʿīl

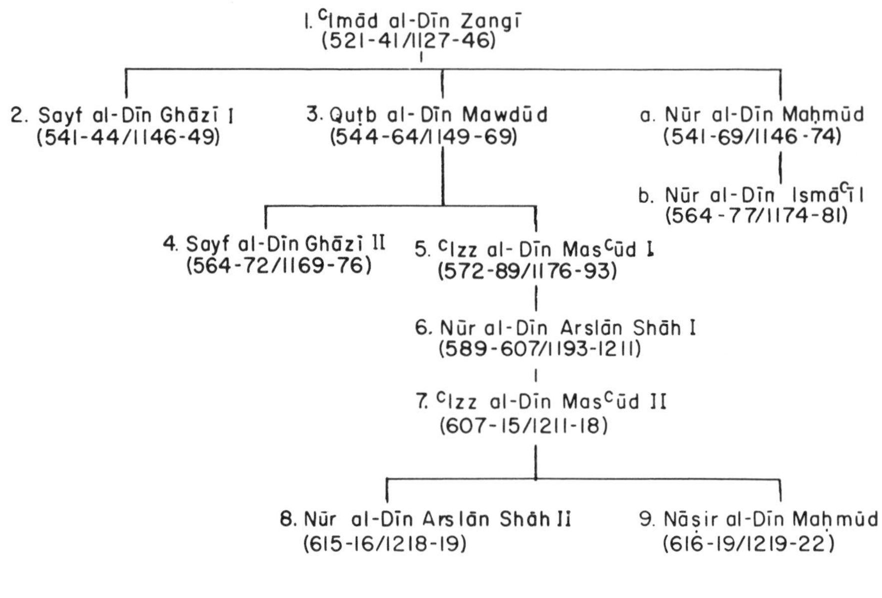

ASIA MINOR AND TURKEY

		Muslim Dates	Christian Dates
*	A. Seljuks of Rūm	470 - 707 A.H.	1077 - 1307 A.D.
	B. Menqüchekids	464 - ca. 650	1071 - 1252
	C. Dānishmandids	464 - 573	1071 - 1177
	D. Isfendiyarids	690 - 866	1291 - 1461
	E. Ṣārū Khānids	700 - 813	1300 - 1410
	F. Aydīnids	708 - 829	1308 - 1425
	G. Germiyāndids	699 - 832	1300 - 1429
	H. Ḥamīdids	700 - 826	1239 - 1423
	I. Menteshādids	700 - 829	1300 - 1426
	J. Eretnaids	736 - 782	1335 - 1380
	K. Ramaḍānids	780 - 819	1378 - 1416
	L. Dhū-l-Qadrids	738 - 928	1337 - 1522
	M. Karamānids	654 - 888	1256 - 1483
*+	N. Ottomans	680 - 1342	1281 - 1924
*+	O. Köprülü Wazīrs	1066 - 1122	1656 - 1710
*	P. Presidents of Turkey		1923 -

A. Seljuks of Rūm

470/1077	Sulaymān b. Quṭlumush	
479/1086	Interregnum	
485/1092	Qilich Arslān I	
500/1107	Malik-Shāh	
510/1116	Rukn al-Dīn Masʿūd I	
551/1156	ʿIzz al-Dīn Qilich Arslān II	
588/1192	Ghiyāth al-Dīn Kay-Khusraw I [1st reign]	
592/1196	Rukn al-Dīn Sulaymān II	
600/1204	ʿIzz al-Dīn Qilich Arslān III	
601/1204	Ghiyāth al-Dīn Kay-Khusraw I [2nd reign]	
607/1210	ʿIzz al-Dīn Kay-Kā'ūs I	
616/1219	ʿAlā' al-Dīn Kay-Qubādh I	
634/1237	Ghiyāth al-Dīn Kay-Khusraw II	
644/1246	ʿIzz al-Dīn Kay-Kā'ūs II	
646/1248	Kay-Kā'ūs II	Jointly
	Rukn al-Dīn Qilich Arslān IV	
647/1249	Kay-Kā'ūs II	Jointly
	Qilich Arslān IV	
	ʿAlā' al-Dīn Kay-Qubādh II	
655/1257	Qilich Arslān IV	
663/1265	Ghiyāth al-Dīn Kay-Khusraw III	
681/1282	Ghiyāth al-Dīn Masʿūd II [1st reign]	
683/1284	ʿAlā' al-Dīn Kay-Qubādh III [1st reign]	
683/1284	Masʿūd II [2nd reign]	
692/1293	Kay-Qubādh III [2nd reign]	
693/1294	Masʿūd II [3rd reign]	
700/1301	Kay-Qubādh III [3rd reign]	
702/1303	Masʿūd II [4th reign]	
704/1305	Kay-Qubādh III [4th reign]	
707/1307	Ghiyāth al-Dīn Masʿūd III	

N. The Ottomans

ca.679/1280	Ertuğrul
680/1281	Osmān
724/1324	Orhān
761/1360	Murād I
791/1389	Bāyezīd I
805/1403	Interregnum
816/1413	Meḥmet I Chelebi
824/1421	Murād II [1st reign]
848/1444	Meḥmet II Fâtiḥ [1st reign]
850/1446	Murād II [2nd reign]
855/1451	Meḥmet II [2nd reign]
886/1481	Bāyezīd II
918/1512	Selīm I Yavuz
926/1520	Süleymān I Kānūnī
974/1566	Selīm II
982/1574	Murād III
1003/1595	Meḥmet III
1012/1603	Aḥmed I
1026/1617	Muṣṭafā I [1st reign]
1027/1618	Osmān II
1031/1622	Muṣṭafā I [2nd reign]
1032/1623	Murād IV
1049/1640	Ibrāhīm
1058/1648	Meḥmet IV
1099/1687	Süleymān II
1102/1691	Aḥmed II
1106/1695	Muṣṭafā II
1115/1703	Aḥmed III
1143/1730	Maḥmūd I
1168/1754	Osmān III
1171/1757	Muṣṭafā III
1187/1774	ʿAbdülḥamīd I
1203/1789	Selīm III
1222/1807	Muṣṭafā IV
1223/1808	Maḥmūd II
1255/1839	ʿAbdülmecīd I
1277/1861	ʿAbdülezīz
1293/1876	Murād V
1293/1876	ʿAbdülḥamīd II
1327/1909	Meḥmet V Reshād
1336/1918	Meḥmet VI
1341-42/1922-24	ʿAbdülmecīd II [caliph only]

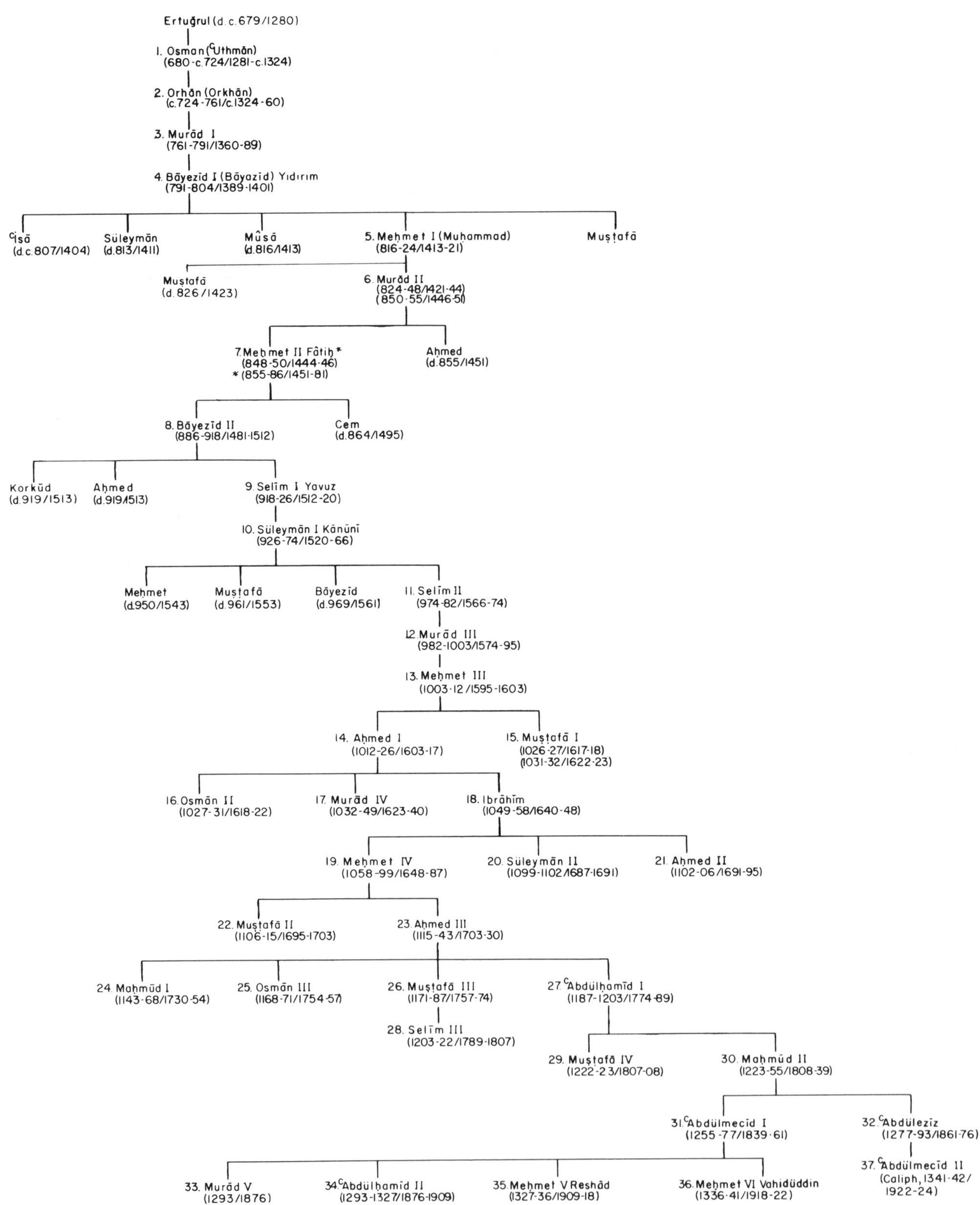

XXIV OTTOMANS (680-1342/1281-1924)

O. Köprülü Wazīrs

1066-72/1656-61	Meḥmet Paşa	1101-02/1689-91	Fāẓil Muṣṭafā Paşa
1072-87/1661-76	Fāẓil Aḥmed Paşa	1109-14/1697-1702	Ḥüseyin Paşa
1087-95/1676-83	Kara Muṣṭafā Paşa [by marriage]	1122/1710	Nu^cmān Paşa

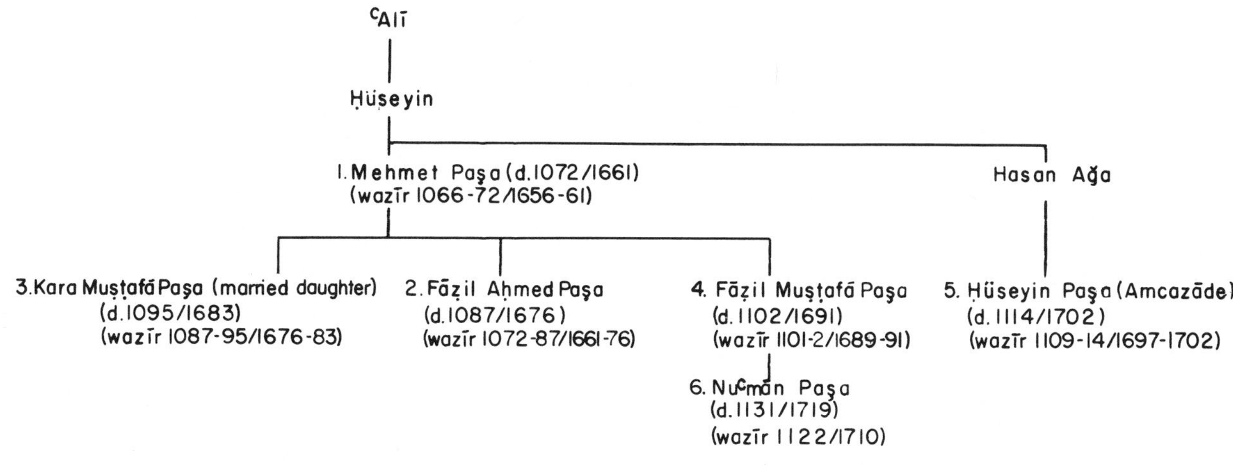

P. Presidents of Turkey

1923	Muṣṭafā Kemal Atatürk	1973	Fahri Korutürk
1938	İsmet İnönü	1980	Ihsan Sabri Çağlayangli [Acting President]
1950	Celal Bayar	1980	Kenan Evren
1961	Cemal Gürsel		
1966	Cevdet Sunay		

MONGOLS

		Muslim Dates	Christian Dates
+	A. Great Mongols	603 - 1043 A.H.	1206 - 1634 A.D.
*+	B. Īl-Khānids	654 - 754	1256 - 1353
	C. Golden Horde	621 - 760	1224 - 1359
	D. White Horde	623 - 831	1226 - 1428
	E. Chaghatayids	624 - 771	1227 - 1370
	F. Khāns of Kazan	841 - 959	1438 - 1552
	G. Khāns of Kasimof	854 - 1089	1450 - 1678
	H. Khāns of Crimea	823 - 1197	1420 - 1783

A. Great Mongols

Descendants of Chingiz Khān

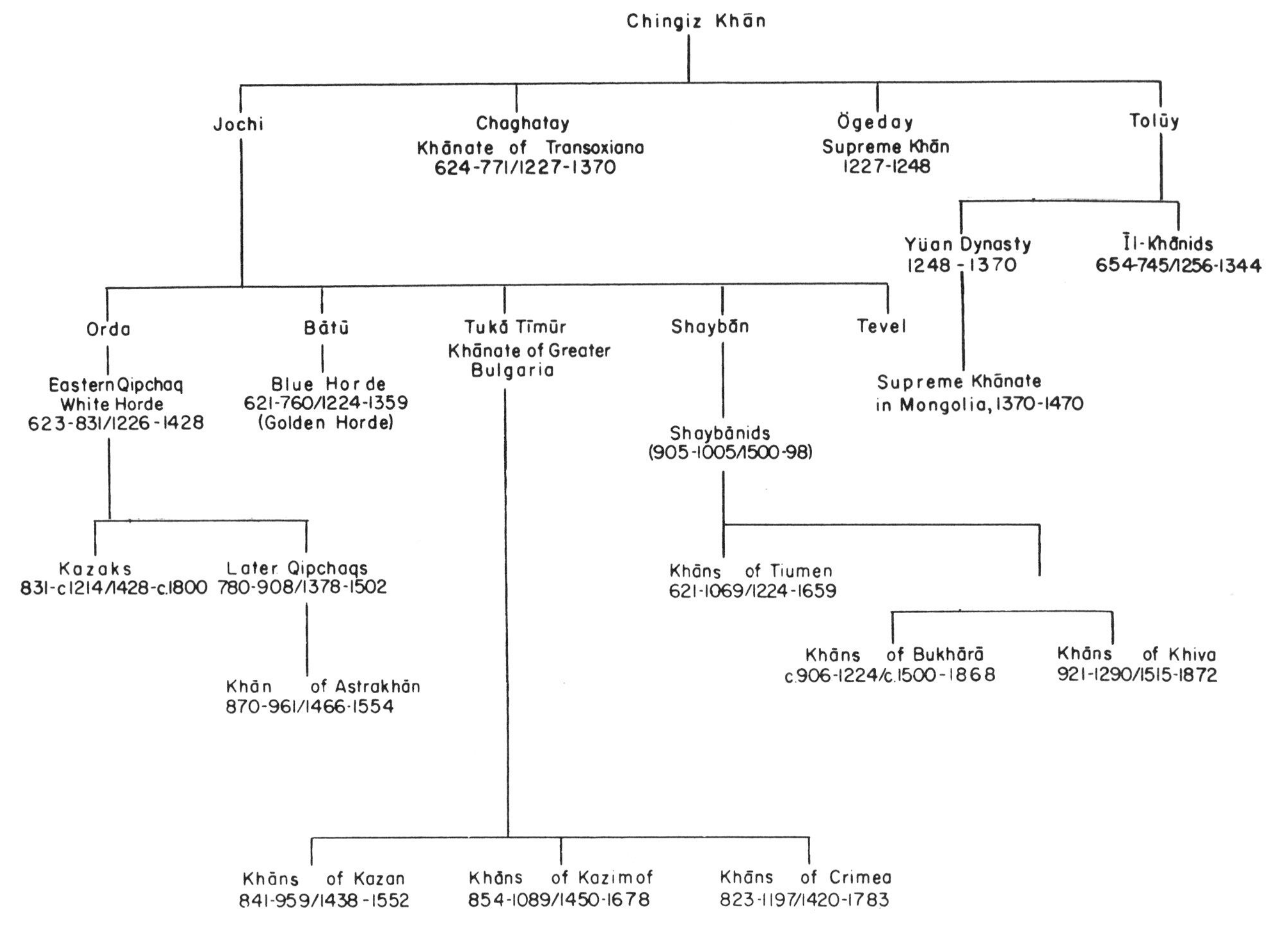

B. Īl-Khānids

654/1256	Hülegü [Hūlagū]	694/1295	Maḥmūd Ghāzān
663/1265	Abaqa	703/1304	Muḥammad Khudābanda Öljeytü [Ūljaytū]
680/1282	Aḥmad Tegüder [Takūdār]	716/1317	Abū Saᶜīd
683/1284	Arghūn	736/1335	Arpa
690/1291	Gaykhatu	737/1336	Mūsā
694/1295	Baydu	[736-54/1336-53	Period of several rival *khāns*]

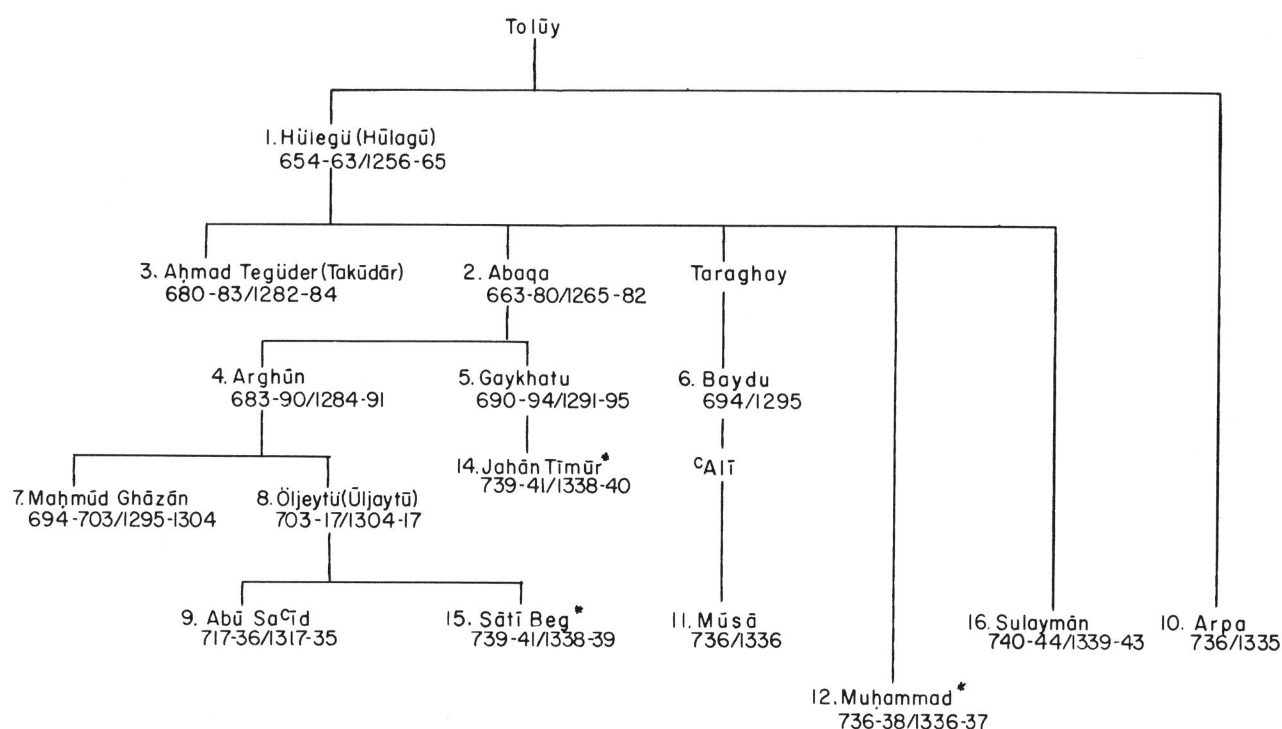

13. Tughiā Tīmūr* (738-52/1337-51)

*Nominated by other powers.

X. IRAN [After the Mongols]

		Muslim Dates	Christian Dates
	A. Jalāyirids	736 - 835 A.H.	1336 - 1432 A.D.
	B. Muzaffarids	713 - 795	1314 - 1393
	C. Īnjūids	703 - 758	1303 - 1357
	D. Sarbadārids	758 - 781	1357 - 1379
	E. Karts	643 - 791	1245 - 1389
	F. Qara Qoyunlu	782 - 873	1380 - 1468
	G. Aq Qoyunlu	780 - 914	1378 - 1508
*+	H. Ṣafavids	907 - 1145	1501 - 1732
*	I. Afshārids	1148 - 1210	1736 - 1795
*	J. Zands	1163 - 1209	1750 - 1794
*+	K. Qājārs	1193 - 1342	1779 - 1924
*	L. Pahlavi	1344 - 1400	1925 - 1979
*	M. Presidents of Islamic Republic of Iran	1400 -	1979 -

H. Ṣafavids

907/1501	Ismā^{c}īl I	1038/1629	Ṣafī I	1145/1732	^{c}Abbās III
930/1524	Ṭahmāsp I	1052/1642	^{c}Abbās II	1163/1749	Sulaymān II
984/1576	Ismā^{c}īl II	1077/1666	Sulaymān I [Ṣafī II]	1163/1750	Ismā^{c}īl III
985/1578	Muḥammad Khudabānda	1105/1694	Ḥusayn I	1166/1753	Ḥusayn II
996/1588	^{c}Abbās I	1135/1722	Ṭahmāsp II	1200/1786	Muḥammad

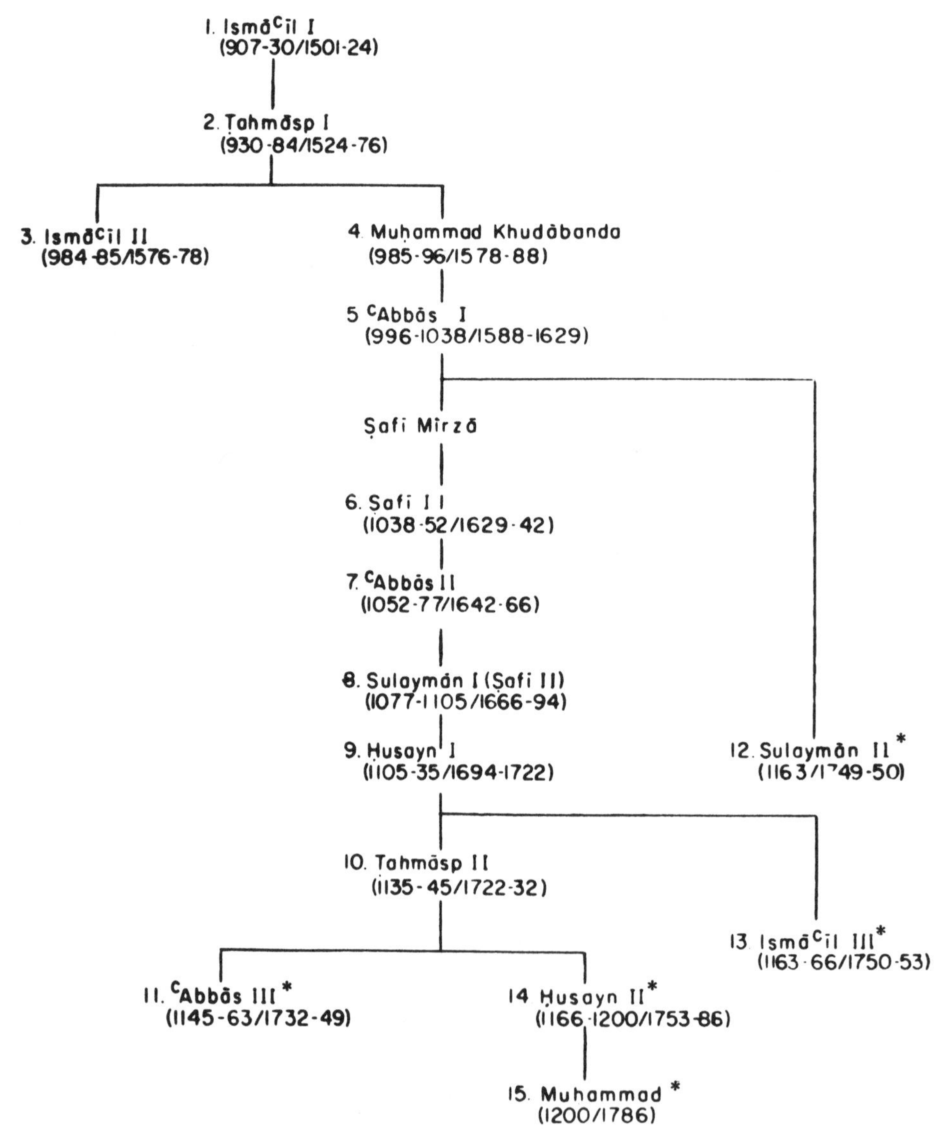

I. Afshārids

1148/1736	Nādir Shāh [Ṭahmāsp Qulī Khān]	1161/1748	Ibrāhīm
1160/1747	^{c}Ādil Shāh [^{c}Alī Qulī Khān]	1161-1210/1748-95	Shāh Rukh [in Khurāsān]

J. The Zands

1163/1750	Muḥammad Karīm Khān
1193/1779	Abū-l-Fatḥ] Joint Rulers Muḥammad ʿAlī]
1193-95/1779-81	Ṣādiq [in Shīrāz]
1193-99/1779-85	ʿAlī Murād [in Iṣfahān]
1199/1785	Jaʿfar
1203-09/1789-94	Luṭf ʿAlī

K. The Qājārs

1193/1779	Āghā Muḥammad
1212/1797	Fatḥ ʿAlī Shāh
1250/1834	Muḥammad
1264/1848	Nāṣir al-Dīn
1313/1896	Muẓaffar al-Dīn
1324/1907	Muḥammad ʿAlī
1327-42/1909-24	Aḥmad

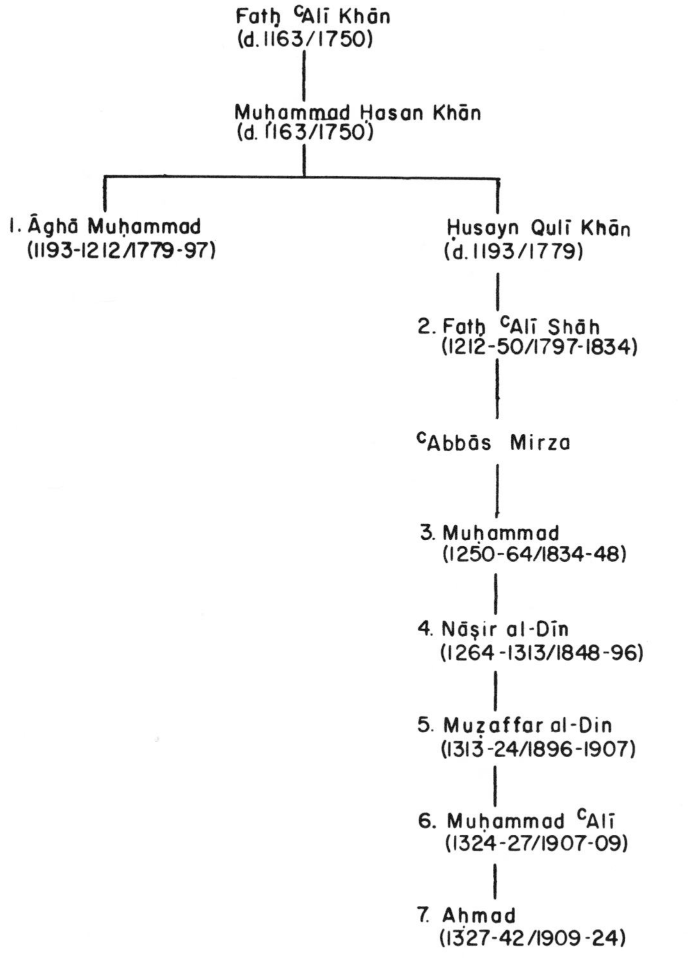

L. Pahlavi Dynasty

1925 - 1941	Reza Shāh
1941 - 1979	Mohammed Reza Shāh

M. Presidents of Islamic Republic of Iran

1980 Abū-l-Ḥasan Banī-Sadr

1981 Muḥammad ^{c}Alī Rajā'i

TRANSOXIANA AND AFGHANISTAN

		Muslim Dates	Christian Dates
*	A. Tīmūrids	771 - 912 A.H.	1370 - 1506 A.D.
	B. Shaybānids	905 - 1007	1500 - 1598
	C. Jānids	1009 - 1199	1559 - 1785
	D. Mangits	1170 - 1339	1757 - 1920
	E. Khāns of Khiva	921 - 1290	1515 - 1872
*+	F. Ghaznavids	366 - 582	977 - 1186
	G. Ghūrids	390 - 612	1000 - 1215

A. Tīmūrids

771/1370	Tīmūr [Temur]	854/1450	^{c}Abdullāh
807/1405	Khalīl [until 812/1409]	855/1451	Abū Sa^{c}īd
807/1405	Shāh Rukh	873/1469	Aḥmad
850/1447	Ulugh Beg	899-906/1494-1500	Maḥmūd b. Abī Sa^{c}īd
853/1449	^{c}Abd al-Laṭīf		

F. Ghaznavids

366/977	Nāṣir al-Dawla Sebüktigīn	444/1053	Qawām al-Dawla Toghril [Usurper]
387/997	Ismā^{c}īl	444/1053	Farrukhzād
388/998	Maḥmūd	451/1059	Ibrāhīm
421/1030	Muḥammad [1st reign]	492/1099	Mas^{c}ūd III
421/1031	Mas^{c}ūd I	508/1114	Shīrzād
432/1041	Muḥammad [2nd reign]	509/1115	Arslān Shāh
432/1041	Shihāb al-Dawla Mawdūd	512/1118	Bahrām Shāh
441/1050	Mas^{c}ūd II	547/1152	Khusraw Shāh
441/1050	^{c}Alī	555-582/1160-86	Khusraw Malik
441/1050	^{c}Abd al-Rashīd		

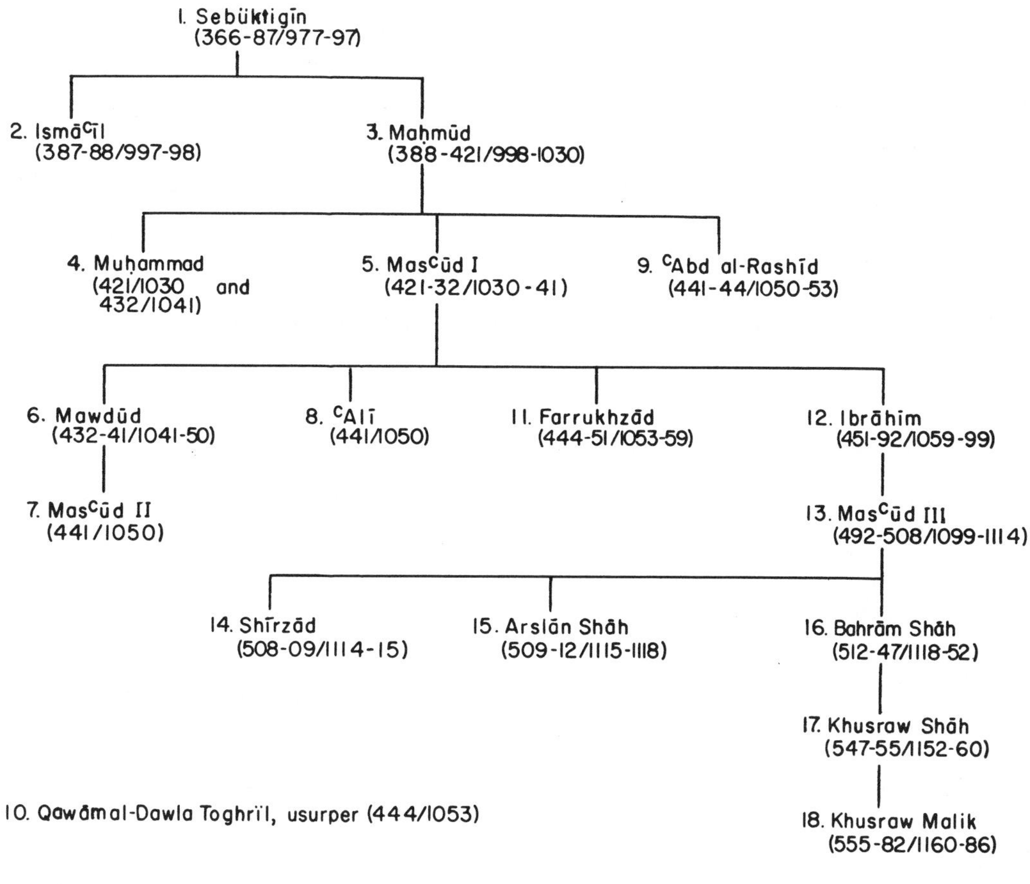

IRAQ AND GREATER SYRIA [Since World War I]

		Christian Dates
*	A. British High Commissioners for Palestine	1920 - 1948 A.D.
	B. French High Commissioners and Delegate Generals:	
*	1. Lebanon	1919 - 1926
*	2. Syria	1923 - 1946
	C. Ḥāshimites:	
*+	1. Hejaz	1908 - 1925
*+	2. Jordan/Transjordan	1921 -
*+	3. Iraq	1921 - 1958
*	D. Presidents of Lebanon	1926 -
*	E. Rulers of Syria	1945 -
*	F. Presidents of Israel	1948 -
*	G. Prime Ministers of Israel	1949 -
*	H. Rulers of Iraq	1958 -

A. Palestine - British High Commissioners

1920	Sir Herbert Samuel	1937	Sir Harold MacMichael
1925	Lord Plumer	1944	Lord Gorst
1928	Sir John Chancellor	1945-48	Sir Alan Cunningham
1931	Sir Arthur Wauchope		

B.1. Lebanon - French High Commissioners and Delegate Generals

1919	Gen. Henri Gouraud	1926	Henri Ponsot

B.2. Syria - French High Commissioners and Delegate Generals

1923	Gen. Maxime Weygand	1940	Gen. Henri-Fernand Dentz
1925	Gen. Maurice Sarrail	1941	Gen. Georges Catroux
1925	Henri de Jouvenal	1943	Yves Chataigneau
1933	Damien de Martel	1943	Jean Helleu
1938	Gabriel Puaux	1944-46	Gen. Paul Emile Beynet

C.1. Ḥāshimites - Hejaz

1908	Ḥusayn [Amīr]	1924-25	ᶜAlī
1916	Ḥusayn [King]		

C.2. Ḥāshimites - Transjordan/Jordan

1921	ᶜAbdallāh [Amīr]	1952	Ḥusayn
1946	ᶜAbdallāh [King]		
1951	Ṭalāl		

C.3. Ḥāshimites - Iraq

1921	Fayṣal I	1939-58	Fayṣal II
1933	Ghāzī		

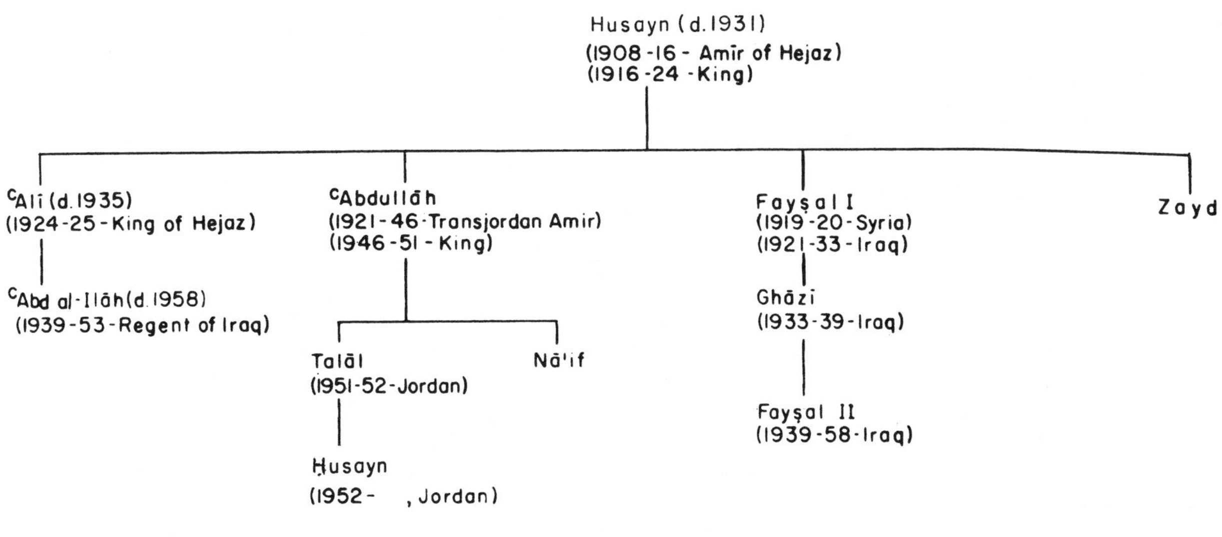

D. Presidents of Lebanon

1926 Sharl Dabbās [Charles Dabbas]
1934 Ḥabīb al-Sa^{c}d [Habib Sa'd]
1936 Imīl Iddi [Emile Edde]
1941 Alfred Naqqāsh [Alfred Naccache]
1943 ^{c}Ayyūb Thābit [Eyub Tabet]
1943 Batru Trād [Petro Trad]
1943 Bishārah al-Khūrī [Bishara Khuri]
1952 Kamīl Shim^{c}ūn [Camille Chamoun]
1958 Fu'ād Shihāb [Gen. Fouad Chehab]
1964 Sharl Ḥilū [Charles Helou]
1970 Sulaymān Franjīyah [Suleiman Franjieh]
1976 Ilyās Sarkīs [Elias Sarkis]
1982 Amīn al-Jumayyil [Amin Gemayel]

E. Rulers of Syria

1945 Shukrī al-Quwatlī
1949 Husnī Za^{c}īm
1949 Sāmī al-Ḥinnāwī
1949 Adīb Shīshaklī
1954 Akram al-Hawranī] Diumvirate
^{c}Abd al-Ḥamīd al-Sarrāj]
1958 United Arab Republic
1961 Naẓīm al-Qudsī [President]
1963 Amīn al-Ḥāfiz
1966 Ṣalāḥ Jadīd
1970 Ḥāfiẓ al-Asad

F. Presidents of Israel

1948 Chaim Weizmann
1952 Itzhak Ben-Zvi
1963 Zalman Shazar
1973 Ephraim Katzir
1978 Itzhak Navon
1983 Chaim Herzog

G. Prime Ministers of Israel

1949 David Ben-Gurion
1953 Moshe Sharett
1955 David Ben-Gurion
1963 Levi Eshkol [d. February 26, 1969]
1969 Golda Meir [d. December 8, 1978]
1974 Yitzhak Rabin
1977 Menachem Begin
1983 Yitzhak Shamir

H. Rulers of Iraq

1958 ^{c}Abd al-Ḥamīd Qāsim
1963 ^{c}Abd al-Ṣalām ^{c}Ārif
1966 ^{c}Abd al-Raḥmān ^{c}Ārif
1968 Aḥmad Ḥasan al-Bakr
1979 Ṣaddām Ḥusayn al-Takrītī

V. Supplementary Charts

Major Ṣūfī Isnāds
Major Arab Tribes: Skeleton Outline
Time Chart, 600-1800 A.D.
Semitic (Afro-Asiatic) Family of Languages
Indo-European and Altaic Families of Languages

MAJOR ṢŪFĪ ISNĀDS

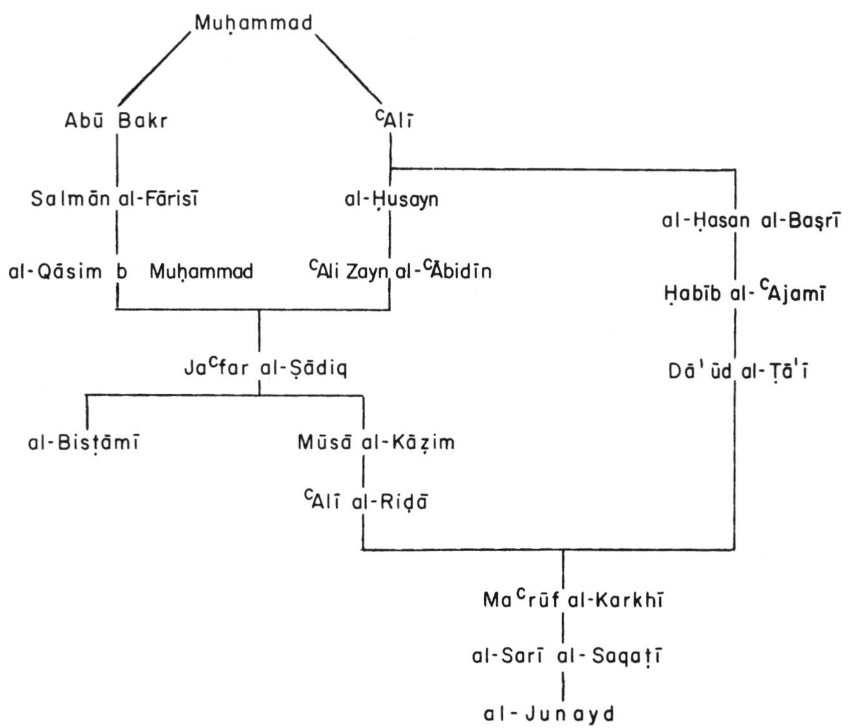

MAJOR ARAB TRIBES: SKELETON OUTLINE

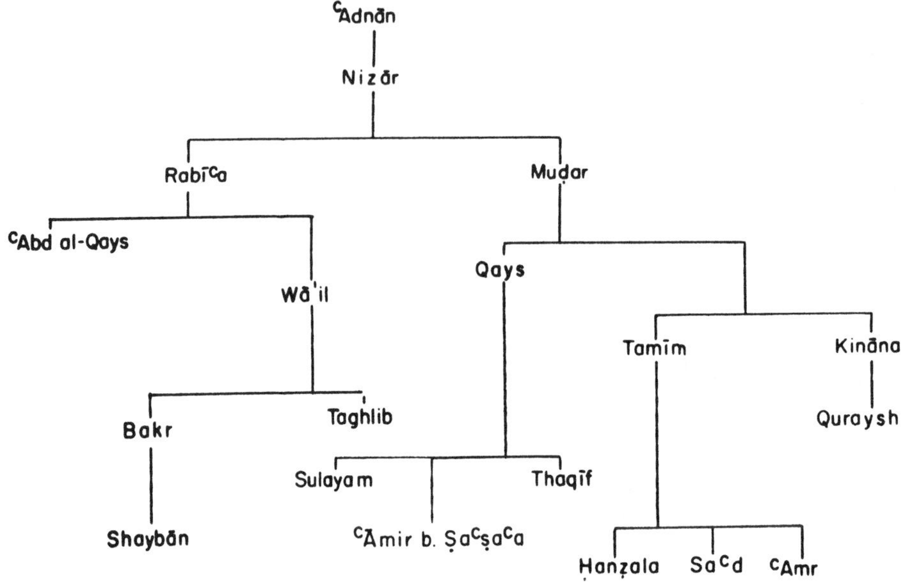

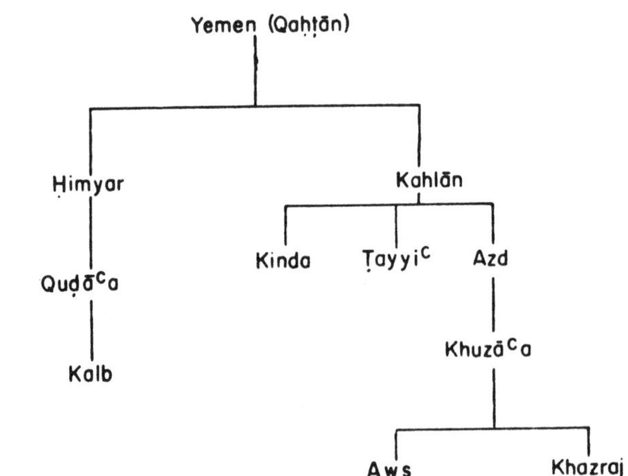

C. TIME CHART, 600 to 1800 A.D.

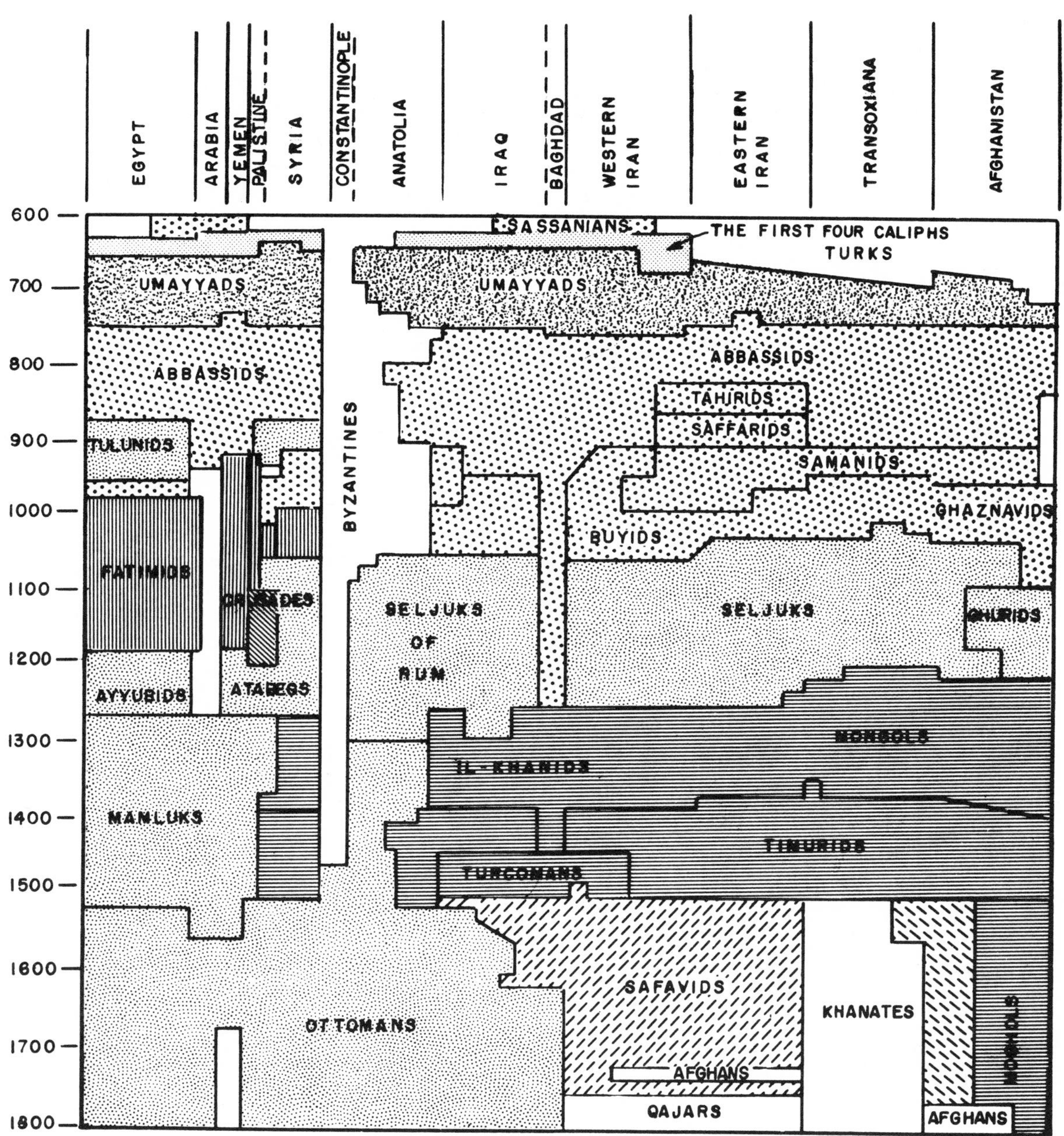

SEMITIC [AFRO-ASIATIC] FAMILY OF LANGUAGES

- Semitic Family
  - East (Akkadian)
    - *I. Old Akkadian
      - *A. Babylonian
      - B. Assyrian
  - West
    - Northwest
      - A. Costal
        - * I. Ugaritic
        - 2. Canaanite
          - * a. Proto-Palestinian
          - * b. Moabite
          - *c. Phoenician
          - d. Hebrew
            - * I. Biblical
            - *2. Mishnaic
            - *3. Medieval
            - 4. Modern
      - B. Inland
        - I. Aramaic
          - *a. Old Aramaic
          - *b. Imperial Aramaic
          - *c. Biblical Aramaic
          - A. Western
            - * I. Jewish Palestinian
            - *2. Christian Palestinian
            - *3. Palmyranean
            - *4. Nabataean
            - 5. Modern Aramaic
          - B. Eastern
            - * I. Jewish Babylonian
            - *2. Mandaean
            - 3. Syriac
              - *a. Western (Jacobite)
              - *b. Eastern (Nestorian)
              - c. Modern Syriac
    - Southwest
      - I. North Arabic
        - A. Pre-Classical
          - * I. Lihyanian
          - *2. Talmudic
          - *3. Safaitic
        - B. Classical
          - I. Modern Literary
        - C. Modern (Spoken)
          - I. Arabian
          - 2. Iraqi
          - 3. Syro-Palestinian
          - 4. Egyptian
          - 5. Maghribi
            - a. Maltese
          - 6. Hassani (Mauretanian)
      - 2. South Arabic
        - A. Ancient
          - * I. Sabaean
          - *2. Minaean
          - *3. Himyaritic
          - *4. Qatabanian
        - B. Modern (Spoken)
          - I. Hadara Group
          - 2. Soqoṭri
        - C. Ethiopic
          - North
          - South

*indicates that language or dialect is extinct

INDO-EUROPEAN and ALTAIC FAMILIES OF LANGUAGES

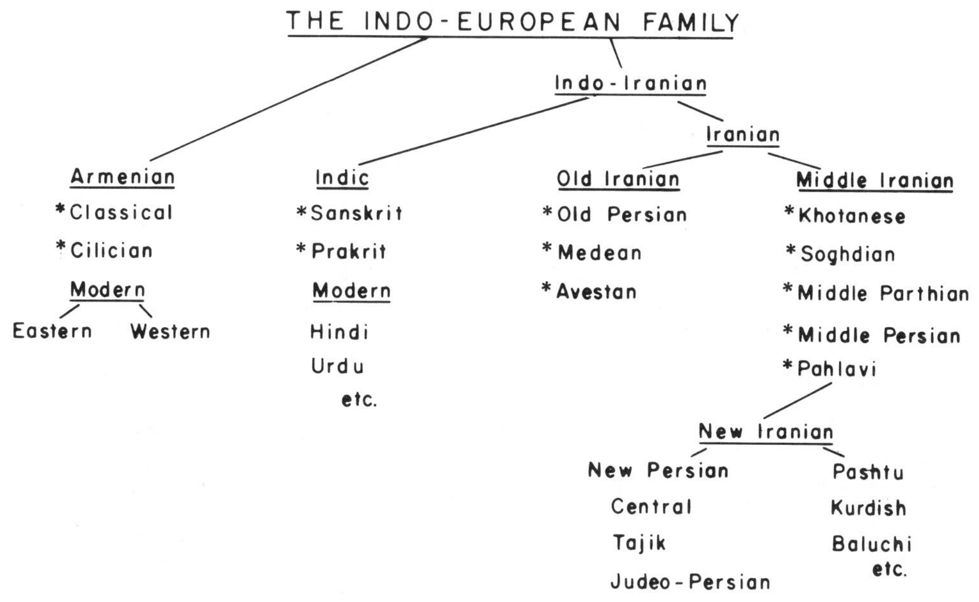

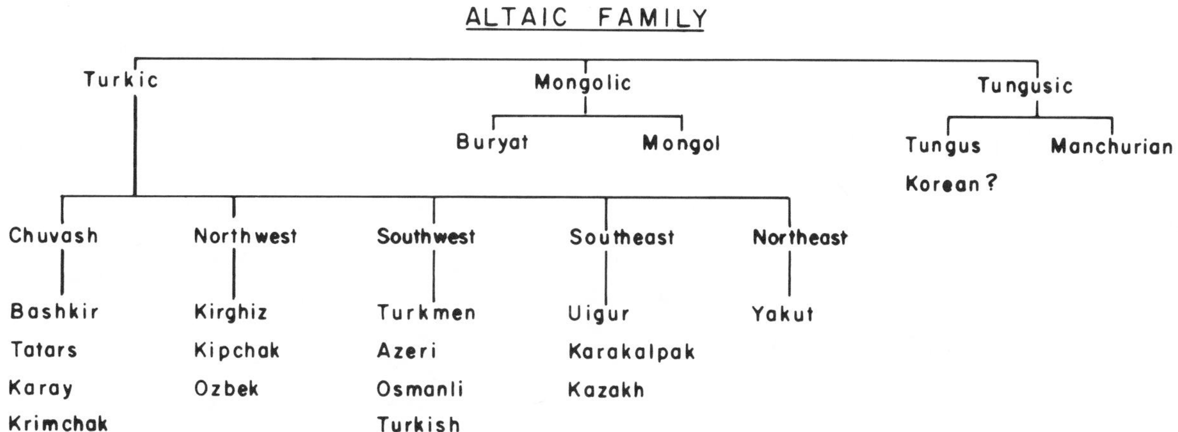

VI. Chronology

The selecting of items for this chonological list is based upon the author's teaching and research experiences. For example, some of the previously listed dynasties, rulers and administrators are listed, but not all of them. In most cases, there is general agreement among scholars as to when events took place, except for incidents during the first three decades of Islam. The foundation dates for the city of al-Kūfa are given in the medieval Arabic sources as A.H. 15, 16, 17 and 18, or any one of four years between 636 and 640 A.D. I have chosen 637. The few other cases of disagreement represent one-year variations between sources.

The most detailed chronology for the period to *circa* 1800 is by Marshall G.S. Hodgson. *The Venture of Islam*, 3 vols. (Chicago: University of Chicago Press, 1974), in his numerous tables. For events since 1947, *MEJ* includes a chronology at the end of each quarterly volume, and they are extremely valuable. Two new annuals are also very helpful:

- Colin Legum, ed., *Middle East Contemporary Survey* (New York: Holmes and Meier), with the first volume covering October 1976 to October 1977.
- David H. Partington, ed., *The Middle East Annual* (Boston: G.K. Hall & Co.), with Volume 1 covering 1981.

There are also various standard references for current events or annual surveys which can be used.

570	Traditional date for birth of Muḥammad.
602	End of Lakhmid dynasty at Ḥīra.
610	Muḥammad received first revelation.
615	Emigration of some Muslims from Mecca to Abyssinia.
622	*Hijra*: Beginning of Muslim calendar.
	Sept. 24: Muḥammad's arrival at Yathrib [Medina/Madīna].
624	Muḥammad's victory at Badr.
625	Muḥammad's temporary defeat at Uḥud.
627	Battle of the Khandaq [Trench] at Medina. Meccans repulsed.
628	Agreement at al-Ḥudaybīyah between Muḥammad and Meccans.
629	Pilgrimage to Mecca.
630	Mecca under Muslim rule.
630-631	"Year of Delegations" of Arab tribal leaders to Muḥammad.
632	March 16 [18 Dhū-l-Ḥijja A.H. 10]: Ghadīr Khumm where, according to Shī^cite tradition, Muḥammad appointed ^cAlī his successor.
632	June 8: Death of Muḥammad.
632-634	Reign of Caliph Abū Bakr.
633	End of al-Ridda Wars. Defeat of Musaylima by Khālid b. al-Walīd.
634	Defeat of Byzantines at Ajnadayn.
	Aug.: Death of Abū Bakr.
634-644	Reign of Caliph ^cUmar.
635	Occupation of Damascus by Khālid b. al-Walīd.
	Expulsion by ^cUmar of Jews from Khaybar and Christians from Najrān.
636	Defeat of Sassanians at Qādisīya.
637	Defeat of Byzantines at Yarmūk.
	Muslim conquest of Ctesiphon, Sassanian capital.
	Kufa [al-Kūfa] and Basra [al-Baṣra] established as garrison bases [*amṣār*].

638 Muslim conquest of Jerusalem.

640 Jan.: ^{c}Amr b. al-^{c}Āṣ entered Egypt.

641 ^{c}Amr b. al-^{c}Āṣ captured Babylon.
Fusṭāt founded.
Defeat of Sassanians at Nihawend and fall of Persia.

644 Nov.: Murder of ^{c}Umar by a non-Muslim slave.

644-656 Reign of Caliph ^{c}Uthmān.

646 Final capture of Alexandria, previously held from 642-645.

649 Conquest of Cyprus by Mu^{c}āwiya, Governor of Syria.

651 Yazdigird III, last Sassanian ruler, murdered at Merv.

656 June: Assassination of ^{c}Uthmān by Muslims.
Dec. 9: Battle of the Camel near Basra; ^{c}Alī defeated al-Zubayr, Ṭalḥa and ^{c}Ā'isha.

656-661 Reign of Caliph ^{c}Alī.
First civil war.

c.658 Battle of Ṣiffīn between ^{c}Alī and Mu^{c}āwiya.

c.659 Arbitration at Adhruh.
Battle between ^{c}Alī and Kharijites at Nahrawān Canal.

661 Jan. 24: ^{c}Alī murdered by a Kharijite.
Ḥasan b. ^{c}Alī renounced claim to caliphate.

661-680 Reign of Caliph Mu^{c}āwiya I.

661-750 Umayyad Dynasty.

662-675 Ziyād ibn Abīhi, Governor of Basra; then of Kufa as well.

667 Arabs cross Amū Darya [Oxus].

670 Establishment of Qayrawān.
^{c}Uqba b. Nāfi^{c} [d. 683] active in North Africa.

674-679 Siege of Constantinople failed.

680 Oct. 10 [10th Muḥarram A.H. 61]: Ḥusayn b. ^{c}Alī martyred at Karbalā'.

680-683 Reign of Caliph Yazīd I.

683-692 *Fitnah* of Ibn al-Zubayr [2nd civil war].

683-684 Reign of Caliph Mu^{c}āwiya II.

684-685 Reign of Caliph Marwān I.

684 July: Battle of Marj Rāḥit.
Victory of Kalb over Qays.

685-687 Revolt of Mukhtār at al-Kūfa.

685-705 Reign of Caliph ^{c}Abd al-Malik.

692 al-Ḥajjāj b. Yūsuf ended *fitnah* of Ibn al-Zubayr; occupied Mecca.

694-714 al-Ḥajjāj b. Yūsuf, Governor of Iraq.

696 Introduction of all-Arabic coinage.

705-715 Reign of Caliph Walīd I.

705 Umayyad mosque of Damascus built.

c.705 Wāsiṭ founded a garrison city.

711 Ṭāriq, subordinate of Mūsā b. Nuṣayr, invaded Spain.

711-713 Conquest of Sind and Transoxiana.

714 Death of al-Ḥajjāj.

717-718 Siege of Constantinople under Maslama failed.

717 First Muslim expedition across Pyrenees.

717-720 Reign of Caliph ^{c}Umar II.

720-724 Reign of Caliph Yazīd II.

720-759 Occupation of Narbonne.

724-743 Reign of Caliph Hishām.

728 Death of mystic, al-Ḥasan al-Baṣrī.

732 Battle of Tours [Poitiers].
Charles Martel defeated Muslims.

739-742 Anti-Arab Berber revolt in North Africa.

740 Failure of Shī^{c}ite revolt.
Death of Zayd.

745-750 Reign of Caliph Marwān II.

747 June: ^{c}Abbāsid revolt begun by Abū Muslim near Merv.
Third civil war.

749 Sept.: ^{c}Abbāsid troops took Kufa.
Nov.: Abū-l-^{c}Abbās [posthumously called al-Saffāḥ] proclaimed caliph at Kufa.

750 Feb.: Marwān defeated at Battle of Greater Zāb.
June: Massacre of most Umayyad family members by ^{c}Abbāsids.

750-1258 ^{c}Abbāsid dynasty.

750-754 Reign of Caliph Abū-l-^{c}Abbās al-Saffāḥ.

754-775 Reign of Caliph Abū Ja^{c}far al-Manṣūr.

755-1031 Umayyad dynasty of Spain.

755 Assassination of Abū Muslim by order of al-Manṣūr.

755-788 ^{c}Abd al-Raḥmān I in Cordoba.

757 Death of translator and author of Arabic prose, Ibn al-Muqaffa^{c}.

762 Founding of Baghdad [Madīnat al-Salām].
Unsuccessful Shī^{c}ite revolt at Medina by Muḥammad b. ^{c}Abdullāh, "The Pure Soul."

763 Death of Shī^{c}ite, Ibrāhīm b. ^{c}Abdullāh.

765 Death of Ja^{c}far al-Ṣādiq, 6th Shī^{c}ite Imām.

767 Death of jurisconsult, Abū Ḥanīfa.
Death of Ibn Iṣḥāq, biographer of Muḥammad.

775-785 Reign of Caliph al-Mahdī.

785-786 Reign of Caliph al-Hādī.

786-809 Reign of Caliph Hārūn al-Rashīd.

792 al-Amīn designated successor to Hārūn al-Rashīd.

795 Death of jurisconsult, Mālik b. Anas.

798 Death of jurisconsult, Abū Yūsuf, of the Hanafite *madhhab*.

799 al-Ma'mūn designated 2nd successor to Hārūn al-Rashīd.

800-909 Aghlabid dynasty of North Africa.

801 Death of female mystic, Rābi^{c}a.

803 Fall of Barmakid family.

805 Death of jurisconsult, al-Shaybānī of the Hanafite *madhhab*.

806 Major Muslim attack against Byzantium.

809-813 Reign of Caliph al-Amīn.
Fourth civil war.

812 Siege of Baghdad by Ṭāhir.

813-833 Reign of Caliph al-Ma'mūn.

816-838 Revolt of Babak, primarily in Azerbaijan.

817 al-Ma'mūn designated ^{c}Alī al-Riḍā [d. 818] as successor.

819 al-Ma'mūn entered Baghdad.

820 Death of jurisconsult, al-Shāfi^{c}ī.

821-873 Ṭāhirid dynasty of Khurāsān.

827 al-Ma'mūn established Mu^{c}tazilite doctrines as "orthodoxy."

829-831 Revolt of Copts in Egypt.

833-842 Reign of Caliph al-Mu^{c}taṣim.

836-889 Samarra ^{c}Abbāsid capital.

842-847 Reign of Caliph al-Wāthiq.

847-861 Reign of Caliph al-Mutawakkil.

855 Death of jurisconsult, Aḥmad b. Ḥanbal.

861-908 Most active period of Ṣaffārid dynasty, led by Ya^{c}qub al-Ṣaffār [d. 879].

864 Zaydī Shī^{c}ite dynasty established in Daylam.

868 Death of writer, al-Jāḥiz.

868-905 Ṭūlūnid dynasty of Egypt founded by Aḥmad b. Ṭūlūn [808-884].

869-892 Reign of Caliph al-Mu^{c}tamid, regent.
al-Muwaffaq took charge of ^{c}Abbāsid army.

869-883 Zanj revolt.

870 Conquest of Malta.
Death of *ḥadīth* collector, al-Bukhārī.

871 Zanj sacked Basra.

873 Death of philosopher, al-Kindī.
Death of translator, Ḥunayn b. Isḥāq.
Disappearance of 12th Shī^{c}ite Imām.

873-940 Lesser or Little Occulation [Ghaybah] for Ithnā ^{c}Asharī.

874-999 Sāmānid dynasty of Transoxiana.

877 Aḥmad b. Ṭūlūn began building mosque in al-Qaṭā^{c}i.

880s Rise of Qarmatians.

883 Death of jurisconsult, Dāwūd b. Khalaf of the Ẓāhirī *madhhab*.

886 Peace agreement between Ṭūlūnid Khumārawayh and Caliph al-Mu^{c}tamid.

890-1008 Major line of Ḥamdānid dynasty of Iraq and Syria.

892 Death of historian, Aḥmad al-Balādhurī.

901 Establishment of Shī^{c}ite Zaydī state in Yemen.

902-908 Reign of Caliph al-Muktafī.

908 Dec. 17: One-day caliphate of Ibn al-Mu^{c}tazz.
Revolt in name of Fāṭimid dynasty in North Africa.

909-1171 Fāṭimid dynasty.

910 Death of mystic, al-Junayd.

922 Death of mystic, al-Ḥallāj.

923 Death of historian, al-Ṭabarī.

925 Death of physician, al-Rāzī.

928 Qarmatians stole Black Stone from Ka^{c}ba; held it until 951.

929 ^{c}Abd al-Raḥmān III [912-961] of Umayyads of Spain took title of "caliph."

932-1062 Būyids of Iraq and Iran.

935-969 Ikhshīdid dynasty of Egypt founded by Muḥammad b. Ṭughj.

935 Death of theologian, al-Ash^{c}arī.

936 Ibn Rā'iq became *amīr al-umarā'*.

940 Beginning of Greater Occulation [Ghaybah] for Ithnā ^{c}Asharī.

944 Peace agreement between Muḥammad b. Ṭughj al-Ikhshīd and Caliph al-Muttaqī.

945-1055 Būyids occupied Baghdad.

950 Death of philosopher, al-Fārābī.

953-975 Reign of al-Mu^{c}izz, Fāṭimid caliph.

956 Death of historian, al-Mas^{c}ūdī.

962-1186 Ghaznavid dynasty.

962 Alptegīn in Ghazna.

965 Death of poet, al-Mutanabbī.

966-968 Kāfūr ruled Egypt.

969 Jawhar conquered Egypt for Fāṭimids and founded Cairo.

973 al-Azhar was founded.

975-996 Reign of al-^{c}Azīz, Fāṭimid caliph.

996-1021 Reign of al-Ḥākim, Fāṭimid caliph.

998-1030 Maḥmūd of Ghazna.

1020 Death of poet Firdawsi, author of "Shāhnāma."

1030 Death of historian, Miskawayh.

1036-1094 Reign of al-Mustanṣir, Fāṭimid caliph.

1037 Death of philosopher, Ibn Sīnā [Avicenna].

1039 Death of optician, Ibn al-Haytham.

1048 Death of savant, al-Bīrūnī.

1055-1063 Ṭughril Beğ entered Baghdad as head of Seljuks.

1058 Death of political theorist, al-Māwardī.

Death of poet, Abū-l-^{c}Alā al-Ma^{c}arrī.

1059 Shī^{c}ite revolt in Iraq, led by al-Basāsīrī.

1063-1072 Reign of Alp Arslān, Seljuk sultan.

1064 Death of philosopher, Ibn Ḥazm.

1065 Establishment of Niẓāmiyyah *madrasa* in Baghdad.

1071 Aug. 26: Battle of Manzikert [Malazgirt] and Byzantine defeat.

1072-1092 Reign of Malik Shāh, Seljuk sultan.

1075 Seljuks of Rūm made Iznik [Nicaea] their capital.

1090 Ḥasan-i Ṣabbāh seized Alamut fortress.

1092 Niẓām al-Mulk murdered by Assassins.

1095 Nov.: Pope Urban at Clermont called for First Crusade.

1097 First Crusade at Constantinople; then took Iznik.

Konya became capital of Seljuks of Rūm.

1098 Crusaders captured Antioch.

1099 July 15: Jerusalem conquered by Crusaders.

1100 Baldwin became King of Jerusalem.

1111 Death of philosopher and mystic, al-Ghazzālī.

1118-1157 Reign of Sanjar, Seljuk sultan.

1123 Death of poet and astronomer, ^{c}Umar Khayyām.

1124 Death of al-Ḥasan b. al-Ṣabbāḥ, leader of Assassins.

1144 Zangī [1127-1146] captured Edessa [Urfa] from Crusaders.

1147 Second Crusade, led by Conrad II and Louis VII.

1148-1215 Ghūrid dynasty of Afghanistan.

1154 Nūr al-Dīn [1146-1174] captured Damascus.

1166 Death of *ṣūfī*, ^{c}Abd al-Qādir Gīlānī.

1169-1193 Ṣalāḥ al-Dīn [Saladin] controlled Egypt.

1171-1250 Ayyūbid dynasty in Egypt.

1171 Ṣalāḥ al-Dīn ended Fāṭimid dynasty and established Ayyūbid dynasty.

1176 Sept.: Kilij Arslān defeated Byzantine forces at Myriokephalon.

1180-1225 Reign of al-Nāṣir, ^{c}Abbāsid caliph.

1187 July 4: Ṣalāḥ al-Dīn victorious over Crusaders at Battle of Ḥaṭṭīn.

1189-1192 Third Crusade, led by Frederick Barbarossa, Philip Augustus and Richard I.

1198 Death of philosopher, Ibn Rushd [Averroës].

---

c.1200 Death of Persian writer, ^{c}Aṭṭār.

1200-1218 Reign of al-Malik al-^{c}Ādil, Ayyūbid sultan.

1203 Death of Persian poet, Niẓami.

1204-1261 Fourth Crusade and Latin occupation of Constantinople.

1206 Temuchin took title of Chingiz Khān.

1218 Fifth Crusade landed at Damietta.

1218-1238 Reign of al-Malik al-Kāmil, Ayyūbid sultan of Egypt.

1220 Khwarazm Shāhs defeated by Chingiz Khān.

1220-1231 Reign of Khwarazm Shāh Jalāl al-Dīn.

1227 Death of Ghengis Khān.

1229 Death of geographer, Yāqūt.

Peace treaty between Sixth Crusade, led by Frederick II, and al-Malik al-Kāmil.

1234 Death of historian, Ibn al-Athīr.

1235 Death of *ṣūfī* poet, Ibn al-Fārid.

1238-1492 Naṣrid dynasty of Granada.

1240 Death of philosopher, Ibn ^{c}Arabī.

1242-1258 Reign of al-Musta^{c}ṣim, last ^{c}Abbāsid caliph of Baghdad.

1243 Mongols defeated Seljuks of Rūm at Kösedagh near Sivas.

1244 Jerusalem taken by Khwarazmian troops.

1249 Seventh Crusade, led by Louis IX, landed at Damietta.

1250-1517 Mamlūk dynasty in Egypt.

1250 Shajar al-Durr, female ruler of Egypt.

1256 Hūlāgū took Assassin stronghold of Alamūt.

1256-1249 Īl-Khānid dynasty of Persia.

1258 Feb.: Hūlāgū sacked Baghdad and ended ^{c}Abbāsid caliphate.

1260 Sept. 3: Mamlūk victory at ^{c}Ayn Jālūt over Mongols.

1260-1277 Reign of Baybars, Mamlūk sultan.

1265 Death of Hūlāgū.

1271 Journey of Marco Polo through Persia to China.

1273 Death of mystic, Jalāl al-Dīn al-Rūmī.

1274 Death of astronomer, Nāṣir al-Dīn al-Ṭūṣī.

1279-1290 Reign of Qalā'ūn, Mamlūk sultan.

1282 Death of biographer, Ibn Khallikān.

1291 Fall of last Crusader stronghold in Levant, during Mamlūk sultanate of al-Ashraf Khalīl [1290-1293].

1291 Death of poet, Sa^{c}dī.

1294 Marco Polo in Persia on return to Europe.

1295-1304 Reign of Ghāzān Khān, Īl-Khānid ruler.

1317-1335 Reign of Abū Sa^{c}īd, Īl-Khānid ruler.

1318 Death of historian, Rashīd al-Dīn.

1324-1360 Reign of Orhān, Ottoman sultan.

1326 Ottomans captured Bursa.

1328 Death of Hanbalite, Ibn Taymīyyah.

1331 Ottoman conquest of Nicaea [Iznik].

1337 Ottoman conquest of Nicomedia [Izmit].

1345 First Ottoman campaign in Europe.

1354 Ottoman conquest of Ankara.

Ottoman occupation of Gallipoli.

c.1360-89 Reign of Murād I, Ottoman sultan.

1361 Murād captured Adrianople [Edirne].

1369 Tīmūr conquered Khurāsān and Transoxiana.

1371 Battle of Chermanon and Ottoman victory over Serbs.

1378-1469 Qara Qoyunlu [Black Sheep] dynasty in Armenia and Azerbaijan.

1378-1502 Aq Qoyunlu [White Sheep] dynasty in Iraq and Armenia.

1382-1517 Circassian or Burjī Mamlūk rule of Egypt and Syria.

1382-1398 Reign of Barqūq, Mamlūk sultan.

1385 Ottoman conquest of Sofia.

1386 Ottoman conquest of Nish.

1387 Ottoman conquest of Salonika.

1389 June 15: Battle of Kosovo and Ottoman victory over Serbs.

Death of poet, Ḥāfiẓ.

1389-1402 Reign of Bāyezīd I, Ottoman sultan.

1391-1398 First Ottoman siege of Constantinople.

1395 June: Wallachia became an Ottoman vassal state.

1396 Sept. 25: Battle of Nicopolis.
Ottoman victory over Venice, Hungary, Byzantium and Crusaders.

1397 Ottomans annexed Karamān lands, including Konya.

1398 Ottoman conquest of Vidin in Europe and Sivas in Anatolia.

1398-1399 Tīmūr attacked India and sacked Delhi.

1400-1401 Tīmūr attacked Syria and Asia Minor.
Captured Sivas.

1402 July 28: Battle of Ankara.
Tīmūr captured Bāyezīd.

1402-1413 Civil war primarily among Bāyezīd's sons: Süleymān, Meḥmed and ᶜĪsā.

1403 Ottomans lost Salonika.
Death of Bāyezīd.

1405 Feb. 18: Death of Tīmūr.

1405-1447 Reign of Shāh Rukh of the Tīmūrids.

1406 Death of Ibn Khaldūn, historian.

1413 Meḥmet I unified Ottoman territories.

1415 Meḥmet reconquered Smyrna [Izmir].

1418-1422 Revolt of Muṣṭafā the False [Düzme Muṣṭafā].

1421-1451 Reign of Murād II, Ottoman sultan.

1422 Second Ottoman siege of Constantinople.

1422-1437 Reign of Barsbāy, Mamlūk sultan.

1425-1430 Ottoman-Venetian War.

1430 Ottomans reconquered Salonika.

1440 Ottomans failed to take Belgrade.

1442 Death of historian, al-Maqrīzī.

1443 Iskender Beğ [Scanderbeğ/Georges Kastriote] rebelled in northern Albania.

1444 Murād II abdicated in favor of Meḥmet II.
Nov. 10: Battle of Varna; Ottoman defeat of Hungarian King Ladislas and John Hunyadi.

1446 Murād II's second accession to Ottoman sultanate.

1448 Oct.17-19: Second Battle of Kosovo.
Ottomans defeated Hungarians.

1449 Death of ruler and astronomer, Ulugh Beğ.

1451 Feb. 3: Death of Murād II.

1451-1481 Reign of Meḥmet II, Ottoman sultan.

1452 Ottoman fortress of Rumeli Hisari erected.

1453 Apr. 6-May 29: Ottoman siege and capture of Constantinople.

1455 Ottomans made Moldavia a tribute state.

1456 Ottomans failed again to take Belgrade.

1459 Ottomans' final defeat of Serbs after death of George Brancovich.

1460 Meḥmet II conquered Morea.

1461 Ottoman conquest of Trebizond.

1463-1479 Ottoman-Venetian War.

1464 Completion of Topkapı Sarayı in Istanbul.

1466-1470 Inconclusive war between Mamlūks and Ottomans.

1468 Meḥmet II re-annexed Karamān lands in Anatolia.
Jan. 17: Death of Iskender Beğ.

1468-1496 Reign of Qāyitbāy, Mamlūk sultan.

1469 Death of historian, Ibn Taghrī Birdī.

1471-1478 Uzun Ḥasan, Aq Qoyunlu ruler, active in European support against Ottomans.

1472 Venetian, Cypriot and Uzun Ḥasan alliance against Ottomans.

1475 Ottoman conquest of Genoese colonies in Crimea.
Ottoman suzerainty over khānate of Crimea.

1479 Ottoman-Venetian peace.

1480-1481 Ottomans occupied Otranto, Italy.

1481 May 3: Death of Meḥmet II.
May 20: Accession of Bāyezīd II.
June 20: Battle of Yenisehir.
Bāyezīd II defeated Cem, his brother and rival.

1481-1512 Reign of Bāyezīd II, Ottoman sultan.

1483 Ottomans annexed Herzegovina.

1484 Ottomans annexed Kilia and Akkerman.

1487	Bartholomew Diaz rounded Cape of Good Hope by vessel.
1492	Fall of Naṣrid dynasty in Granada to Christians.
	Death of *ṣūfī* poet, Jāmī.
1495	Feb. 25: Death of Ottoman, Prince Cem, in Naples.
1497	Bābur, eventual founder of Mughal dynasty, captured Samarqand.
1499	Ismāʿīl established Ṣafavid dynasty in Iran.
	Ottoman conquest of Lepanto.
1499-1502	Ottoman war with Venice.
1500-1516	Reign of Qānṣūh al-Ghawrī, Mamlūk sultan.
1502	Ṣafavid capital established at Tabriz.
1504	Ṣafavid Shāh Ismāʿīl took Baghdad.
1505	Bābur established Mughal dynasty in India.
	Death of encyclopedist, al-Suyūtī.
1506	Death of painter, Bihzād.
1507	Portuguese attacked Hormuz.
1509-1513	Increasing struggle for power primarily among Bāyezīd's sons: Korkūd, Aḥmed and Selīm.
1511	Rebellion of Shāh Kuli in Anatolia.
1512-1520	Reign of Selīm I, Ottoman sultan after deposing his father, Bāyezīd II.
1512	Withdrawal of Bābur from Central Asia.
1514	Aug. 23: Selīm I defeated Shāh Ismāʿīl and his Qizilbash troops at Chāldirān.
1516	Portuguese, under d'Albuquerque, took Hormuz.
	Aug. 24: Ottoman victory over Mamlūks at Marj Dābiq.
1517	Jan.: Ottoman conquest of Egypt.
1520-1566	Reign of Süleymān I, Ottoman sultan.
1521	Ottoman conquest of Belgrade.
1522	Ottoman conquest of Rhodes.
1524-1525	Revolt of Aḥmad Pāshā in Egypt; suppressed by Ibrāhīm, Ottoman Grand Wazīr.
1524-1576	Reign of Ṭahmāsp, Ṣafavid shah.
1526	Aug. 29: Ottoman victory over Hungarians at Battle of Mohács.
1528	Ottomans captured Buda.
1529	Sept.-Oct.: Ottoman siege of Vienna.
1530	Death of Bābur.
1533	Armistice of Istanbul between Süleymān and Hapsburg Archduke Ferdinand.
	War between Ṣafavids and Ottomans.
	Barbarossa made Ottoman Grand Admiral.
1534	Ottomans captured Tabriz and Baghdad.
1535	Ottoman-French alliance.
1537-1540	Ottoman-Venetian War.
1538	Ottomans annexed Hungary; third capture of Buda.
1547	Ottoman-Hapsburg peace.
1548	Ottoman-Ṣafavid War.
1550	Süleymāniye mosque built by Sinan in Istanbul.
1551-1562	Ottoman-Austrian War.
1552	Ottomans failed to dislodge Portuguese from Hormuz.
1553-1555	Ottoman war with Ṣafavids.
1555	May 29: Ottoman-Ṣafavid Peace Treaty at Amasya.
	Revolt against Süleymān in name of executed son, known as the second Düzme [False] Muṣṭafā.
1558-1560	Struggle for power between Süleymān's sons, Selīm and Bāyezīd.
1561	Ṭahmāsp made Qazvīn Ṣafavid capital.
1566	Sept. 6: Süleyman's death before fortress of Szigetvar.
1566-1574	Reign of Selīm II, Ottoman sultan.
1569	Ottoman campaign against Russians.
	Ottoman campaign in Yemen.
1571	Ottoman conquest of Famagusta, Cyprus.
	Oct. 7: Ottoman naval loss to Holy League at Lepanto.
1578	Ottomans annexed Georgia and Derbent.
1578-1639	Ottoman-Ṣafavid wars.
1588-1629	Reign of ʿAbbās I, Ṣafavid shah.
1590	Ottoman-Ṣafavid peace.
1593-1606	Ottoman-Austrian War.
1596-1610	Major problem with *celali* in Anatolia.

1600 Shāh ᶜAbbās made Iṣfahān the Ṣafavid capital.
Death of Ottoman poet, Bāzī.
1602 Shāh ᶜAbbās captured Baḥrain from the Portuguese.
1603 Shāh ᶜAbbās captured Tabriz.
1606 Ottoman-Austrian Peace Treaty at Zsitva-Török.
1622 English captured Hormuz.
1623 Shāh ᶜAbbās I captured Baghdad.
1638 Ottomans recaptured Baghdad.
1639 Ottoman-Ṣafavid Peace Treaty of Zuhāb [Qaṣr-i Shīrīn].
1645 Ottomans attacked Crete.
1645-1670 Ottoman-Venetian War.
1656 Venice conquered Lemnos.
1656-1661 Meḥmet Köprülü, Ottoman Grand Wazīr.
1661-1676 Aḥmed Köprülü, Ottoman Grand Wazīr.
1663 Austria joined Venice against Ottomans.
1664 Ottomans defeated at St. Gotthard.
20-year truce concluded at Vasvár with Austria.
1669 Conclusion of Ottoman-Venetian conflict by capitulation of Qandiya.
1672-1676 Ottoman-Polish War.
1676 Peace of Zurawno.
Ottomans gained Podolia and Eastern Ukraine from Poland.
1676-1683 Kara Muṣṭafā, Ottoman Grand Wazīr.
1677-1681 First Ottoman-Russian War.
1679 Death of Ottoman traveler, Evliya Chelebi.
1681 Peace of Radzyn.
Ottomans lost Eastern Ukraine.
1682-1699 Ottoman-Austrian War.
1683 July-Sept.: 2nd siege of Vienna.
Ottoman defeat.
1684 Holy League of Papacy, Austria, Poland and Venice against Ottomans.
1686 Ottomans lost Buda to Austria.
Venice captured most of Morea.
Russia joined the Holy League.
1687 Ottomans lost Battle of Mohács to Austrians.
First Russian siege of Azov.
1688 Ottomans lost Belgrade.
1689 Ottomans lost Szigetvár and Vidin.
F. Muṣṭafā Köprülü, Ottoman Grand Wazīr.
1690 Ottomans gained land against Austria, including Belgrade.
1691 Battle of Szalánkamén.
Ottomans lost to Austria.
Death of Fāẓil Muṣṭafā Köprülü.
1696 Russians, under Peter the Great, took Azov.
1697 Ottomans defeated at Zenta by Prince Eugene of Savoy.
1699 Jan. 26: Peace of Carlowitz.
First permanent loss of territory by Ottomans to Europeans.

1703 July-Aug.: Edirne [Adrianople] Affair [*vaqᶜasi*] against Sulṭān Muṣṭafā II, forcing his abdication.
1710-1711 Ottoman-Russian War.
1711 Ottomans won Battle of Pruth against Russians; regained Azov.
Peace of Pruth.
1716 Ottoman-Austrian War.
1716-1718 War with Venice; Ottomans retook Morea.
1717 Austrian conquest of Belgrade.
1718 Peace of Passarowitz.
Ottomans lost lands to Austria.
1718-1730 Tulip Period [Lâle Devri] in Ottoman Empire.
1722 Mar. 8: Battle of Gulnābād. Ṣafavid forces routed by Afghan Maḥmūd.
Peter the Great took Derbent.
Afghan Maḥmūd took Iṣfahān.
Effective end of Ṣafavid dynasty.
1725-1730 Ismāᶜīl Pāshā al-ᶜAẓm, Governor of Damascus.
1726-1729 Ottomans attacked Persia, but peace was arranged by Ashrāf, Afghan shah of Persia.
1729-1730 Nādir Khān Afshār drove Afghans from Persia.
1729 First Turkish printing press.
1736-1739 Ottoman war with Austria and Russia.

1736 Russia retook Azov.

1736-1747 Nādir Khān became Nādir Shāh.

1739 Treaty of Belgrade with Austria. Ottomans acquired Belgrade.
Nādir Shāh attacked Delhi in India.

1740 Nādir Shāh attacked Bukhara.

1745 Establishment of Wahhābī Reform Movement in Dar^{c}īya, Arabia.

1747 Assassination of Nādir Shāh.

1750-1779 Karīm Khān Zand, sole ruler in southern Iran.

1757-1773 Reign of Muṣṭafā III, Ottoman sultan.

1758-1779 Karīm Khān Zand, undisputed ruler of Persia.

1768-1774 Ottoman-Russian War.

1769 Russians captured Jassy and Bucharest.

1770 Russian naval victory over Ottomans at Chesme.

1770-1773 ^{c}Alī Bey active in Egypt.

1770-1789 Yūsuf Shihāb, Amīr of Lebanon.

1773-1789 Reign of ^{c}Abdülhamīd I, Ottoman sultan.

1774 Treaty of Küçük Kaynarci between Russia and Ottomans.

1775 Aḥmad Pāshā al-Jazzār [d. 1804], Governor of Sidon; later of Acre.

1783 Russia annexed Crimea.

1787-1792 Ottoman-Russian War.

1788 Austria joined Ottoman-Russian War.

1789 Austria invaded Bosnia and Serbia.
Russia invaded Moldavia and Wallachia.

1789-1807 Reign of Selīm III, Ottoman sultan.

1789-1840 Bashīr II Shihāb, Amīr of Lebanon.

1791 Peace of Sistova between Austria and Ottomans re-establishing 1788 borders.

1792 Peace of Jassy between Russia and Ottomans, with Dniester as new Russian-Ottoman border.

1796 Āghā Muḥammad Qājār became Shāh of Persia.

1797-1834 Reign of Fatḥ ^{c}Alī, Qājār ruler.

1798 July: Bonaparte's victory at Battle of Pyramids outside Cairo.
July: Admiral Nelson destroyed French fleet at Abū Qir.

1799 Napoleon invaded Palestine, but failed to capture Acre.

1800 Russia annexed Georgia.

1801 French evacuation of Egypt.

1802 Wahhābī raid on Karbala.

1803-1804 Wahhābīs captured Mecca and Medina.

1804 Serbian revolt.

1805-1848 Muḥammad ^{c}Alī, Viceroy of Egypt.

1806-1812 Ottoman-Russian War.

1807 Treaty of Finkenstein between Persia and Russia.
Treaty of Tilsit between Napoleon and Russia.
British occupation of Alexandria.

1808-1839 Reign of Maḥmūd II, Ottoman sultan.

1811 Mar. 1: Massacre of Egyptian Mamlūks by Muḥammad ^{c}Alī.

1811-1818 Muḥammad ^{c}Alī's campaigns against the Wahhābīs.

1813 Treaty of Gulistan between Persia and Russia.

1815-1817 Second Serbian uprising.

1816-1831 Dā'ūd Pāshā, Governor of Baghdad.

1818 Persian attack on Afghanistan.

1820s British pacts with Persian Gulf *shaykhs*.

1820-1821 Sudanese campaigns of Muḥammad ^{c}Alī.

1821 Insurrections in Wallachia.

1821-1823 Ottoman-Persian War.

1821-1830 Greek War of Independence.

ca.1822 Establishment of Būlāq press in Egypt.

1823 Khartoum founded.

1824-1827 Muḥammad ^{c}Alī's campaigns in Greece led by Ibrāhīm.

1825-1828 Persian-Russian War.

1826 June 15: Massacre of Janissaries in Istanbul.

1827 Establishment of medical schools in Istanbul and Cairo.
July 6: Treaty of London [Britain, France, Russia] on their support of Greece against Ottomans.
Oct. 20: Battle of Navarino.
Ottoman-Egyptian navy defeated by

Admiral Codrington and Western forces.

1828 Egyptians evacuated Greece.
Treaty of Turkmanchai between Persia and Russia.

1828-1829 Ottoman-Russian War.

1829 Sept.: Treaty of Adrianople between Ottomans and Russians.

1830 French invaded Algeria.

1832 Battle of Konya.
Ottomans defeated by Egyptians.

1832-1841 Egyptian involvement in Syria under Ibrāhīm.

1833 Apr. 8: Convention of Kütahya between Ottomans and Egyptians.
July 8: Treaty of Unkiar Skelessi between Ottomans and Russians.

1834 Arabic press in Beirut established.

1837-1838 Persian siege of Herat.

1839 June 24: Battle of Nezib.
Ibrāhīm's victory over Ottoman forces trained by von Moltke.

1839 Nov. 3: Promulgation of Hatt-i Sherif Gülhane in Istanbul.

1839-1861 Reign of ᶜAbdülmecīd, Ottoman sultan.

1840 July: Treaty of London [Britain, Austria, Prussia, Russia] on Eastern question.

1841 Feb.: Hereditary viceroyalty of Egypt for Muḥammad ᶜAlī.
July: Straits Convention [Britain, France, Prussia, Russia, Austria].

1842 Shihābī amirate of Lebanon ended.

1842-1858 Stratford de Redcliffe, British ambassador in Istanbul.

1843 Dual Qaimaqamate in Lebanon established.

1844 Sayyid Muḥammad ᶜAlī of Persia proclaimed himself the Bāb. This is considered the beginning of the Bahā'i Movement.

1848-1854 ᶜAbbās Ḥilmī I, Viceroy of Egypt.

1848-1896 Nāṣir al-Dīn, Qājār shah.

1850 Execution of the Bāb.
Bābī uprisings.

1852 Persecution in Iran of Bābīs, who fled to the West.

1853 Oct.: Ottomans declared war on Russia.

1854-1856 Crimean War [Ottoman-Russian War], with a number of European states participating on the Ottoman side.

1854 Oct. 25: Battle of Balaklava and "Charge of the Light Brigade."
Nov.: Ferdinand de Lesseps received concessions to build Suez Canal.

1854-1863 Saᶜīd, Viceroy of Egypt.

1855 Sept.: Sebastopol taken from Russia.

1856 Feb. 18: Hatt-i Hümayun promulgated in Istanbul.
Feb.-Mar.: Treaty of Paris ending Crimean War.
Persian occupation of Herat.

1857 Alexandria-Cairo railroad completed.
Afghanistan's independence recognized by Britain and Persia.

1860 Robert College founded in Istanbul.

1860-1861 Civil war in Lebanon.
French expeditionary force in Lebanon.

1861 Organic Regulation of Lebanon that established semi-autonomous self-government in Mt. Lebanon area.

1861-1876 Reign of ᶜAbdülezīz, Ottoman sultan.

1863-1879 Ismāᶜīl, Viceroy and then Khedive of Egypt.

1864 Ottoman Law of Vilayets.

1865 Establishment of Ottoman National Debt Administration.

1866 Ismāᶜīl of Egypt acquired "Khedive" title from Ottoman sultan.
American University of Beirut, originally called Syrian Protestant College, founded.

1866-1868 Uprising on Crete against Ottomans.

1869 University of Istanbul founded.
Nov. 17: Suez Canal officially opened.

1869-1872 Midhat Pāshā, Governor of Baghdad.

1872 Sweeping Persian concessions to Baron Julius de Reuter revoked by Qājār government.

1874-1879 Gen. Charles Gordon, Governor of Sudan.

1875 Establishment of Mixed Courts in Egypt.
Britain acquired Khedive's shares in the Suez Canal Company.

1875	Uprisings in Herzegovina and Bosnia.
1876	May: Establishment of *Caisse de la Dette* and dual control in Egypt.
	ʿAbdülezīz, Ottoman sultan, deposed.
	Aug.: Murād V, Ottoman sultan, deposed.
	Dec. 23: ʿAbdülḥamīd, Ottoman sultan, promulgated a Constitution.
1876-1909	Reign of ʿAbdülḥamīd, Ottoman sultan.
1877	Feb.: Midhat Pāshā dismissed from Ottoman government.
	Mar.: Opening of Ottoman Parliament.
1877-1878	Ottoman-Russian War.
1878	Feb. 13: Ottoman Parliament dismissed; Constitution suspended.
	Mar.: Treaty of San Stefano between Ottomans and Russians.
	June-July: Congress of Berlin modified Treaty of San Stefano.
	Uprising in Crete.
	Russians organized Cossack Brigade in Persia.
1879-1892	Muḥammad Tawfīq, Khedive of Egypt.
1881	French occupied Tunisia.
	Outbreak of Sudanese Mahdia.
	First Zionist *Aliya* to Palestine.
1881-1882	ʿUrābi revolt in Egypt.
1882	Jan. 8: British-French Gambetta Note on developments in Egypt.
	July: British bombarded and occupied Alexandria.
	Sept.: British defeated Egyptians at Battle of Tall al-Kābir.
1883	Nov.: General Hicks and Egyptian forces defeated by Mahdī.
1883-1907	Lord Cromer, British Consul General in Egypt.
1885	Fall of Khartoum.
	Death of General Gordon.
1888	Convention of Constantinople concerning Suez Canal.
1889	Uprising in Crete.
	Imperial Bank of Persia founded.
1890-	Persian tobacco concession.
1890-1897	Armenian revolts against Ottomans.
1890-1898	Reconquest of the Sudan by Kitchener.
1892-1914	Reign of ʿAbbās Ḥilmī II, Khedive of Egypt.
1896-1897	Uprising in Crete.
1896-1907	Muẓaffar al-Dīn, Qājār ruler.
1897	Ottoman-Greek War.
1898	Fashoda Incident.
1899	Anglo-Egyptian Condominium established in the Sudan.
	Concessions by Ottomans to Germans to build railroads.
	British agreement with *shaykh* of Kuwait.
______	
1900	First Persian oil concession to d'Arcy.
1900-1908	Hejaz railroad built.
1901	Ibn Saʿūd and Wahhābīs took Riyadh.
1902	Congress of Ottoman Liberals met in Paris.
1902-1903	Uprising in Macedonia.
1904	Apr.: Entente Cordiale between Britain and France.
1905	Persian Revolution.
	Death of Muḥammad ʿAbdūh.
1906	May: Sinai officially part of Egypt after Taba-Aqaba frontier dispute between Ottomans and Britain.
	Jun. 13: Dinshawāy Incident in Egypt.
	Aug.: Qājār ruler, Muẓaffar al-Dīn, promulgated a Constitution.
	Dec.: Persian Constitution ratified.
1907	Anglo-Russian Convention divided Persia.
	Young Turk movements united under name of Committee of Union and Progress.
1907-1909	Muḥammad ʿAlī, Qājār ruler.
1907-1911	Gorst, British Consul General in Egypt.
1908	Revolt of Ottoman Third Army Corps in Salonika.
	ʿAbdülḥamīd reactivated 1876 Constitution.
	Crete annexed by Greece.
	Death of Egyptian political leader, Muṣṭafā Kāmil.
1909	Apr.: Ottoman Third Army deposed ʿAbdülḥamīd II.

1909 Formation of Anglo-Persian Oil Company to exploit d'Arcy concession.
Russian intervention in Persia.

1909-1924 Aḥmad, Qājār ruler.

1910 Assassination of Buṭrus Ghālī in Egypt.
Uprising in Albania against Ottomans.

1911 Shuster, American financial expert, appointed as Persian Treasurer General; dismissed after Russian intervention.
Abadan refinery completed.

1911-1912 Ottoman-Italian War over Libya and Ottoman loss.

1911-1914 Kitchener, British Consul General in Egypt.

1912 Proclamation of Albanian independence.

1912-1913 First Balkan War.

1913 Committee of Union and Progress [CUP] took over direct control of Ottoman government.
Arab Congress in Paris.
Second Balkan War.
Sept.: Treaty of Constantinople between Ottomans and Bulgaria.

1914 Formation of Arab *al-ᶜAhd*, Nationalist secret society.
Aug.: Secret treaty between CUP and Germany.
Aug.: Outbreak of World War I.
Nov. 1: Ottomans declared war on Britain, France and Russia.
Nov. 5: Britain declared war on Ottomans and annexed Cyprus.
Nov. 22: British forces landed at Fao, Iraq.
Dec. 18: British declared a protectorate over Egypt.

1914-1917 Ḥusayn Kāmil, Sultan of Egypt.

1915 Feb.: Ottomans attacked Suez Canal.
Mar. 18: Constantinople Agreement among Britain, France and Russia on division of Ottoman lands.
Apr. 25: Allied landing on Gallipoli Peninsula.
Apr. 26: Treaty of London among Britain, France, Russia and Italy.
July: Ḥusayn-MacMahon correspondence began.
Sep. 28: Turks laid siege to British at Kūt al-Amāra, Iraq.
Oct. 24: Major British reply to Ḥusayn's proposals.
Dec.: Agreement between Britain and Ibn Saᶜūd.

1916 Jan. 9: Allied withdrawal from Gallipoli Peninsula.
Apr. 29: British surrendered to Turks at Kūt al-Amāra, Iraq.
May: Sykes-Picot Agreement.
Jun. 5: Arab Revolt, popularly associated in the West with T.E. Lawrence [Lawrence of Arabia].
Jul. 19: 2nd Ottoman campaign against Suez Canal.
Dec. 15: British recognized Ḥusayn as King of the Hejaz only.

1917 Mar. 11: British occupied Baghdad.
Mar.-Apr.: British battled Ottomans in Gaza.
Apr.: Agreement of St. Jean de Maurene among Britain, Italy, France.
Nov. 2: Balfour Declaration.
Nov. 7: Bolshevik Revolution in Russia.
Dec. 5: Soviets renounced all claims to Ottoman lands.
Dec. 9: Allenby took Jerusalem.

1917-1936 Aḥmad Fuᶜād, King of Egypt.

1918 Mar. 3: Treaty of Brest Litovsk between Soviets and Central Powers.
Oct. 1: British and Arabs captured Damascus.
Oct. 7: French troops landed at Beirut.
Oct. 26: Aleppo captured by British and Arabs.
Oct. 30: Mudros Armistice concluded between Ottomans and Allies.
Nov. 11: Armistice in Europe.
Nov.: Zaghlūl, Egyptian leader, led

wafd to British High Commissioner.

Nov. 13: Allied fleet arrived in Istanbul.

1919 Jan.: Peace conference opened in Paris.

Feb.: Greek Premier Venizelos issued claims to Izmir and part of Anatolia.

Mar. 8: Zaghlūl deported from Egypt. Popular uprising.

Mar.: Italians landed in Anatolia.

May: Ibn Saʿūd defeated troops of Ḥusayn of Mecca.

May 15: Greeks landed at Izmir [Smyrna].

May 19: Muṣṭafā Kemal [b. 1880] arrived at Samsun.

Jul.23: Turkish Nationalist Congress at Erzurum.

Aug. 9: Anglo-Persian Agreement; never ratified by Persian *majlis*.

Sep.13: Turkish National Pact at Sivas; declaration of National Pact.

Oct.: General Gouraud, French High Commissioner for Lebanon and Syria.

Dec.: Lord Milner's mission to Egypt.

1920 Mar. 20: Syrian National Congress proclaimed Fayṣal King of Syria and Palestine.

Apr.: Provisional Turkish government established in Ankara.
San Remo Conference,

May: Soviets in Gilan.

July: Sir Herbert Samuel, High Commissioner for Palestine.
French occupation of Damascus.

Jul.-Aug.: Major Arab insurrection in Iraq.

Aug.: Ibn Saʿūd annexed ʿAsīr.

Aug. 20: Ottoman government in Istanbul signed Treaty of Sevrés.

Aug. 31: French High Commissioner created Greater [Modern] Lebanon.

1921 Jan. 20: Turkish Fundamental Law adopted by Grand National Assembly in Ankara.

Feb. 21: Persian *coup d'étāt*, led by Reza Khān.

Feb. 26: Russo-Persian Treaty signed.

Mar.: Cairo Conference run by Winston Churchill.

Mar. 13: Italians agreed to withdraw from Turkey.

Mar. 16: Treaty of Moscow between Soviets and Muṣṭafā Kemal.

Apr. 1: ʿAbdullāh, ruler of newly created State of Transjordan.

May: Major anti-Zionist riots in Palestine.

Aug. 23: Fayṣal proclaimed King of Iraq.

Aug.24-Sep.16: Battle of Sakarya between Turks and Greeks.

Oct. 20: French agreed to withdraw from Turkey.

1922 Feb. 28: Britain declared Egyptian independence.

Mar. 15: Fuʿād took title of King of Egypt.

July: Churchill's White Paper for Palestine.

Jul. 24: League of Nations approved British and French mandates for Palestine, Transjordan, Iraq, Lebanon and Syria.

Sep. 11: Turks retook Izmir.

Nov. 1: Muṣṭafā Kemal abolished the sultanate.

Nov. 20: Lausanne Conference began, with Turkish delegation headed by İsmet.

1922-1927 First Millspaugh mission to Iran.

1923 Apr.: Egyptian Constitution promulgated.

Jul. 24: Treaty of Lausanne signed with Turkey.

Sep. 29: Mandate system came into official effect.

Oct. 13: Ankara made Turkey's capital.

Oct. 29: Turkish republic formally proclaimed.

1924 Mar. 3: Caliphate abolished.
Oct. 3: Ḥusayn of Mecca abdicated in favor of his son, ᶜAlī.
Nov. 22: Sir Lee Stack murdered in Egypt.
Allenby's ultimatum.

1924-1927 Druze rebellions in Syria.

1925 Apr.: Hebrew University in Jerusalem opened.
Aug.: Polygamy abolished in Turkey.
Oct.: Persian *majlis* deposed last Qājār shāh.
Nov.: Wearing of *fez* in Turkey forbidden.
Dec. 12: Reza Khān became Reza Shāh, founder of Pahlavi dynasty of Iran.
Dec. 19: ᶜAlī, King of the Hejaz, abdicated.

1926 Jan.: Ibn Saᶜūd proclaimed King of the Hejaz.
Apr.: Reza Shāh crowned himself.

1927 Death of Zaghlūl.
Egyptian *wafd*, headed by al-Naḥḥās.
European dress required for men in Iran.
May: British recognized Ibn Saᶜūd's kingdom.

1928 Apr.: Turkey declared a secular state.
Nov.: Turkey adopted Latin alphabet.
Abolition of capitulations in Iran.

1929 Aug.: Wailing Wall Incident.
Riots in Palestine.

1930 Mar.: Official "Turkification" of all Turkish city names.
May: Shaw Report for Palestine.
Oct.: Passfield's White Paper for Palestine.

1931 Feb.: British Prime Minister MacDonald's letter on Palestine.

1932 Aug.: Turkey joined League of Nations.
Sep.: Saudi Arabia's new, official name of Kingdom of the Hejaz and Nejd.
Oct.: Iraq joined League of Nations.

1933 Sep.: Death of Fayṣal of Iraq.

1933-1939 Reign of Ghāzī, who succeeded Fayṣal in Iraq.

1934 Jan. 1: Muṣṭafā Kemal became Atatürk.
Jan. 1: Family names required of all Turkish citizens.

1935 Mar. 21: Iran became official name for Persia.
Oct. 3: Italians invaded Ethiopia.

1936 Apr.-Oct.: General strike of Arabs in Palestine.
July: Montreaux Convention gave Turkey complete control of Straits of Dardanelles.
Aug. 26: Anglo-Egyptian Treaty.
Sept. 9: Franco-Syrian Treaty; never ratified.
Oct. 29: First military *coup d'état* in Iraq, led by Bakr Ṣidqī.

1936-1952 Reign of King Fārūq of Egypt, including period of his minority.

1937 Jul. 8: Peel Commission Report on Palestine.
Jul. 9: Saadabad Pact among Iran, Iraq, Afghanistan and Turkey.
Sep. 8: Pan-Arab Congress at Bludan.

1938 Nov. 9: Woodhead Commission Report on Palestine.
Nov.10: Atatürk died; succeeded by İsmet Inönü as president of Turkey.

1939 Feb.: Anglo-Arab Conference on Palestine, held in London.
May 17: British White Paper on Palestine.
Jun. 23: Alexandretta [Hatay] Province incorporated into Turkey.
Sept.: Outbreak of World War II with German attack on Poland.

1940 Jun. 22: Franco-German armistice.

1941 Apr.-Jun.: Rashīd ᶜAlī in power in Iraq; ended with British occupation.
June: Allies occupied Syria and Lebanon; governed by Vichy administrators.
Aug. 25: Anglo-Soviet troops moved into Iran.

1941 Sep. 16: Reza Shāh of Iran forced to abdicate; succeeded by his son, Mohammed [Muḥammad] Reza Shāh.

1942 Feb. 4: Britain forced Egyptian government to accept al-Naḥḥās as Prime Minister.

May 11: Zionist Biltmore program.

Jul. 1: Rommel's German army reached al-Alamayn, Egypt.

Oct.: Germans defeated at al-Alamayn.

1943 Jan.: Germans defeated at Stalingrad.

National Pact between Sunnī and Maronite leaders of Lebanon.

Dec. 1: Tehran Declaration by Churchill, Roosevelt and Stalin.

1943-1945 Millspaugh [American financial expert] mission to Iran.

Oct. 5: "Protocol of Alexandria," issued by Arab leaders, laid basis for Arab League.

Nov. 4: Lord Moyne assassinated in Cairo by "Stern Gang."

Dec.: Jebel Druze absorbed into Syrian state.

1945 Mar. 22: Arab League created.

Nov.: Anglo-American Committee of Inquiry formed to investigate Palestine's future.

Dec. 12: Proclamation of Autonomous Republic of Azerbaijan.

1946 Jan.: Democratic Party of Turkey founded.

Jan. 19: Iran appealed to UN Security Council to have Soviet troops withdraw from Azerbaijan.

Mar. 19: 2nd Iranian appeal to Security Council.

May 1: Report issued by Anglo-American Committee of Inquiry on Palestine.

May 9: Soviet troops evacuated from Iran.

Dec.11: Collapse of Autonomous Republic of Azerbaijan.

1947 Mar.12: Truman Doctrine to maintain governments in Greece and Turkey.

May: UN Security Council on Palestine [UNSCOP] created.

Oct. 22: Iranian *majlis* rejected Soviet-Iranian oil concession.

Nov. 27: UN Partition Plan for Palestine passed by UN General Assembly.

1948 Apr. 10: Massacre of Arabs at Deir Yassin.

May 14: State of Israel established.

May 14-15: End of British Mandate for Palestine.

May 15-Jun. 11: Open warfare between Arabs and Israelis.

Jul. 8-18: 2nd phase of open warfare between Arabs and Israelis.

Sep. 17: Count Bernadotte assassinated by Stern Gang in Palestine.

Nov. 19: Establishment of UNRPR.

Dec. 1: ʿAbdullāh renamed his state Ḥāshimite Kingdom of Jordan.

1949 Jan. 31: Jordan joined United Nations.

Feb. 24: Israeli-Egyptian armistice.

Mar. 7: Israeli-Lebanese armistice.

Mar. 11: Israel joined United Nations.

Mar. 30: Syrian *coup d'état*; civilian government of Shukrī al-Quwatlī replaced by Col. Ḥusnī Zaʿīm.

Apr. 3: Israel-Jordan armistice.

Jul. 20: Israel-Syria armistice.

Aug. 14: Syrian *coup d'état*, led by Col. Sāmī al-Ḥinnawī.

Dec. 20: Syrian *coup d'état*, led by Col. Adīb Shīshaklī.

1950 Mar.: National Front, led by Dr. Mosaddeq, made significant gains in election for Iranian *majlis*.

May 1: Democratic Party replaced People's Republic Party in Turkish election: Menderes as Prime Minister and Bayar as President.

May 25: Britain, France and U.S. issued Tripartite Declaration.

Sep. 19: Turkey joined North Atlantic Organization.

1951 Mar. 7: Iranian Prime Minister Razmara shot to death.

1951 Apr. 29: Dr. Muḥammad Mosaddeq became Iranian Prime Minister.

May 2: Shāh of Iran signed oil nationalization bill.

Jul. 20: King ^{c}Abdullāh of Jordan assassinated.

Dec. 24: Libya became independent.

1952 Jan. 25: British involved in Battle of Ismā^{c}īlīya against Egyptian police.

Jan. 26: "Black Saturday" in Cairo.

Jul. 23: Egyptian Revolution, led by Gamāl ^{c}Abd al-Nāṣir [Nasser] and RCC.

Jul. 26: Fārūq compelled to abdicate.

Aug. 3: Iranian *majlis* gave Prime Minister Muṣaddiq [Mosaddeq] unlimited powers for 6 months.

Aug. 11: Ḥusayn [Hussein] became King of Jordan; replaced his father, Talāl.

Sept.: Major Land Reform Act promulgated in Egypt.

1953 Jan. 19: Iranian *majlis* voted to extend Mosaddeq's [Muṣaddiq's] power for a year.

Feb.: Angl-Egyptian agreement on British evacuation of Sudan.

Jun. 18: RCC abolished Egyptian monarchy.

Aug. 13: Iranian Shāh dismissed Mosaddeq.

Aug. 16: Iranian Shāh fled to Iraq.

Aug. 22: Iranian Shāh returned to power in Iran.

Aug. 22: Mosaddeq placed under arrest.

Nov. 3: Moshe Sharett became Prime Minister of Israel; replaced Ben-Gurion.

Nov. 9: ^{c}Abd al-^{c}Azīz b. Sa^{c}ūd died.

Nov. 9: Sa^{c}ūd became King of Saudi Arabia.

1954 Feb. 24: Shīshaklī removed from power in Syria by military.

Aug. 5: Compensation Agreement between Iran and AIOC.

Oct. 19: Egyptian-British agreement on evacuation of British Suez bases.

Oct. 26: Muslim Brotherhood attempted to assassinate Nasser.

Nov. 1: Algerian rebellion began.

1955 Feb. 17: Ben-Gurion became Israel's Defense Minister.

Feb. 24: Iraq-Turkey Agreement. Start of Baghdad Pact.

Feb. 28: Israeli raid on Gaza.

April: Britain joined Baghdad Pact.

Apr. 18-24: Afro-Asian Conference at Bandung.

Sept.: Pakistan joined Baghdad Pact.

Sep. 27: Nasser announced Russian arms deal.

Oct. 11: Iran officially joined Baghdad Pact.

Nov. 3: Ben-Gurion became Prime Minister of Israel.

1956 Jan. 1: Proclamation of Sudanese independence.

Mar. 1: Ḥusayn of Jordan removed Gen. John Glubb from command of Arab Legion.

May 16: Egypt recognized government of Mainland China.

Jul. 19: Secretary of State Dulles announced no U.S. aid to build Egyptian Aswan High Dam.

Jul. 26: Nasser nationalized Suez Canal.

Oct. 11: Major Israeli raid against Jordan.

Oct. 24: Jordan joined Egypt and Syria in a defense pact.

Oct. 29: Israel invaded Sinai.

Oct. 30: Anglo-French ultimatum issued to Egypt and Israel.

Oct. 31: Britain bombed Egyptian military bases.

Nov. 5: Israeli military operations in Sinai effectively ended.

Nov. 5: Anglo-French force invaded Canal Zone.

Nov. 6: Eden and Mollet accepted cease-fire, effective next day.

Dec. 22: Withdrawal of Anglo-French contingents from Suez completed; replaced by UNEF troops.

1957 Jan. 5: Eisenhower Doctrine announced.

Mar. 7: Last Israeli troops withdrew from

Sinai and Gaza Strip.

Mar. 13: Jordan terminated 1948 Anglo-Jordanian Treaty.

1958 Feb. 1: United Arab Republic [UAR] of Egypt and Syria created.

Apr.: Amīr Fayṣal came to power in Saudi Arabia.

May: Increasing internal turmoil in Lebanon.

Jul. 14: Iraqi Revolution, led by al-Qāsim [Kaseem].

Jul. 15: U.S. Marines landed in Lebanon.

Oct. 25: U.S. troops withdrew from Lebanon.

Nov. 17: Ibrāhīm ^{c}Abbūd led *coup* in Sudan.

1960 May 27: Turkish military, led by General Gürsel, overthrew government of Celal Bayar and Adnan Menderes; established NUC.

1961 Jun. 19: Kuwait declared free and independent of British control.

Jun. 25: Iraqis threatened Kuwait.

July: Major socialization and nationalization laws promulgated in Egypt.

Sep. 28: Syria withdrew from UAR.

Oct. 25: 2nd Turkish republic established under President Gürsel.

1962 July: Algeria became independent.

July: Shāh of Iran announced White Revolution for internal reform.

Sep. 19: Muḥammad al-Badr became Imām of Yemen.

Sep. 26: Beginning of Yemeni Civil War, with Republican forces led by ^{c}Abdullāh Sallāl.

1963 Jan.: Aden joined Federation of South Arabia.

Feb. 8: *Coup d'état* in Iraq, led by ^{c}Abd al-Salām ^{c}Arīf.

Mar. 8: *Coup d'état* in Syria, led by Ba^{c}thists.

Jun. 16: Levi Eshkol became Israeli Prime Minister.

1964 May 28: PLO established, with Aḥmad Shuqayri as head.

Nov. 2: Fayṣal officially replaced Sa^{c}ūd as Saudi Arabian king.

1965 Oct.: Süleymān Demirel, head of Justice Party, became Turkish Prime Minister.

1966 Feb. 23: Military *coup* in Syria, led by Gen. Ṣalāḥ Jadīd.

Mar. 28: Gen. Cevdet Sunay became President of Turkey.

Apr. 13: ^{c}Abd al-Salām ^{c}Arīf of Iraq died in helicopter crash; succeeded by his brother, Maj. Gen. ^{c}Abd al-Raḥmān ^{c}Arīf.

Oct.: Intra Bank of Beirut failed.

Nov. 13: Palestinian *fidā'iyīn* land mine killed Israelis near Hebron.

Nov. 13: Israeli reprisal attack on Jordanian border village of al-Samu.

1967 Apr. 7: Israeli-Syrian air clash.

May 14: Nasser reinforced Sinai forces.

May 16: Egyptian troops replaced UNEF in Sinai.

May 21: Partial mobilization of Israeli and Egyptian troops.

May 22: Nasser announced blockade of Straits of Tiran.

May 30: Jordan joined Arab Defense Pact of Egypt and Syria.

June 1: Moshe Dayan was made Israeli Defense Minister.

June 5: Arab-Israeli War began with Israeli air strikes.

Jun. 10: End of 3rd Arab-Israeli War [Six-Day War].

Jul. 28: Israel "annexed" Old Jerusalem.

Aug. 29-Sep. 1: Arab summit meeting at Khartoum.

Oct. 21: Egypt sank Israeli naval destroyer, *Elath*.

Oct. 22: Israel attacked Egyptian Suez oil refineries.

Nov. 4: ^{c}Abd al-Raḥmān al-Iryānī led *coup* in Yemen against ^{c}Abdullāh Sallāl.

Nov. 22: UN Resolution 242 on Arab-Israeli problem.

Nov. 30: Last British troops left Aden.

Dec. 24: Aḥmad Shuqary resigned as head of PLO.

1968 Mar. 21: Israel attacked Karameh, Jordan; fought against Palestinian and Jordanian troops.

Jul. 17: *Coup d'état* in Iraq.

Jul. 17: Gen. Aḥmad Ḥasan al-Bakr became President.

Jul. 23: El-Al Israel airliner hijacked to Algeria.

Oct. 26: Gen. Ḥāfiẓ al-Asad became Syrian leader in a bloodless *coup*.

Oct. 27: Israeli raided deep into Egyptian territory.

Dec. 26: PLO attacked El-Al Israel airliner in Athens.

Dec. 28: Israel raided Beirut airport; destroyed 13 planes.

1969 Feb. 3: Yāsir [c]Arafāt became head of the PLO.

Feb. 18: PLO attacked Israeli airliner in Zürich.

Feb. 28: Gen. Ḥāfiẓ al-Asad took over direct control of Syrian government.

Mar. 8: Intensive fighting along the Suez Canal.

Mar. 8: War of Attrition began; lasted until August 1970.

Mar. 17: Golda Meir became Israel's Prime Minister.

May: Gen. Ja[c]far al-Numayrī seized power in Sudan.

June: PFLP blew up tapline in Golan Heights.

July 1: Israel moved major government offices to Old Jerusalem.

Aug. 11: Israel attacked Lebanese villages, which Israel claimed were *fidā'īyīn* bases.

Aug. 21: Fire at al-Aqsa Mosque in Jerusalem.

Aug. 29: TWA airliner hijacked by PLO *fidā'īyīn*.

Sep. 1: Revolution in Libya, led by Col. Mu[c]ammar al-Qadhdhāfī [Qaddafi].

Oct.: Palestinian-Lebanese clashes.

Nov.: Cairo Agreement between Lebanon and Palestine.

Dec. 9: U.S. Secretary of State Rodgers proposed Middle East peace plan.

1970 Feb. 12: Israeli jets raided Cairo suburbs.

Mar. 11: Major agreement between Iraqi government and the Kurds.

June: Widespread fighting in Jordan between Palestinian *fidā'īyīn* and Ḥusayn's troops.

Jul. 21: Aswan High Dam completed.

Jul. 26: Qabus b. Sa[c]īd overthrew his father in palace *coup* in Oman.

Aug. 7: Cease-fire along Suez Canal between Egypt and Israel, ending the War of Attrition.

Sept.: Civil war in Jordan between Ḥusayn and Palestinian *fidā'īyīn*.

Sep. 6-12: PFLP hijacked and blew up U.S. and Swiss airlines in Jordan and Egypt.

Sep. 23: Süleymān Faranjiya became President of Lebanon.

Sep. 27: Truce in Jordan signed between Ḥusayn and Palestinian leader, [c]Arafāt.

Sep. 28: Gamāl [c]Abd al-Nāṣir died.

Sep. 28: Anwar al-Sādāt became President of Egypt.

Sep. 29: Last hostages released from the September 6th hijacking.

Oct. 13: Second truce between Ḥusayn and [c]Arafāt signed.

Nov. 13: Gen. Ḥāfiẓ al-Asad consolidated his power in Syria.

1971 Mar. 7: Sadat ceased renewing Egyptian-Israeli Cease-Fire Agreement.

May 27: Soviet-Egyptian Treaty of Friendship signed.

Jul. 18: Last *fidā'īyīn* positions eliminated in Jordan.

Jul.19-22: *Coup d'état* in Sudan, led by Ḥāshim al-[c]Atā, fell to counter-*coup*, led by Numayrī.

1972 Apr. 6: Soviet-Iraqi Treaty of Friendship signed.

May: Marxist-oriented, urban guerillas active in Turkey.

1972 May 30: 3 Japanese men, in name of Palestinian movement, opened fire on civilians at Lod Airport, Tel Aviv; killed 26 persons.

Jul. 18: President Sadat of Egypt ordered Soviet advisers and experts to leave Egypt.

Sep. 5: 11 members of Israeli Olympic team in Munich were killed while hostages of Palestinian *fidā'īyīn*.

Oct. 5: OPEC set goal of 51% ownership in oil companies.

1973 Feb. 21: Israel shot down Libyan civilian airliner over Sinai.

Mar. 1: Palestinian "Black Septemberists" seized Saudi embassy in Khartoum; 3 American diplomats ultimately killed.

Mar. 26: Sadat announced Soviet-Egyptian relations were again solid.

Apr. 6: Fahri Korutürk elected President of Turkey.

Apr. 10: Israeli commandos raided Sidon and Beirut against PLO.

May: Malkert Agreement between PLO and Lebanon on halting PLO raids from Lebanon.

July 1: Attempted overthrow of al-Bakr's Iraqi government failed.

July 5: President Ḥāfiẓ al-Asad of Syria inaugurated Euphrates Dam at al-Tabqa, which was renamed Madīnat al-Thawra.

Sep. 13: Air clashes between Israel and Syria.

Oct. 6: Egyptian and Syrian troops attacked Israeli forces; detachments from other Arab states eventually joined in.

Oct. 14: U.S. began resupplying Israel to balance continuing Soviet aid to Arabs.

Oct. 16: Israelis crossed Suez Canal.

Oct. 18: OAPEC announced cutback in oil production; oil price was raised during this period.

Oct. 22: UN Security Council passed Resolution 338, calling for a cease-fire "in place."

Oct. 23: UN Security Council passed Resolution 339, reconfirming call for cease-fire; Israel and Egypt accepted it, while Syria accepted it "with conditions."

Oct.25-31: United States troops on alert.

Oct. 27: UN observers on Suez front.

Oct. 28: Israeli-Egyptian negotiations began at Kilometer 101 on Suez-Cairo Road.

Nov. 5: OAPEC announced embargo of all oil to U.S. and Netherlands.

Nov.6-9: U.S. Secretary of State, Henry Kissinger, traveled back and forth between Cairo and Jerusalem.

Nov. 11: Israel and Egypt signed a Cease-Fire Accord; continued negotiations.

1974 Jan. 18: Israel and Egypt signed a Disengagement Agreement.

Mar. 5: Israel completed withdrawal from area west of Suez Canal.

Mar. 11: War of Attrition began between Israel and Syria.

Mar. 18: Arab oil embargo of U.S. lifted.

May 29: Israel and Syria agreed to a Disengagement Agreement.

Jun. 13: Bloodless *coup* in Yemen, led by Ibrāhīm al-Ḥamīdī.

Oct. 28: Arab League meeting at Rabat recognized PLO as sole, legitimate representative of Palestinian people.

Nov. 13: ᶜArafāt spoke before UN General Assembly.

1975 Mar. 6: International Border and Good Neighborly Relations Treaty concluded by Ṣaddām Ḥusayn and M. Reza Shāh.

Mar. 22: Collapse of Kissinger's "shuttle diplomacy" mission.

Mar. 25: Saᶜūdī King Fayṣal assassinated.

Mar. 25: Khālid became king.

Apr. 13: Symbolic beginning of Lebanese Civil War.

June 5: Suez Canal reopened after 8 years.

Sep. 1: Egyptian-Israeli Interim Agreement.

1975 Nov. 10: UN General Assembly resolution declared: "Zionism is a form of racism."

1976 Mar. 14: Sadat terminated 1971 Soviet-Egyptian Treaty.

June: First official units of Syrian-dominated Arab Deterrent Force arrived in Lebanon.

July 1: Abortive *coup* in Sudan against Numayrī.

July 3: Israeli rescue raid on Entebbe Airport, Uganda.

Aug. 12: Tall al-Za^c tar Palestinian refugee camp fell to Phalangists after 54-day siege.

Sep. 23: Elias Sarkis became Lebanese President amidst civil war.

Dec. 20: Yitzhak Rabin resigned as Prime Minister of Israel.

1977 May 18: Victory of Likud Party, with Menachem Begin as Israeli Prime Minister.

July: Brief border war between Egypt and Libya.

July: Shutra Agreement between PLO and Lebanon to restrict PLO activities and weapons in Lebanon.

Nov. 9: Anwar al-Sādāt, Egypt's President, flew to Israel.

Dec.25-26: Begin and Sadat met in Ismā^c īlīya.

1978 Jan. 8: Major incident in Iran between demonstrators and police.

Feb.17-21: Major riots in Tabriz against government.

Mar. 11: Major Palestinian raid into Israel from southern Lebanon.

Mar. 14: Large-scale military operation by Israel into Lebanon.

Apr. 27: Hafizullāh Amīn and Nūr Muḥammad Tarakī overthrew government of Muḥammad Dā'ūd in Afghanistan.

Apr. 27: Tarakī became President.

June: Withdrawal of Israelis from southern Lebanon completed.

Aug. 20: Movie house burned in Abadan; over 400 died.

Sep. 8: "Black Friday" in Tehran, with deaths of large number of protestors.

Sep. 17: Camp David accords for peace in Middle East; framework for conclusion of a peace treaty between Egypt and Israel.

Oct. 6: Ayatollāh Rūḥallāh Khumaynī [Khomeini] expelled from Iraq.

Nov.: Arab summit meeting rejected Egyptian-Israeli accord.

1979 Jan. 16: Shāh Mohammed Reza Pahlavi left Iran.

Jan. 31: Ayatollāh Khumaynī returned to Iran.

Mar. 26: Peace treaty between Israel and Egypt signed in Washington, D.C.

Mar. 31: Islamic republic established by referendum in Iran.

Jul. 16: Ṣaddām Ḥusayn replaced Aḥmad Ḥasan al-Bakr as President of Iraq.

Sep. 16: Hafizullāh Amīn overthrew government of Nūr Muḥammad Tarakī in Afghanistan.

Nov. 4: U.S. Embassy in Iran taken over, including a number of U.S. hostages.

Nov. 6: Mehdi Bazargan, Iranian Prime Minister, resigned; Revolutionary Council took over Iran.

Nov. 20: Revolt in Grand Mosque, Mecca.

Dec. 27: Babrak Karmal made President of Afghanistan.

Dec. 27: Hafizullāh Amīn assassinated.

Dec. 27: Soviets invaded Afghanistan.

1980 Feb. 4: Banī-Ṣadr became first President of the Islamic Republic of Iran.

Apr. 7-Sep. 12: Ihsan Sabri Çağlayangli, Acting President of Turkey.

Apr. 24: U.S. military operation in Iran aborted.

Jul. 9: Major Israeli air raid on Lebanon.

Jul. 27: Mohammed Reza Shāh died in Egypt.

Jul. 30: Israeli Knesset declared all of

Jerusalem to be the united capital of Israel.

1980 Sep. 12: Gen. Kenan Evren led military *coup* in Turkey.

End of 2nd Turkish republic.

Sep. 22: Iraq invaded Iran.

Oct.: Soviet-Syrian Treaty of Friendship and Cooperation signed.

1981 Jan. 20: Iran released American hostages after 444 days of captivity.

Jan.25-28: Arab summit meeting at Tā^{c}if repudiated UN Resolution 242, advocated a *jihād* for the delivery of Jerusalem as the capital of a Palestinian state, and extended the Arab boycott of Israel.

Mar.-Apr.: Tensions increased along the Israeli-Lebanese border.

Apr. 1: Fighting in Zahla, Lebanon; beginning of Syrian-Israeli "missile crises."

Jun. 7: Israeli aircraft destroyed an Iraqi nuclear reactor near Baghdad.

Jun.17-19: Large-scale clashes in Egypt between Muslims and Christians.

Jun. 21: Banī-Ṣadr, President of Iran, formally stripped of office by *majlis*.

Jun. 28: IRP headquarters in Tehran bombed; victims included Ayatollāh Bihishti [Beheshti].

Jun. 30: Likud Party, under Menachem Begin, won Israeli election.

Jul. 28: Banī-Ṣadr, ex-President, and Mas^{c}ūd Rajavī, head of Mujahidīn-i Khalq, fled Iran to Europe.

Aug. 8: Fahd's Eight-Point Plan for Peace in the Middle East presented.

Oct. 6: Anwar al-Sādāt assassinated.

Oct. 6: Ḥusnī Mubārak became President of Egypt.

Oct. 29: U.S. Senate upheld sale of AWACs to Saudi Arabia.

Nov.: Israeli Knesset made Israeli laws applicable to the Golan Heights.

Nov. 25: Arab summit meeting at Fez rejected Fahd's peace plan.

1982 Apr. 25: Israel completed withdrawal from the Sinai Peninsula.

Jun. 13: King Khālid of Saudi Arabia died; replaced by Crown Prince Fahd. Abdullāh became Crown Prince.

Jun. 6: Israelis invaded Lebanon, which they called "Operation Peace for Northern Galilee."

Aug. 21: PLO began evacuation from Beirut.

Aug. 23: Bashīr al-Jumayyil [Gemayel] became President-Elect of Lebanon.

Aug. 25: U.S. Marines arrived in Beirut port area, followed by French and Italian troops. They left September 10.

Sep. 1: U.S. President, Ronald Reagan, presented peace plan for Middle East.

Sep.5-8: Fez Peace Plan proposed at Arab summit meeting.

Sep. 14: Bashīr al-Jumayyil [Gemayel] President-Elect of Lebanon, assassinated.

Sep.16-18: Massacres in Sabra and Shatila Palestinian refugee camps by Christian Phalangists.

Sep. 21: Amīn al-Jumayyil [Gemayel] elected President of Lebanon.

Sep. 25: Large-scale political demonstration in Tel Aviv that called for inquiry into Beirut massacres.

Sep. 27: French, Italian and, on the 29th, U.S. troops returned to Beirut.

Sep. 28: Kahan Commission established in Israel to investigate Sabra and Shatila massacres.

Nov. 9: Kenan Evren elected as 7th President of Turkey after referendum on new Constitution on November 7th.

1983 Feb. 8: Report given by Israeli Kahan Commission on Beirut massacres.

May 7: Revolt within al-Fatah against ^{c}Arafāt leadership, led by Abū Mūsā [Mūsā Sa^{c}īd].

May 27: Agreement between Israel and Lebanon for withdrawal of foreign troops from Lebanon.

1983 Sep. 14: Israelis withdrew from Central Lebanon to Awali River.

Sep. 15: Begin submitted his resignation as Israel's Prime Minister. Yitzhak Shamir replaced Begin as head of Herut political party.

Oct. 10: Shamir was confirmed by Knesset as Prime Minister.

Oct. 23: American and French forces in Lebanon suffered significant losses from truck bombs.

Oct. 30: Lebanese reconciliation meeting in Geneva.

Nov. 6: Turgut Ozal, head of Motherland Party, was elected Turkish Prime Minister.

Nov. 14: Turkish Republic of Northern Cyprus declared by Rauf Denktash, Turkish Cypriot leader.

Nov. 29: Major U.S.-Israel agreement announced on military cooperation and economic issues.

Dec. 4: U.S. bombing raid into Lebanon.

Dec. 20: Evacuation of pro-ᶜArafāt Palestinians from Tripoli completed.

Dec. 29: Sporadic fighting in and around Beirut among numerous groups continued.

VII. Acronyms of Twentieth-Century Organizations

There is no single, extensive collection of abbreviations dealing with the political, social and economic groups formed in the 20th century. Each new resistance movement, military *junta*, political party, oil company, interstate organization, etc. brings with it a new abbreviation. The easiest way to locate the full name of an undefined abbreviation — which, by context, is connected with 20th-century Southwest Asia and Egypt — is to turn to the index of any of the standard works on the Modern Era, such as:

- Abid A. Al-Marayati (Ed.), *The Middle East: Its Government and Politics* (Belmont, CA: Duxbury Press, 1972); and
- Tareq Y. Ismael, *Governments and Politics of the Contemporary Middle East* (Homewood, IL: The Dorsey Press, 1970).
- Yaacov Shimoni and Evyatar Levine (Eds.), *Political Dictionary of the Middle East in the Twentieth Century* (New York: Quadrangle [The New York Times Book Co.; rev. ed.], 1974), does not list groups by abbreviations.
- Clio Dictionaries in Political Science has announced L. Zering, *The Middle East Political Dictionary*, as Volume 5 of their series, and it may be helpful.

ADF Arab Deterrent Force [1976-]: The multinational, Syrian-dominated Arab force sent in 1976 into Lebanon to end the internal strife.

AIOC Anglo-Iranian Oil Co. [1935-51]: British-controlled oil company; superseded APOC.

AL Arab League [1945-]: Members, as of 1983, were Algeria, Bahrain, Egypt, Iraq, Jordan, Kuwait, Lebanon, Libya, Morocco, Qatar, Saudi Arabia, South Yemen, Sudan, Syria, Tunisia, United Arab Emirates, Yemen, Oman, Somalia, Mauritania, and the PLO. Also known as League of Arab States.

ALESCO Arab League Educational, Cultural and Scientific Organization [1970-]: Its divisions include education, social sciences, humanities and culture, science, documentation and information, and the Institute of Arab Manuscripts.

ALF Arab Liberation Front [1969-]: A Palestinian *fidā'īyīn* group sponsored by Iraq.

ANM Arab Nationalist Movement [1950s-]: An Arab, particularly Palestinian, group dominated by George Habash. Precursor to PFLP.

APOC Anglo-Persian Oil Co. [1930-35]: Earliest Western oil company in the area.

ARAMCO Arabian-American Oil Co.[1946-]: Owned by Standard Oil of California, Standard Oil of New Jersey, Mobil Oil and Texaco Oil.

ARE Arab Republic of Egypt [1971-]: Official name of Egypt.

ASU Arab Socialist Union [1962-]: The only

legal Egyptian political party.

BP British Petroleum [1951-]: Superseded AIOC.

CENTO Central Treaty Organization [1958-]: Members, as of 1976, were Britain, Iran, Pakistan and Turkey. Previously called Baghdad Pact [1955-58] and included Iraq.

CUP Committee of Union and Progress [1908-18]: Known as "Young Turks." This group of Turkish military leaders ran the Ottoman government and reinstated the 1876 Constitution.

DFLP Democratic Front for Liberation of Palestine [1969-]: Radical Palestinian *fidā'īyīn* group founded by Nayif Hawatmeh. Broke off from PFLP. Formerly Popular Democratic Front for Liberation of Palestine [PDFLP].

DP Democratic Party [1946-60]: A Turkish political party during first republic, dominated by Adnan Menderes, and was in power from 1950 to 1960.

EGPC Egyptian General Petroleum Co. [1960-]: Egyptian national oil company.

FLOSY Front for Liberation of Occupied South Yemen [1966-67]: Radical group opposed to British occupation of Aden and South Yemen.

GCC Gulf Cooperation Council [1981-]: Saudi Arabia, Kuwait, Bahrain, Qatar and UAE joined a regional economic and defense pact on March 10, 1981.

GE Gush Emmunim ["Group of those who keep faith"; 1973-]: An Israeli pressure group, begun after 1973 elections, whose program includes an active settlement policy in a Greater Israel.

IBRD International Bank for Reconstruction and Development [1944-]: Created to provide and facilitate international investments.

IDF Israel Defense Forces [1948-]: Official name for Israeli military forces.

INOC Iraq National Oil Co. [1958-]: Iraqi national oil company.

IPC Iraq Petroleum Co. [1929-58]: Composed of APOC [BP], Shell Oil, Compagnie Française, Standard Oil of New Jersey, Mobil Oil and Gulbenkian interests in oil consortium. Superseded TPC.

IRP Islamic Republican Party, Iran [1979-]: Dominates *majlis*, judicial system and cabinet.

JNF Jewish National Fund [*Keren Kayemeth*; 1901-]: Concerned with fund-raising and acquisition of land in Palestine, and then Israel, for Jewish people.

JP Justice Party [1961-81]: A major Turkish political party in the 2nd Turkish republic, led by Süleymān Demirel.

KNPC Kuwait National Petroleum Co. [1960-]: National oil company financed by State of Kuwait.

KOC Kuwait Oil Co. [1933-]: Western oil consortium of APOC [BP] and Gulf Oil Corporation.

MEPL Middle East Pipeline, Ltd. [1947]: A company controlled by the AIOC and American oil companies who sought to build a pipeline from Iran to the Mediterranean, but failed.

MFO Multinational Force and Observers [1981-]: An international force—U.S., Fiji, Colombia, Great Britain, France, Italy, Australia and New Zealand—supervising Treaty of Peace between Egypt and Israel on the Sinai. It replaced UNEF II.

NATO North Atlantic Treaty Organization [1949-].

NF National Front [1951-53]: A nationalist Iranian political group dominated by Mosaddeq.

NF National Front [1964-]: A major, radical political party in South Yemen.

NIOC National Iranian Oil Company [1951-]: Iranian national oil company.

NLF National Liberation Front [1954-64]: A radical, anti-British political party in Aden. Later became only legal party of PDRY, the British having transferred power to them.

NSC National Security Council [Turkish; 1980-]: Military leadership under Kenan Evren, which ran Turkey from *coup* of September 12, 1980.

NUC National Unity Committee [1961-62]: The military group that ran Turkey for the period between the two republics.

OAPEC Organization of Arab Petroleum Exporting Countries [1968-]: Membership, as of 1982, was Algeria, Bahrain, Egypt (suspended '79), Iraq, Kuwait, SA, Syria, Tunisia, Libya, Qatar, UAE.

OAU Organization of African Unity [1963-]: Organization of African states, excluding European-controlled areas, to further African unity and solidarity.

OPEC Organization of Petroleum Exporting Countries [1960-]: Membership, as of 1982, was Algeria, Ecuador, Iran, Iraq, Indonesia, Gabon, Kuwait, Libya, Nigeria, Qatar, Saudi Arabia, Venezuela and UAE.

PDFLP See DFLP above.

PDRY People's Democratic Republic of Yemen [1970-]: The official name for the government of South Yemen. From 1967-70, it was known as PRSY [People's Republic of South Yemen].

PFLO Popular Front for the Liberation of Oman [1974-]: A group opposed to the existing government of Oman. Formerly PFLOAG.

PFLOAG Popular Front for Liberation of Oman and the Arabian Gulf [1968-74]: A group opposed to the existing governments of Oman, UAE and other Gulf states sponsored by the PDRY.

PFLP Popular Front for Liberation of Palestine [1968-]: Marxist Palestinian *fidā'īyīn* group founded by George Habash.

PFLP-GC Popular Front for Liberation of Palestine - General Command [1968-]: A radical Palestinian *fidā'īyīn* group founded by Aḥmad Jibrīl. Later broke off from PFLP.

PLA Palestine Liberation Army [1964-]: The official army of the PLO.

PLF Palestine Liberation Front [1965?-68]: A Palestinian *fidā'īyīn* group founded by Aḥmad Jibrīl. Later merged with part of ANM and other groups to form PFLP.

PLO Palestine Liberation Organization [1964-]: Umbrella organization of various Palestinian groups.

PNC Palestine National Council [1965-]: Established in 1965 with 182 members. In 1977 it increased to 292.

POLP Popular Organization for Liberation of Palestine [1969-]: Maoist Palestinian *fidā'īyīn* group.

PPS Parti Populaire Syrien [1932-]: Syrian national party founded by Anṭun Sa^c^ada. Also known as SSNP.

PSP Progressive Socialist Party [1949-]: A major Lebanese Druze political party associated with Kamāl Jumblāṭ.

RCC Revolutionary Command Council [1952-56]: Egyptian military group, led by Gamāl ^c^Abd al-Nāṣir, which planned the 1952 *coup* and then ran the government under leadership of Muḥammad Naguib.

RPP Republican People's Party [1923-81]: A

major Turkish political party founded by Muṣṭafā Kemal Atatürk.

SAR Syrian Arab Republic [1961-]: Official name of Syria.

SAVAK Sāzeman-e Attilᶜāt va Amniyat-e Keshvar [Organization for the information and security of the country]: Iranian security forces combine the roles of the FBI and CIA.

SSNP Syrian Social Nationalist Party: See PPS.

TAPline Trans-Arabian Pipeline Co. [1947-]: A subsidiary of Aramco that built a 1,068.2-mile pipeline from Saudi Arabia to Sidon.

TPC Turkish Petroleum Co. [1912-29]: Western-dominated oil company that became basis for IPC.

UAA Union of Arab Amirates: Also known as UAE [United Arab Emirates].

UAE Union of Arab Emirates [1971-]: Members, as of 1974, include: Abu Dhabi, Dubai, Sharjah, Ahman, Umm al-Qaywayn, al-Fujayrah and Ras al-Khaymah [also United Arab Emirates].

UAR United Arab Republic [1958-61]: Union of Egypt and Syria, with the former keeping the name until 1971, when it became the ARE.

UJA United Jewish Appeal: A major, pro-Israeli Jewish fund-raising group in the United States.

UNCC United Nations Conciliation Commission [1948-49]: Commission composed of France, Turkey and U.S. It aimed to achieve a peace settlement between Israel and the Arab States.

UNDOF United Nations Disengagement Observer Force [1974-]: An international military force established in June 1974 to patrol the buffer region separating Israeli and Syrian forces on the Golan Heights.

UNEF United Nations Emergency Force [1957-67; 1974-79]: An international military force established after the 1956 Suez War between Egypt and Israel and reactivated after the 1973 War.

UNEF II See UNEF. Re-established UNEF after 1973 War.

UNESCO United Nations Educational, Scientific and Cultural Organization.

UNGA United Nations General Assembly.

UNIFIL United Nations Interim Force in Lebanon [1978-]: Established after March 1978, when Israel initiated military actions in southern Lebanon.

UNMAC United Nations Mixed Armistice Commission [1949-]: International groups to supervise and investigate truce violations between Egypt and Israel [UNEIMAC], Jordan and Israel [UNJIMAC], Syria and Israel [UNSIMAC], and Lebanon and Israel [UNLIMAC].

UNOGIL United Nations Observer Group in Lebanon [1958]: International group to investigate possible Syrian interference during Lebanese Civil War.

UNRPR United Nations Relief for Palestinian Refugees [1948-49]: Established to provide immediate relief for Palestinian refugees; superseded by UNRWA.

UNRWA United Nations Relief and Works Agency [1949-]: International group to feed, house and train Palestinian refugees temporarily.

UNSCOP United Nations Special Committee on Palestine [1947]: UN committee whose majority recommended partition of Palestine.

UNTSO United Nations Truce Supervision Organization [1948-49]: Established to supervise the Arab-Israeli armistice.

UNYOM United Nations Yemen Observation Mission [1963-64]: A small international force to oversee the truce in the Yemen Civil War. Unsuccessful and was withdrawn after 15 months.

WZO World Zionist Organization [1897-]: A major Zionist body.

YAR Yemen Arab Republic [1962-]: Official name of Northern Yemen.

VIII. Historical Atlas

The lack of an adequate historical atlas has been a major lacuna in Islamic studies. Dr. R. Roolvink and others compiled the *Historical Atlas of the Muslim Peoples* (Amsterdam: Djambatan, 1957), which has almost 50 multicolored maps covering the area from Spain to Indonesia, and from the pre-Islamic period to the 20th century. Many of them concentrate on particular areas and specific chronological periods. However, the lack of an index is a serious weakness.

But the weakness of Roolvink's work is the strength of Harry W. Hazard's *Atlas of Islamic History*, 3rd ed. (Princeton: Princeton University Press, 1954). His index is not only thorough, but, in many cases, includes the Arabic, Persian, Ottoman and European spellings of a place's name. Each map is accompanied by a list of the dynasties and their dates for all the areas covered. The weakness is in the maps. The first 13 out of 18 cover a fixed area: Spain through Iran, and each deals with a century of changes. They are, therefore, limited in detail and each covers a very long chronological period.

A work limited to the Arab world, from Iraq and Arabia through Spain, is Rolf Reichert's *A Historical and Regional Atlas of the Arab World, [Maps and Chronological Survey]*, (Rio de Janeiro: Sedegra Sociedade Editora e Grafica, Ltd., 1969), in English and Portuguese. The 68 black-and-white maps of fair quality cover the Arabian Peninsula, Syria and Mesopotamia, Northeast Africa and Northwest Africa (Maghrib), on a century-by-century basis. Each map is accompanied by a text covering the major historical events, as well as six genealogy tables. An index is lacking.

An example of an excellent historical atlas is the *Historical Atlas of Iran*, published by Tehran University in 1971, under the editorship of Seyyid Hossein Naṣr, Aḥmad Mostofi and Abbās Zaryab. Of the very large, colored maps, 20 are of use for students of Islamic Iran. Each map, with locations in Persian and English/French, includes all the major cities, many minor ones, general political lines, provinces and bodies of water. Each map is accompanied by a brief historical survey in Persian, French and English. All locations are indexed.

Another specialized publication is the posthumous work of Donald E. Pitcher: *An Historical Geography of the Ottoman Empire from Earliest Times to the End of the Sixteenth Century* (Leiden: E.J. Brill, 1972). As the title indicates, the 36 multicolored maps cover the years from the rise of the Ottomans to 1612. The political and provincial divisions are given in great detail. This work also includes an historical survey which stresses the dates of the territorial acquisitions and an index.

In the decade since the first edition of *A Near East Studies Handbook* was prepared, a number of atlases have appeared or have been announced, which will alleviate many of the problems facing those needing historical atlases. The almost 60 maps in William C. Brice, ed., *An Historical Atlas of Islam* (Leiden: E.J. Brill, 1981), cover the Islamic world from the Atlantic to the Philippines. Each map, in color, gives a sense of the topography and identifies major geographical features. These maps are best for indicating military campaigns, trade routes, and general political boundaries. There are maps of Mecca [Makka], Medina [al-Madīna] and Istanbul, which are very helpful. There is also an index.

Francis Robinson, *Atlas of the Islamic World Since 1500* (New York: Facts on File, Inc., 1982), is an excellent, extensive essay on Islamic political, cultural and religious history with magnificent photographs. The well-drawn, colored maps — limited in number — are outstanding and are particularly valuable for religious developments. There is an index. Unfortunately, the same high praise cannot be given for *Atlas of the Arab World*, compiled by Michael Dempsey (New York: Facts on File, Inc., 1983), whose maps are brightly colored, but give only the most general economic and political information.

Throughout Marshall G.S. Hodgson, *The Venture of Islam*, 3 vols. (Chicago: University of Chicago Press, 1974), there are black-and-white maps reflecting political developments throughout the Islamic world. As with the Robinson book, they supplement the text and are not the focus of the work. There is no index for the maps.

The finest historical atlas is being prepared by the German Research Council and the University of Tübingen. It is *Tübingen Atlas des Vorderen Orients* [*TAVO*], (Wiesbaden: Dr. Ludwig Reichert Verlag, 1977-). This atlas is being produced in large, unbound sheets measuring approximately 20" by 28" which, when finished, should number over 300 sheets. One-third of the series will be on physical geography, including climate, vegetation, population, etc. The historical maps go from the Stone Age to the Modern Age, and will include detailed maps of Islamic cities, locations of major religious movements, etc. An excellent review of this work was written by Michael Bonine in the *MESA Bulletin*, XVII.1 (July 1983):103-105.

Computer-generated maps are being developed for classroom use and could be on the market in the near future. Justin McCarthy, Department of History (University of Louisville), has developed one system that can be adjusted to meet the needs of a particular teacher. Herbert Bodman, Department of History (University of North Carolina), is editing a massive, computer-generated historical atlas entitled *Atlas of the Islamic Peoples*, which is being funded in part by a grant from the National Endowment for the Humanities. It should be available in 1984.

It is also possible for individuals to produce their own computer-generated maps, using the World Data Bank II, a data base of the world's coastlines, developed by the Central Intelligence Agency and now distributed by the National Technical Information Service. The data base includes islands, lakes, rivers, canals and international political boundaries. It is also possible to mark the locations of cities by including their coordinates.

More surprising than some of the inadequacies of the historical atlases for the pre-1900 period is the lack of a good collection dealing with 20th-century political histories. Over half the maps in this book reflect proposed and actual divisions of the Middle East for this century because they are not readily available elsewhere.

For a fuller discussion of all of these resources, the reader may consult Gerry A. Hale's "Maps and Atlases of the Middle East," *MESA Bulletin*, III.3 (October 1969):17-39. The Hale survey is being updated by Douglas L. Johnson, Mary A. Powers, and Charlotte A. Slocum of Clark University, in a 1984 edition of the *MESA Bulletin*.

Cost has been the major factor for limiting the number of maps included within this atlas — a number which could easily have been doubled under somewhat less inflationary circumstances. The Muslim conquests and political changes in North Africa and Spain have not been included in order to be consistent with the geographical limits of this book. The spellings of place names have usually followed the accepted English form rather than a transliterated one; e.g.: Aleppo for Ḥalab, although the index includes these transliterated forms as cross-references. As indicated in the Introduction, line drawings have been used for financial reasons.

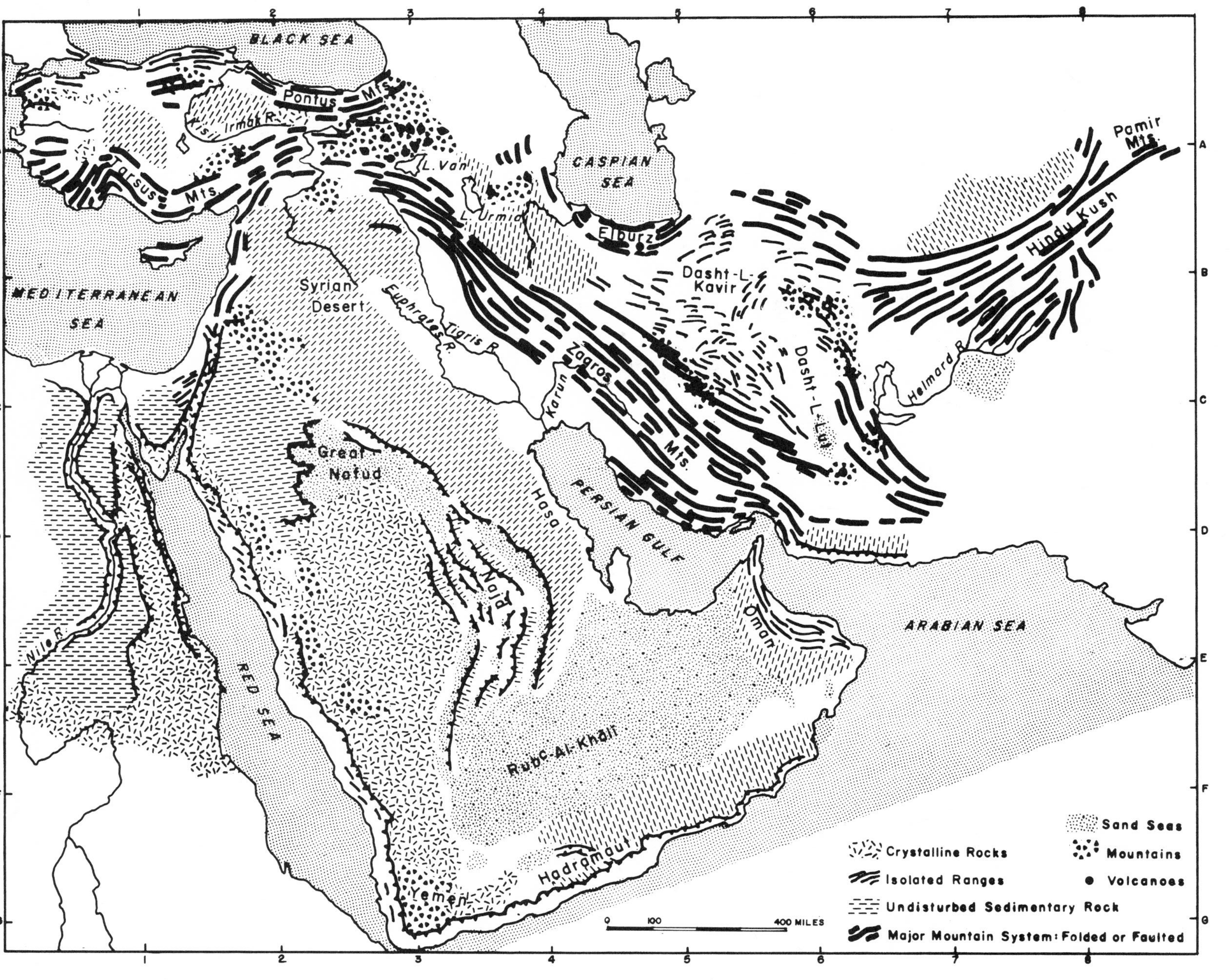

1. EGYPT AND SOUTHWEST ASIA, PHYSICAL CHARACTERISTICS

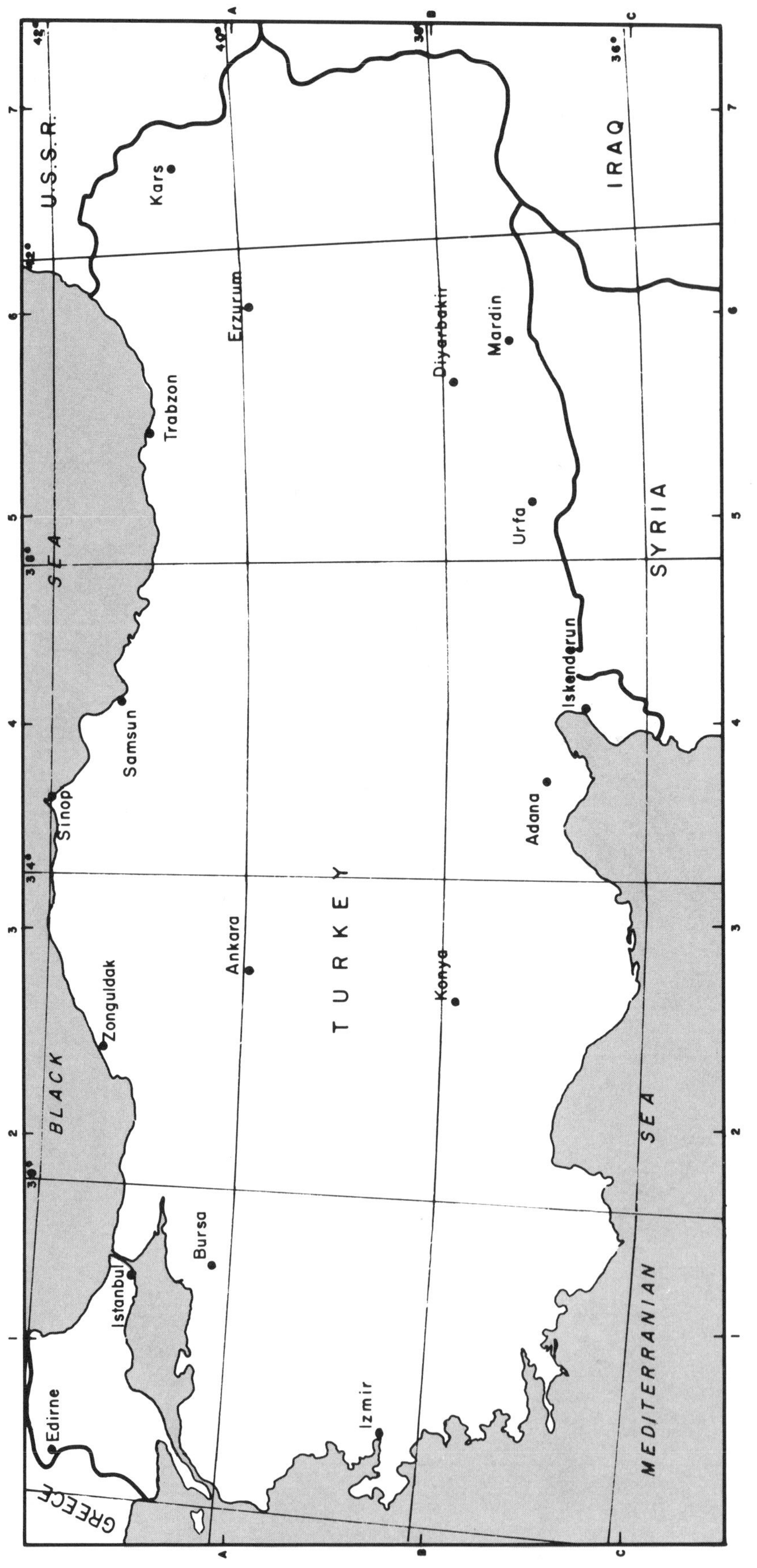

2. CITIES OF TURKEY

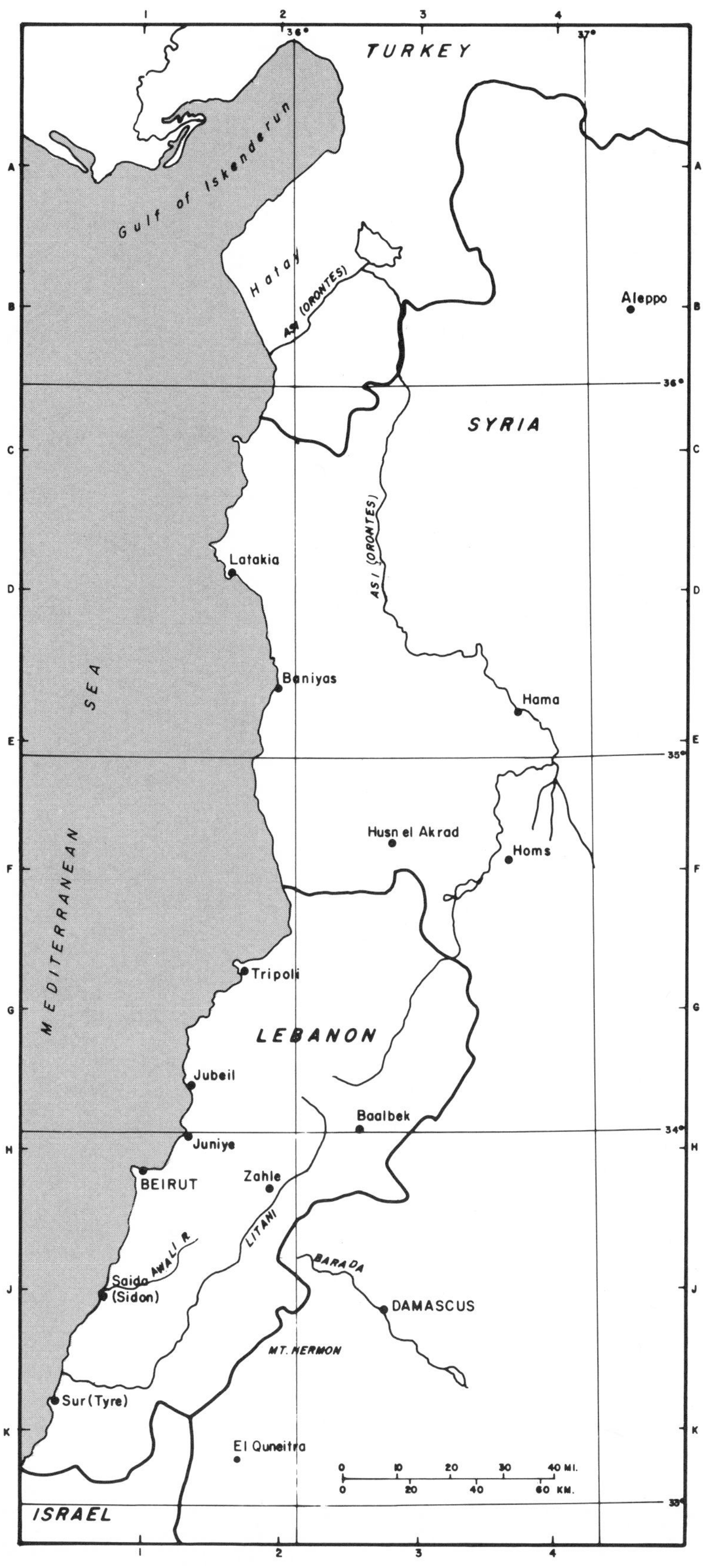

3. CITIES OF LEBANON AND WESTERN SYRIA

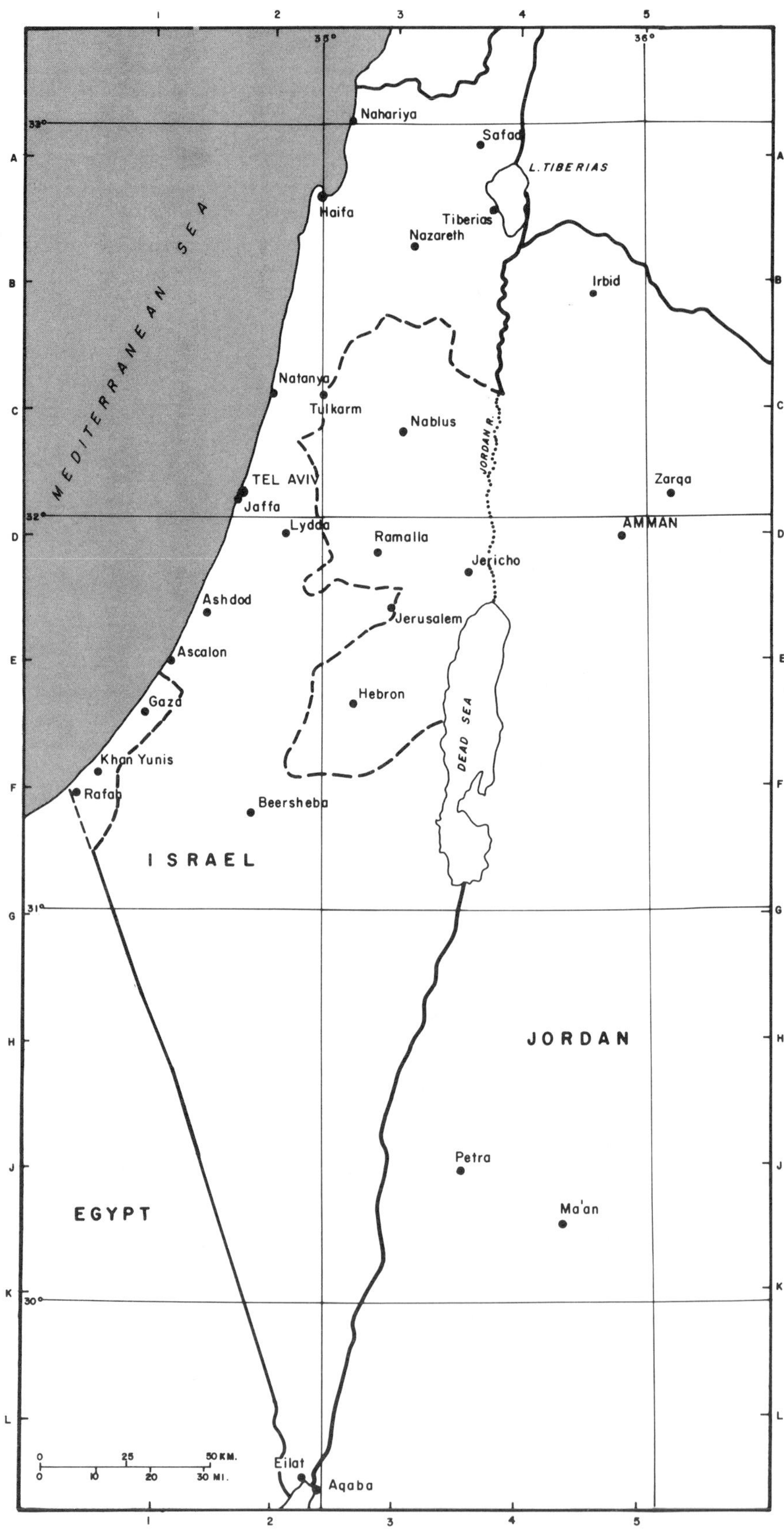

4. CITIES OF ISRAEL, GAZA, WEST BANK, AND WESTERN JORDAN

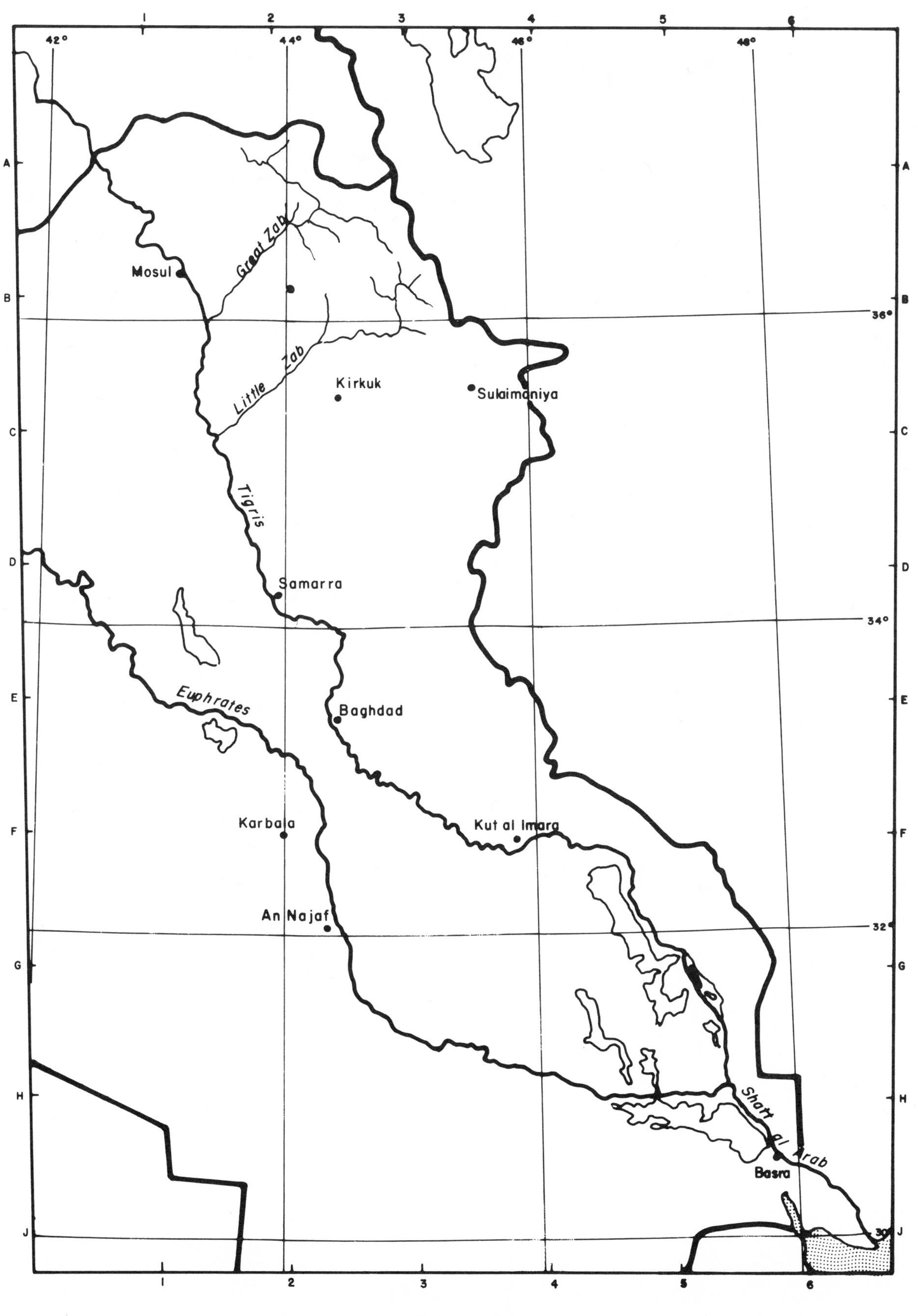

5. CITIES OF IRAQ

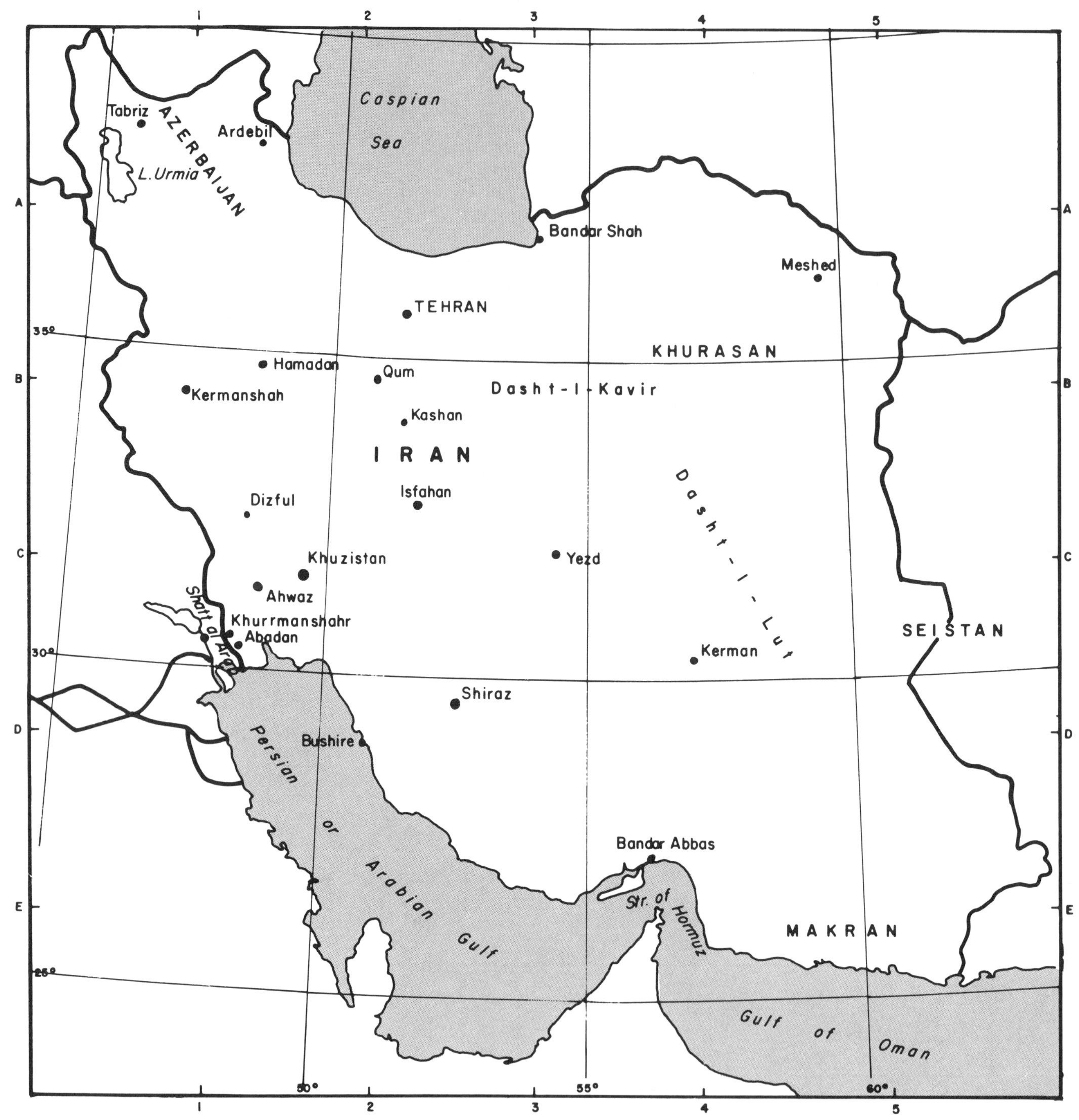

6. CITIES OF IRAN

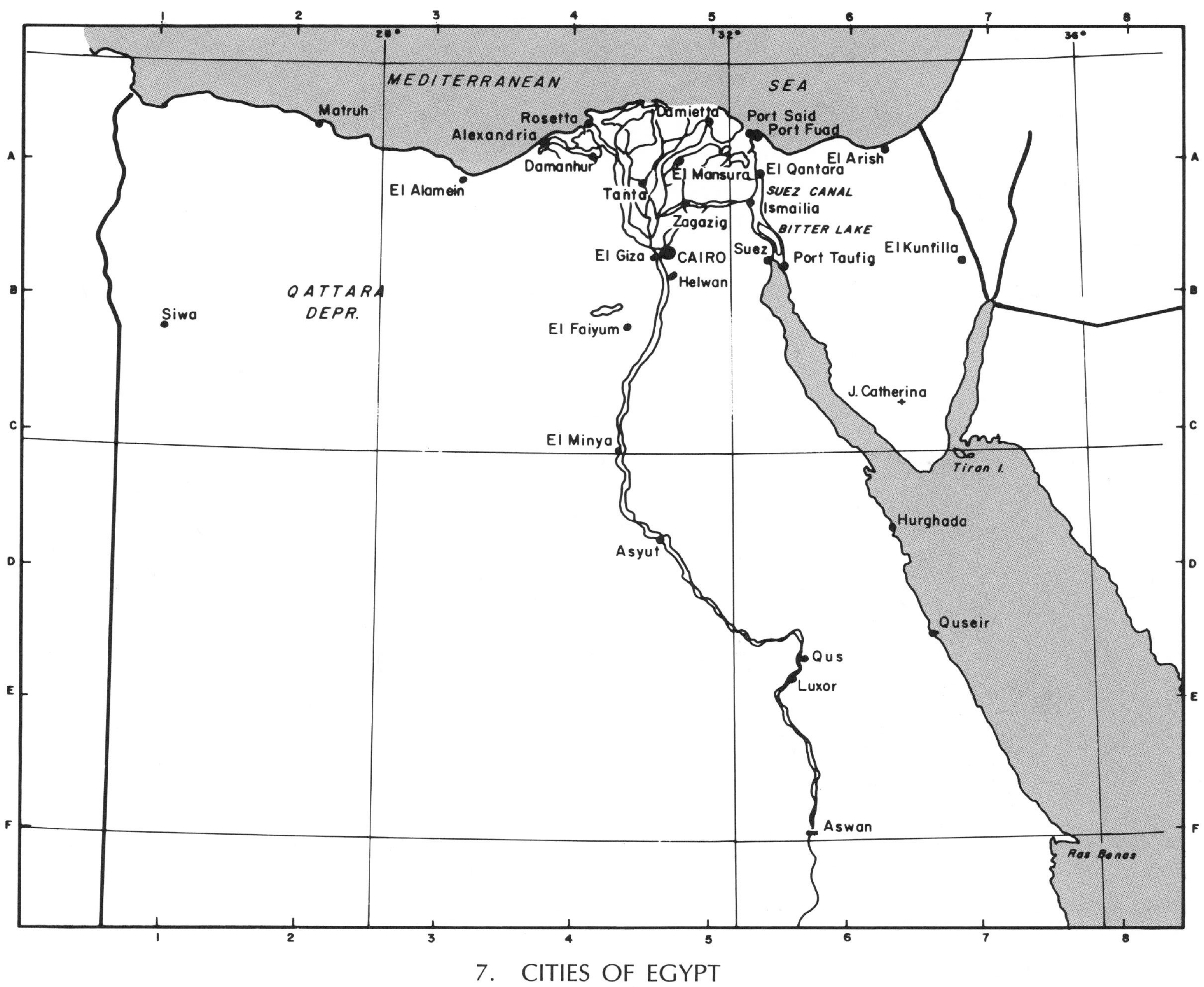

7. CITIES OF EGYPT

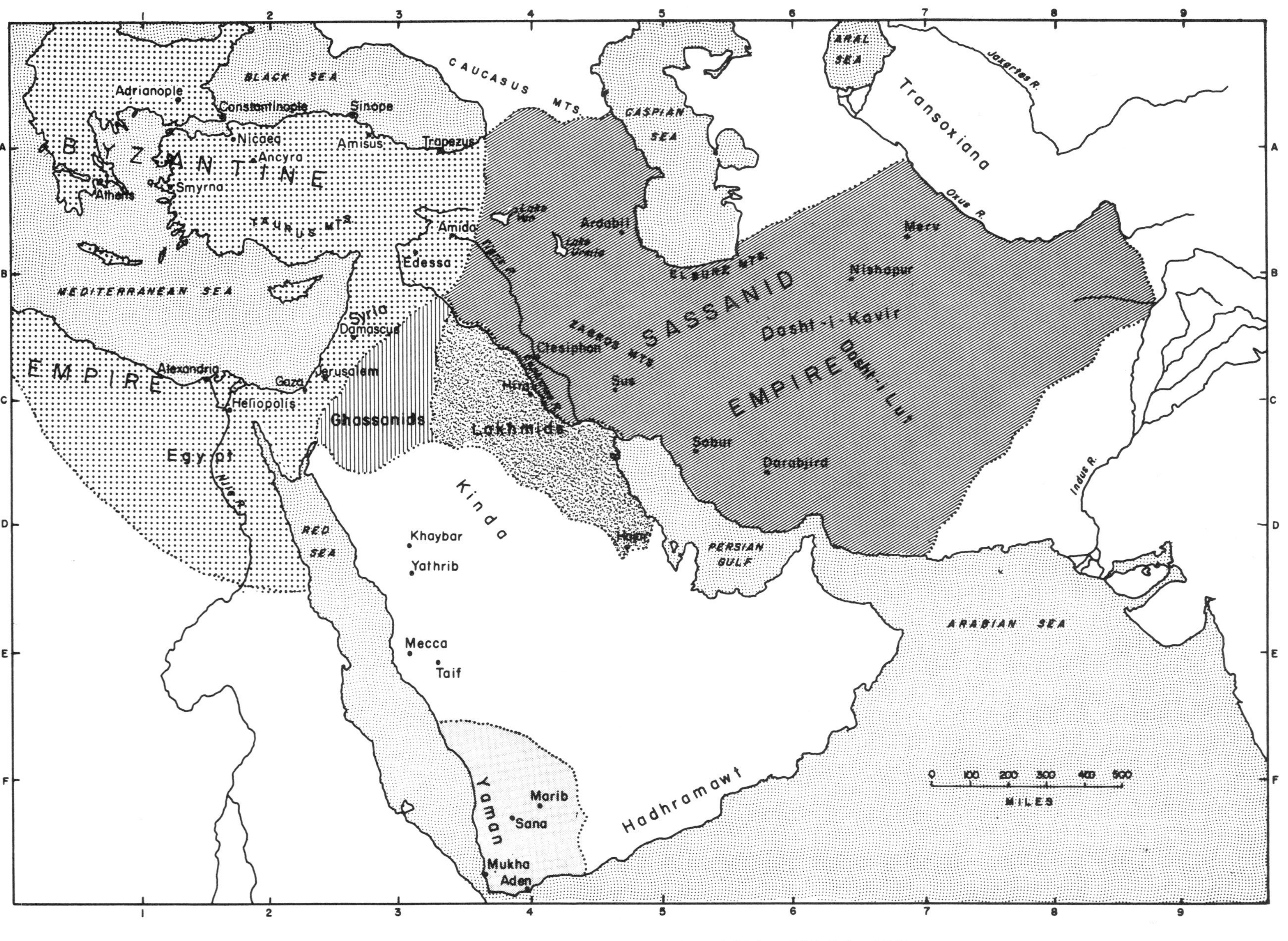

8. EGYPT AND SOUTHWEST ASIA, CIRCA 600

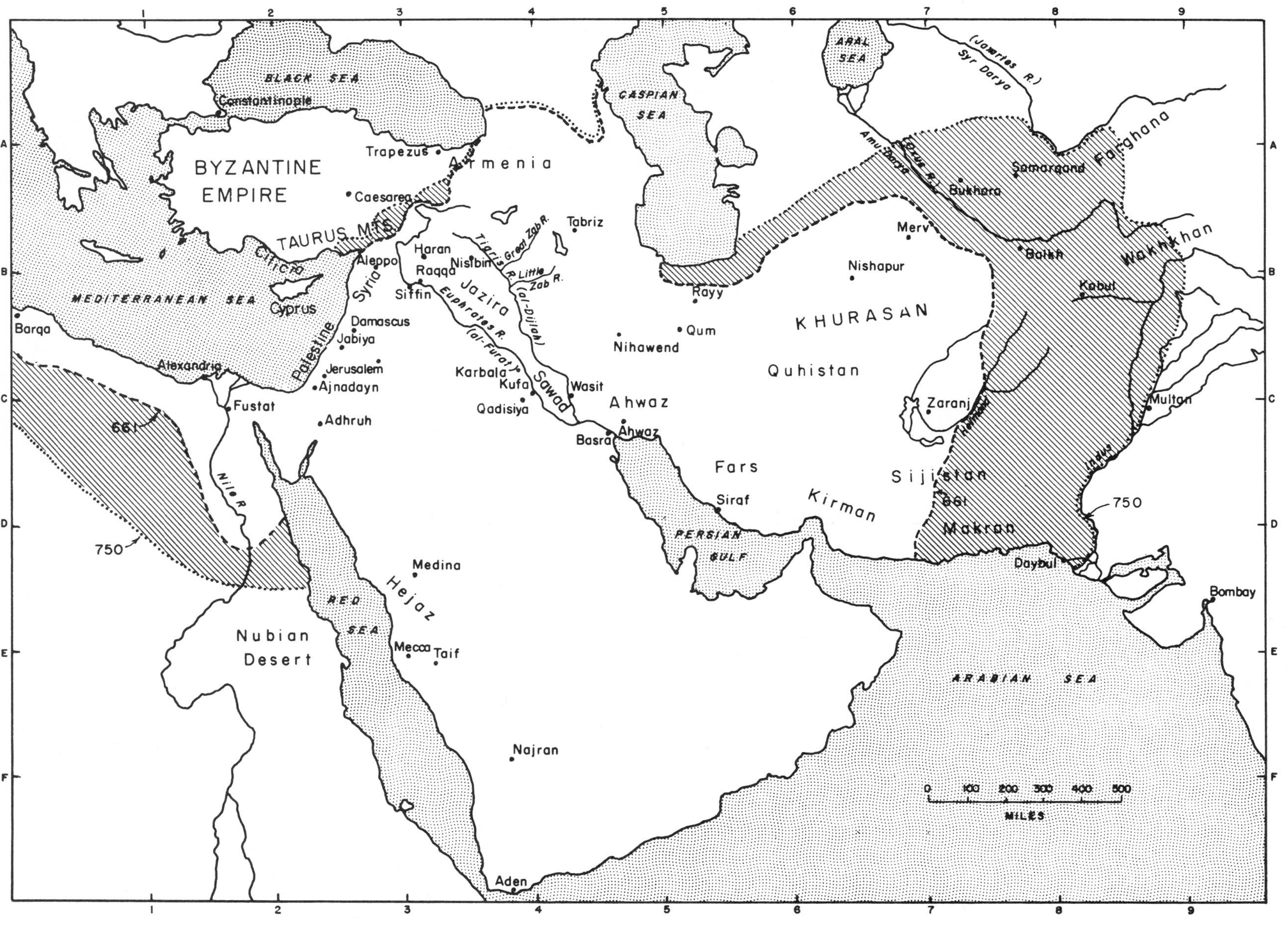

9. CONQUESTS, RĀSHIDŪN AND ʿUMAYYAD PERIODS

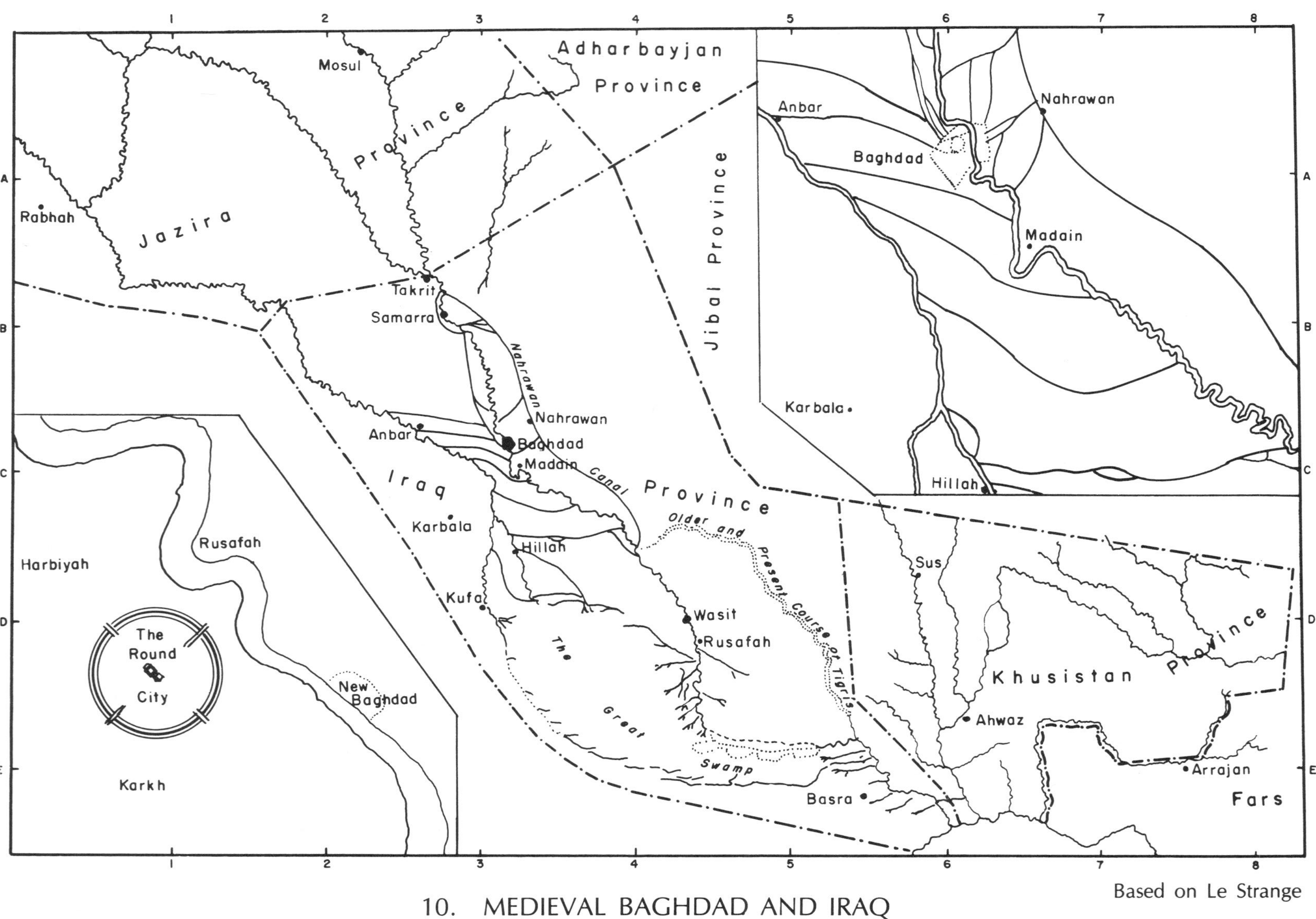

Based on Le Strange

10. MEDIEVAL BAGHDAD AND IRAQ

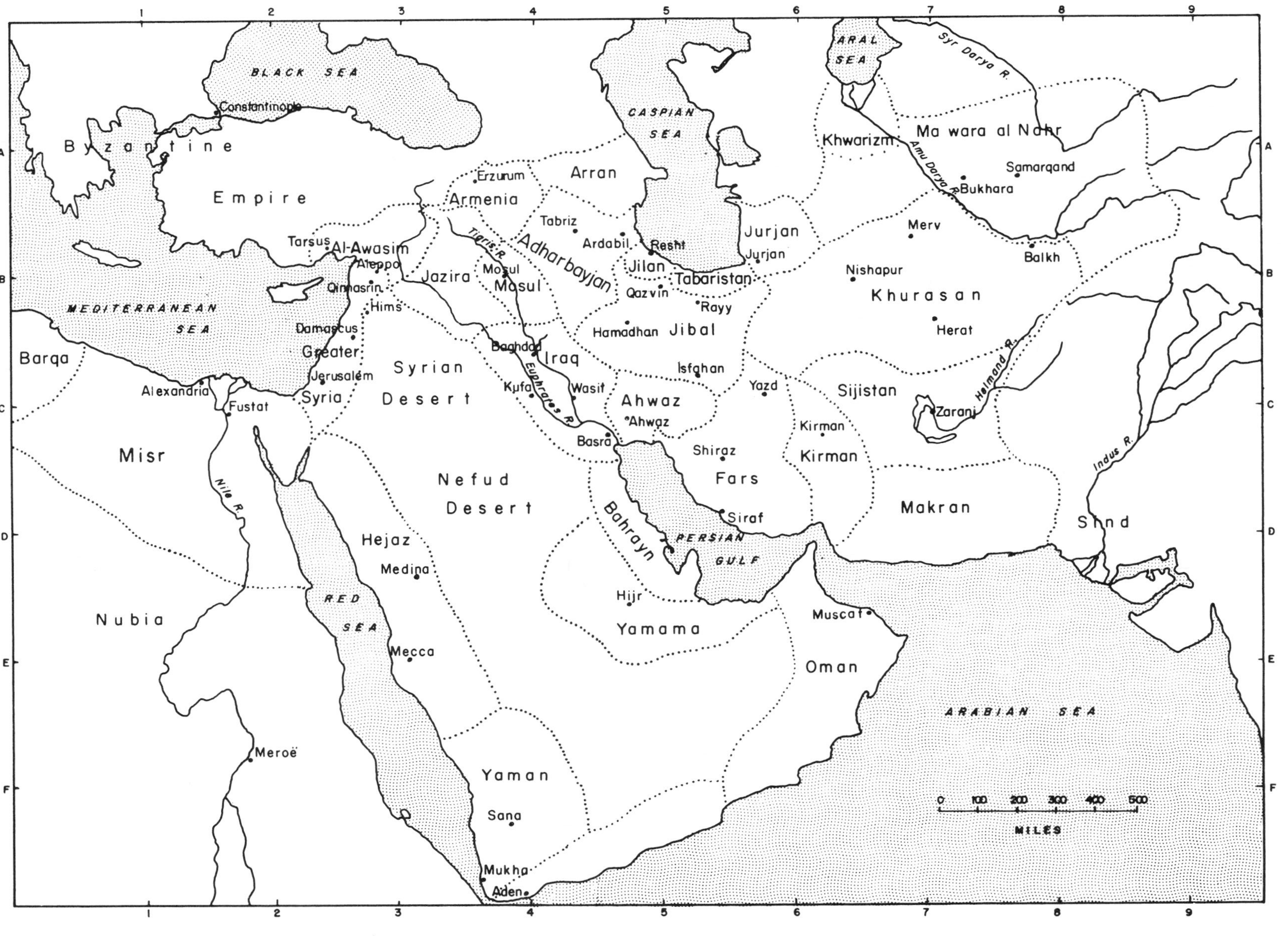

11. ᶜABBĀSID PROVINCES

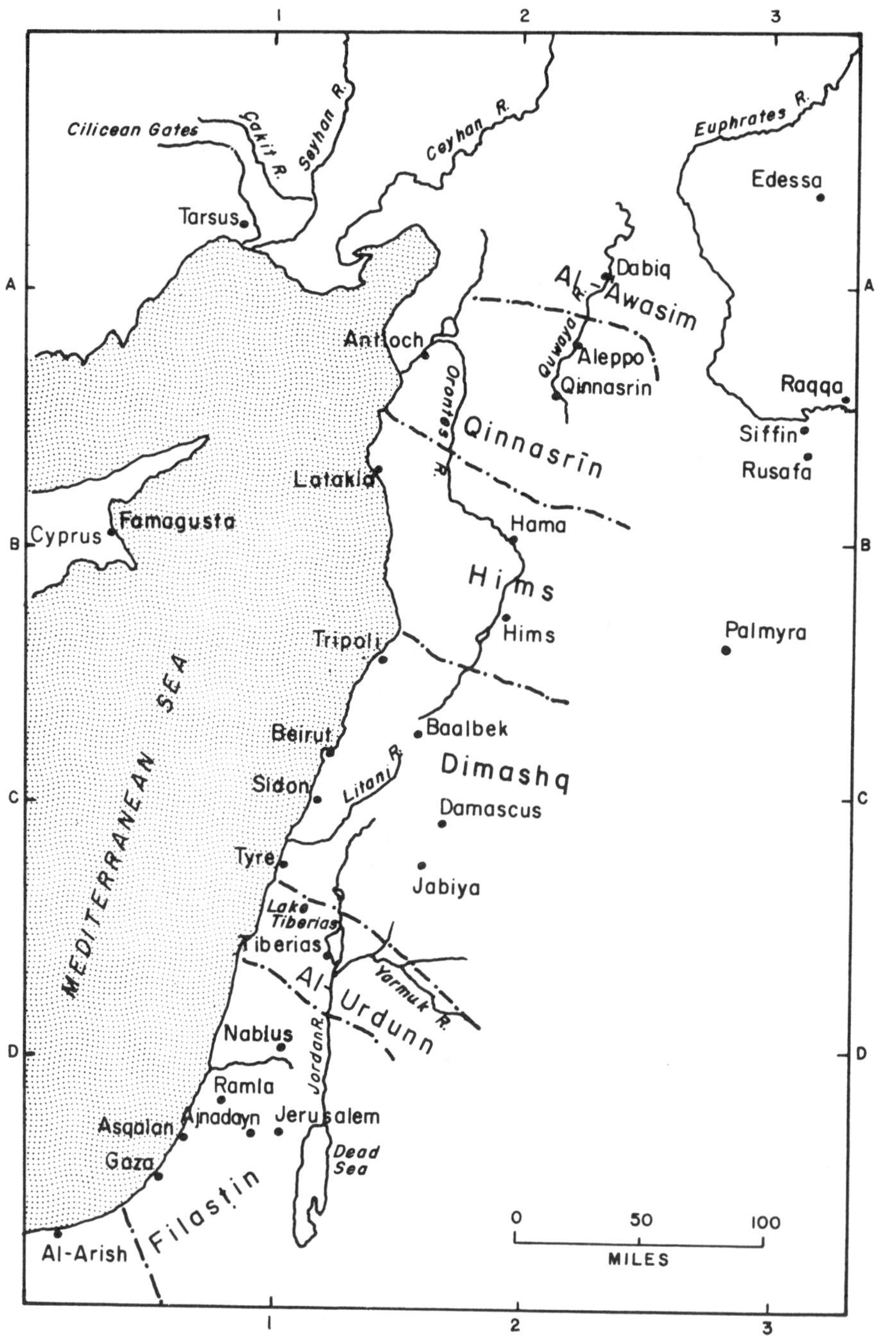

12. SYRIAN PROVINCES, ᶜABBĀSID PERIOD

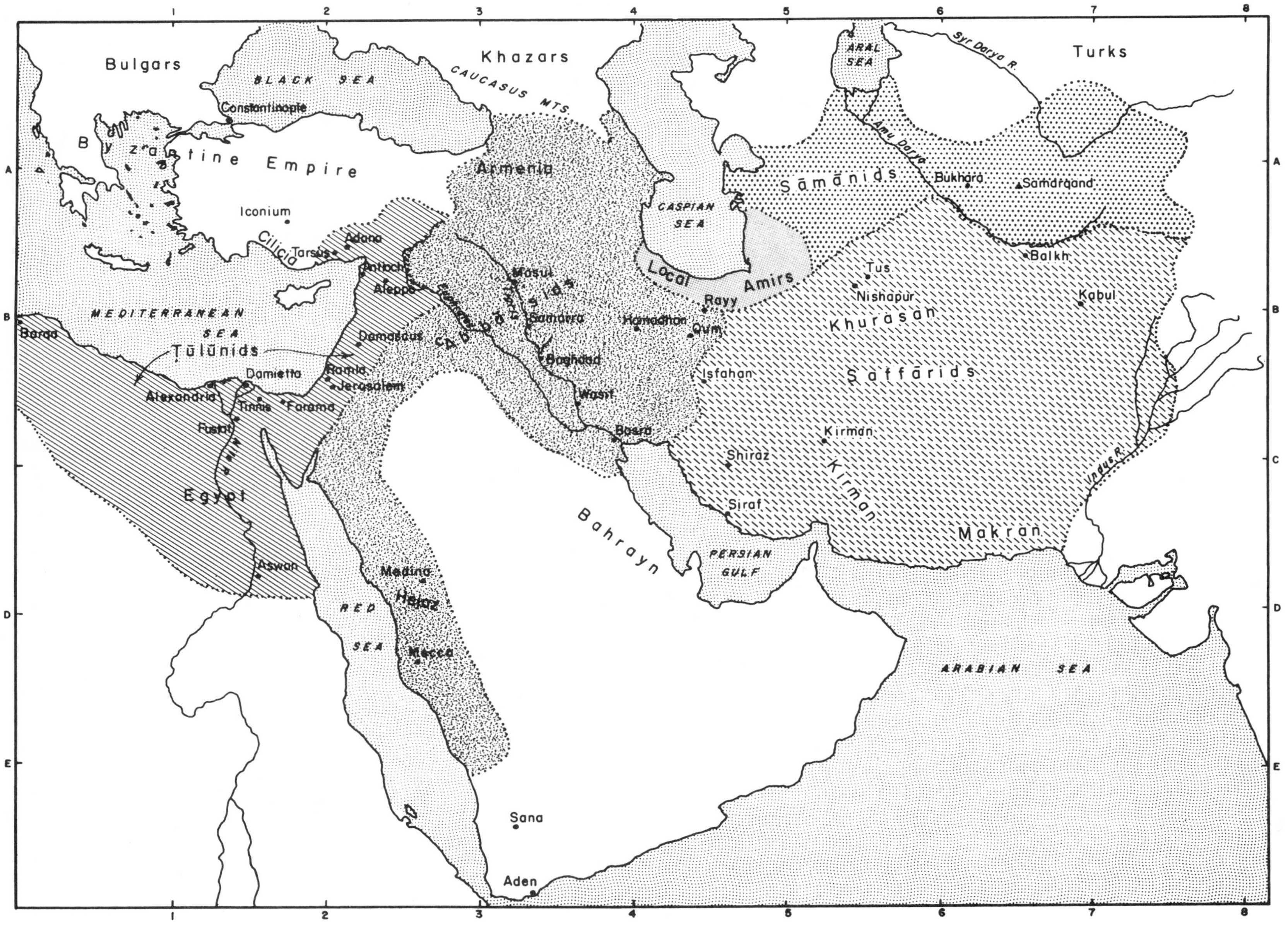

13. EGYPT AND SOUTHWEST ASIA, LATE 9th CENTURY

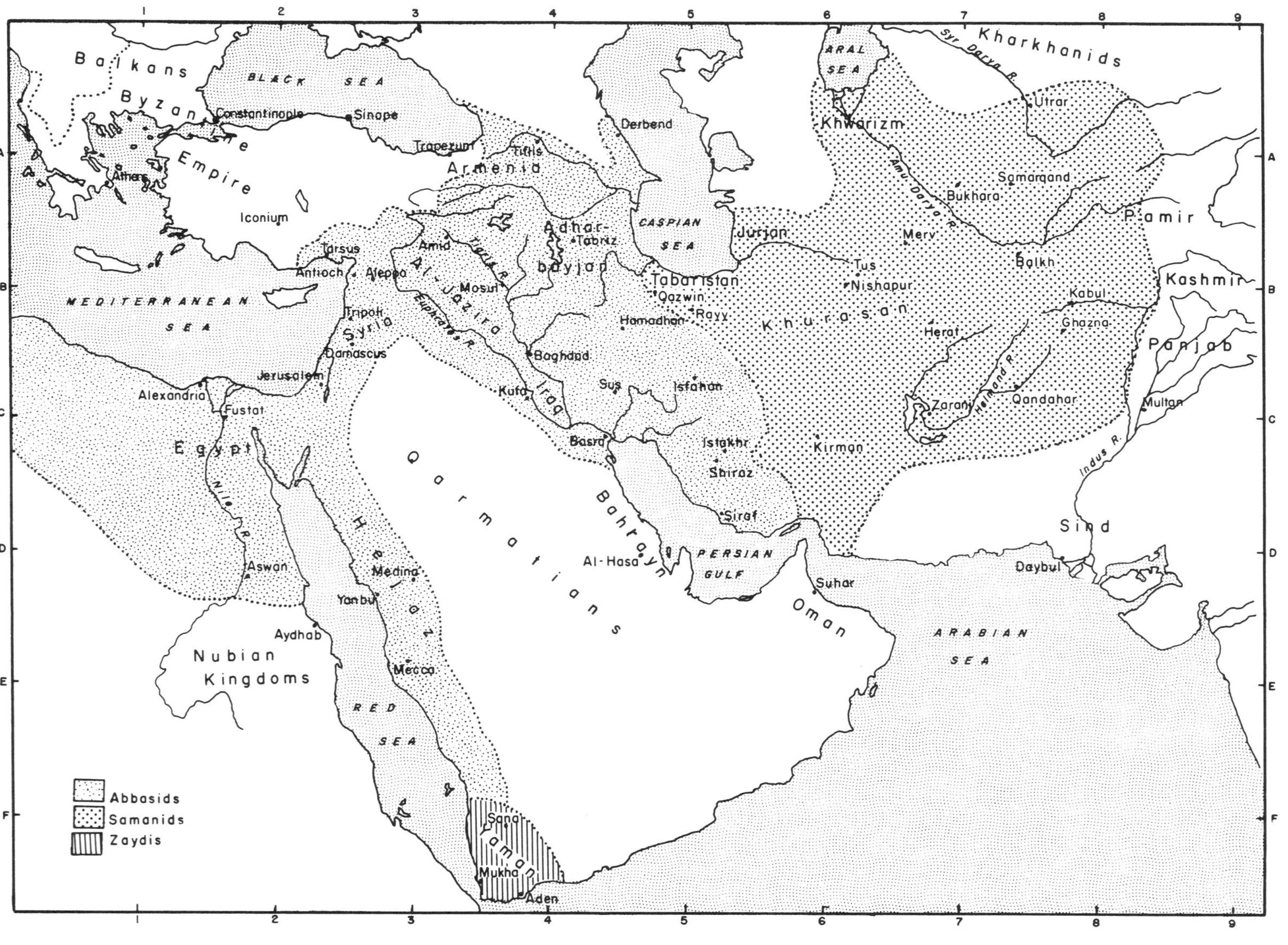

14. EGYPT AND SOUTHWEST ASIA, EARLY 10th CENTURY

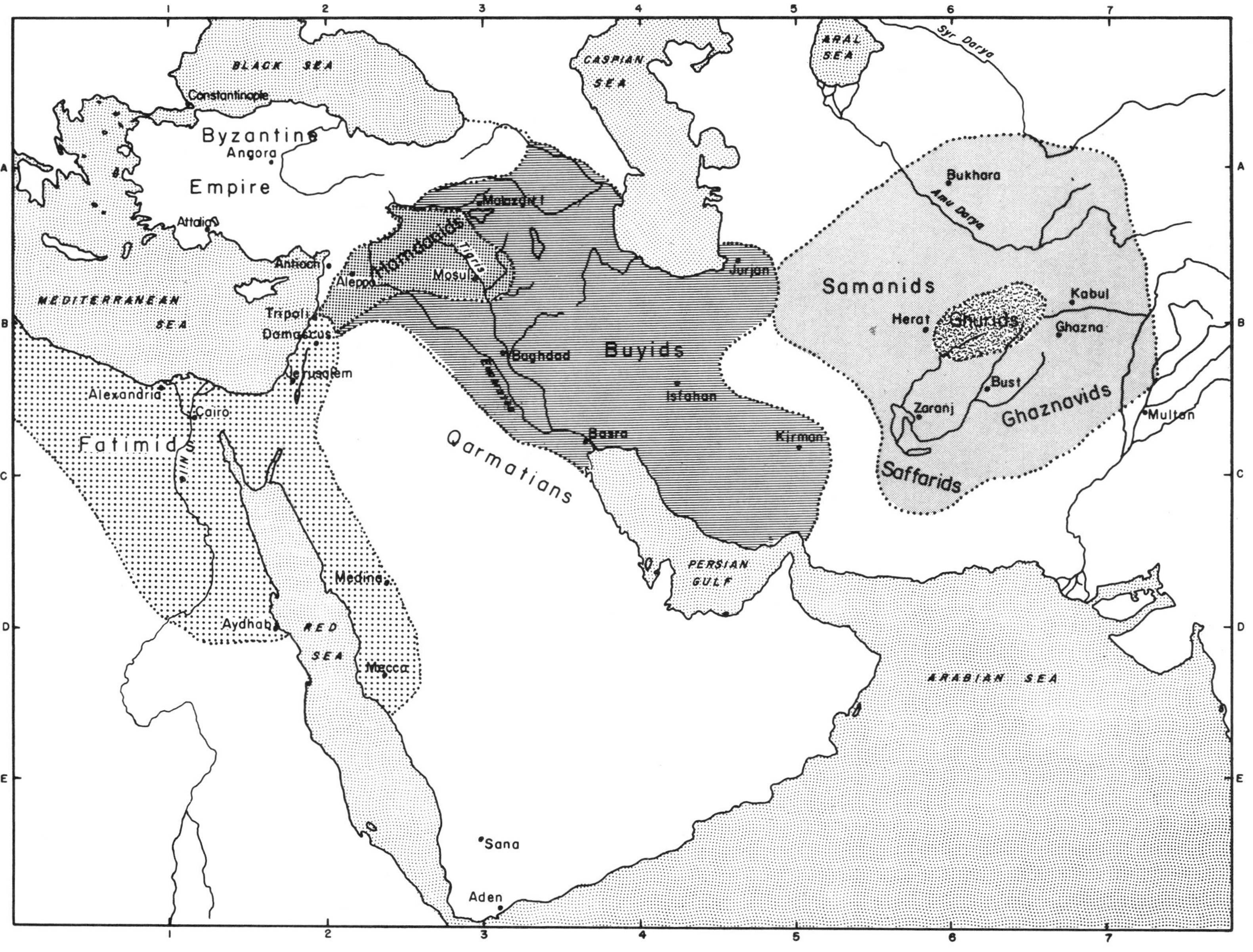

15. EGYPT AND SOUTHWEST ASIA, LATE 10th CENTURY

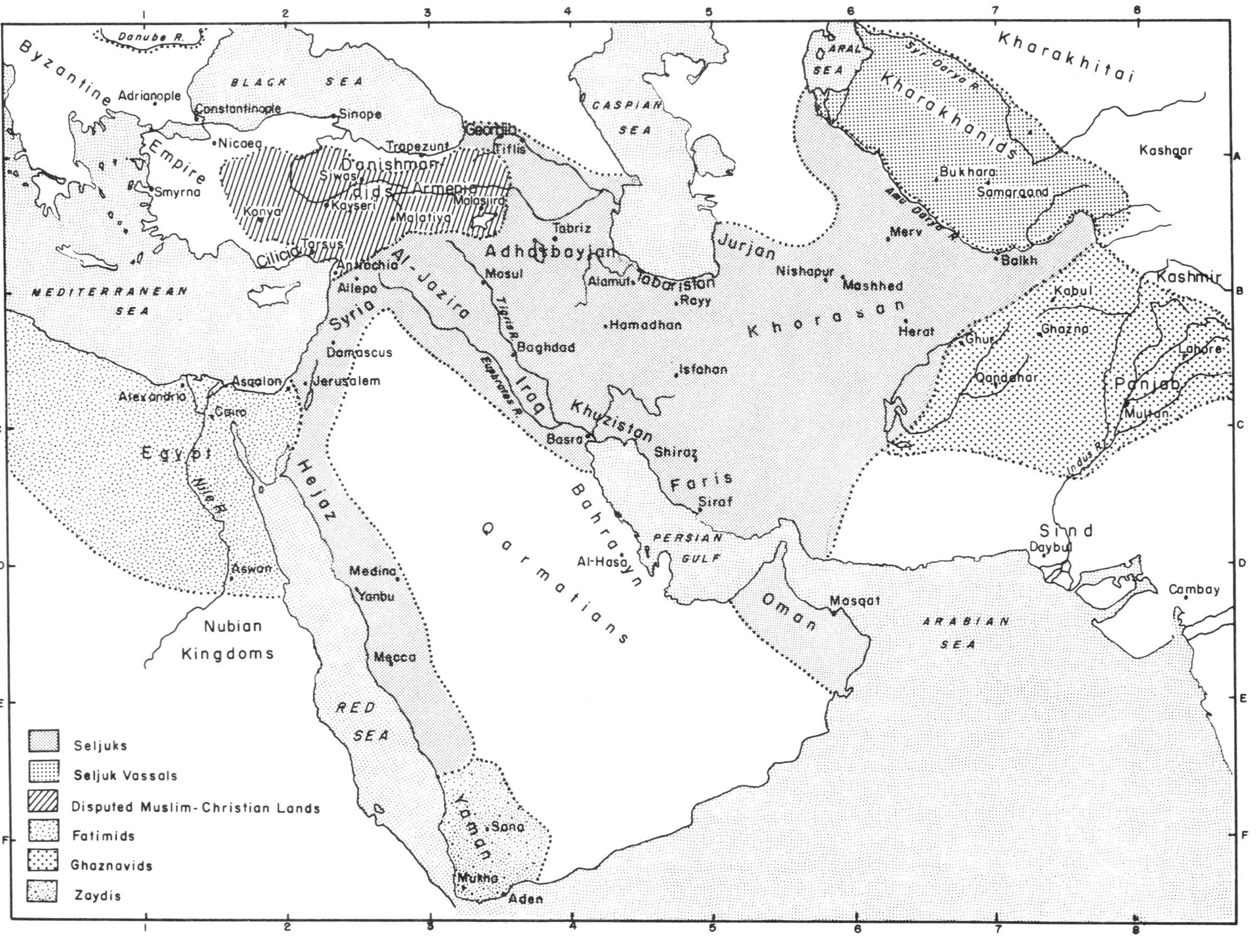

16. EGYPT AND SOUTHWEST ASIA, LATE 11th CENTURY

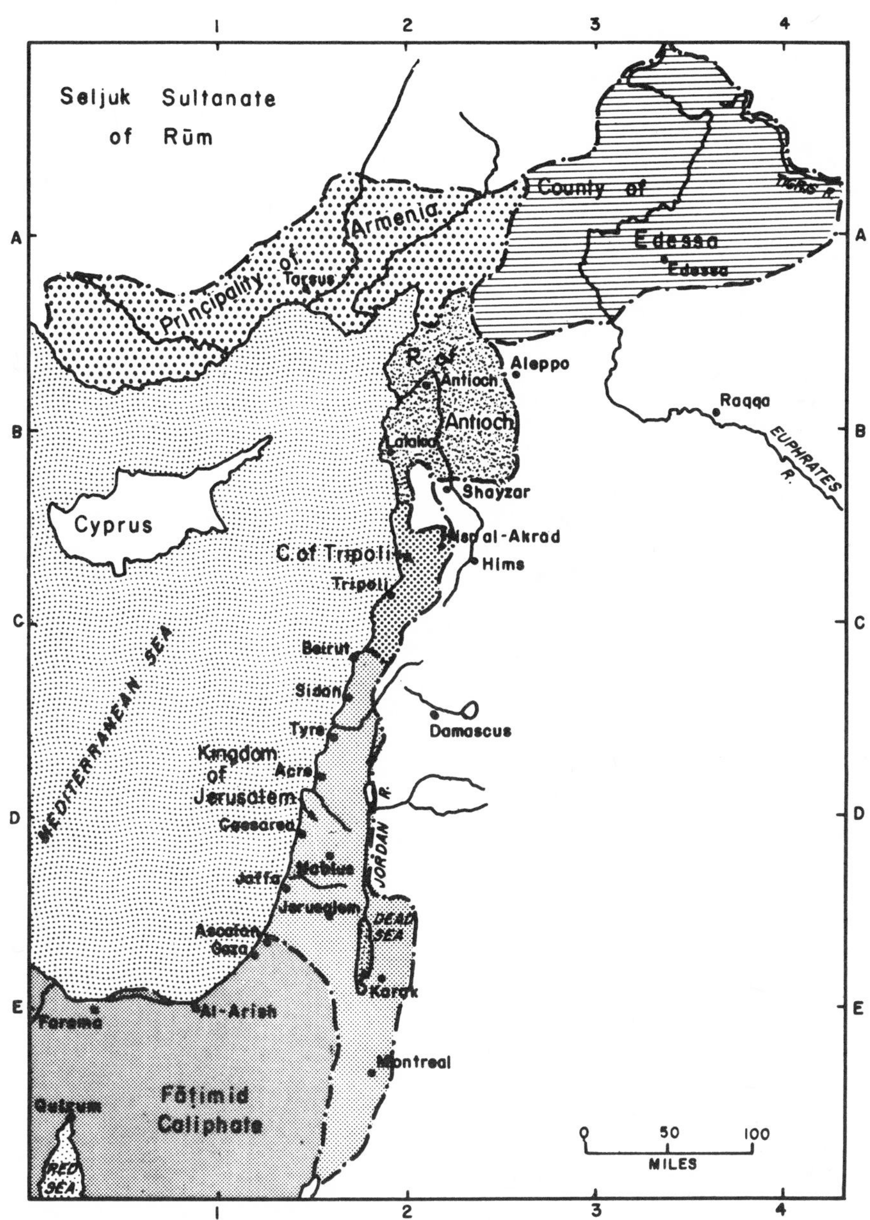

17. CRUSADING STATES, CIRCA 1130

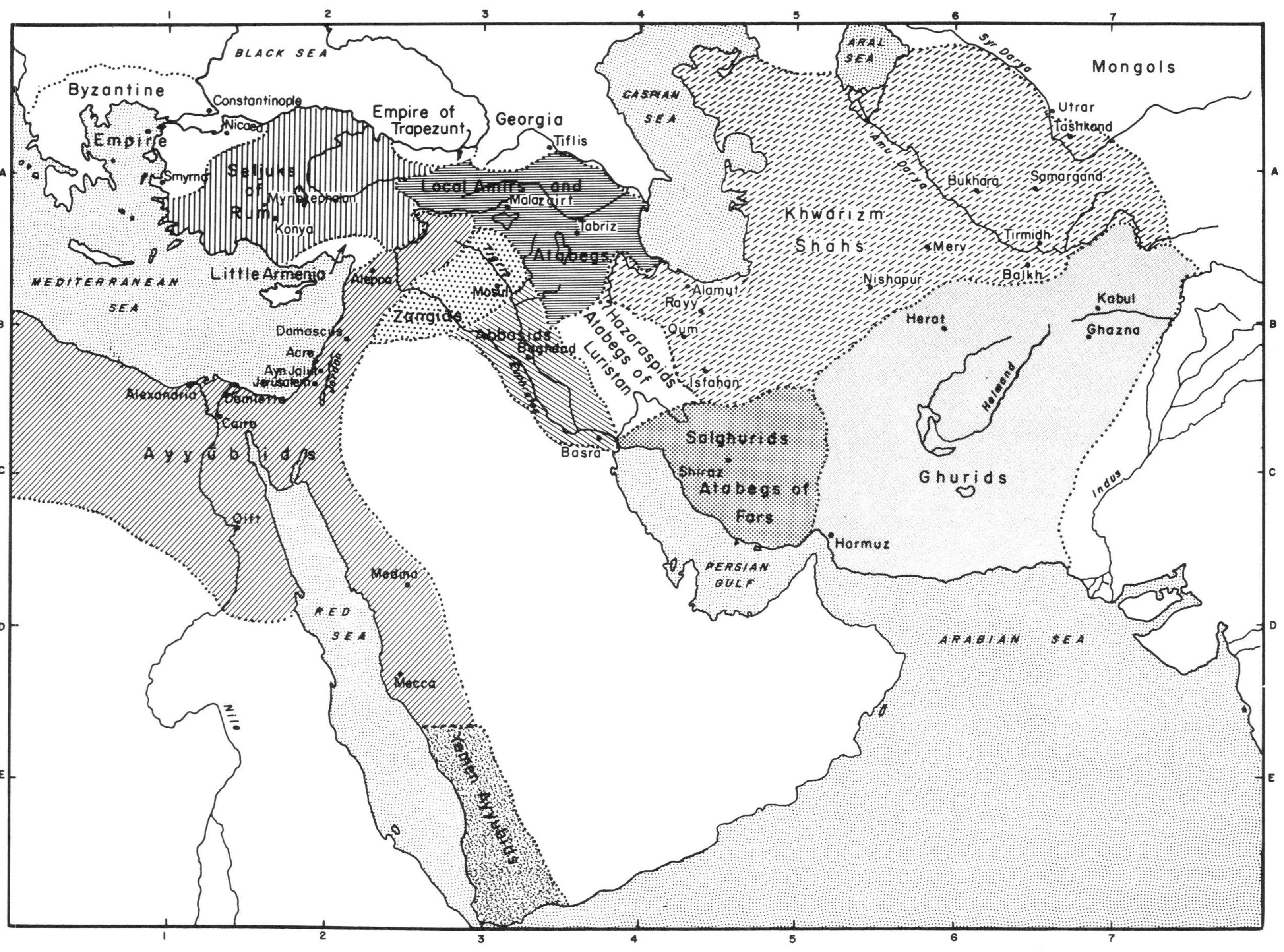

18. EGYPT AND SOUTHWEST ASIA, LATE 12th CENTURY

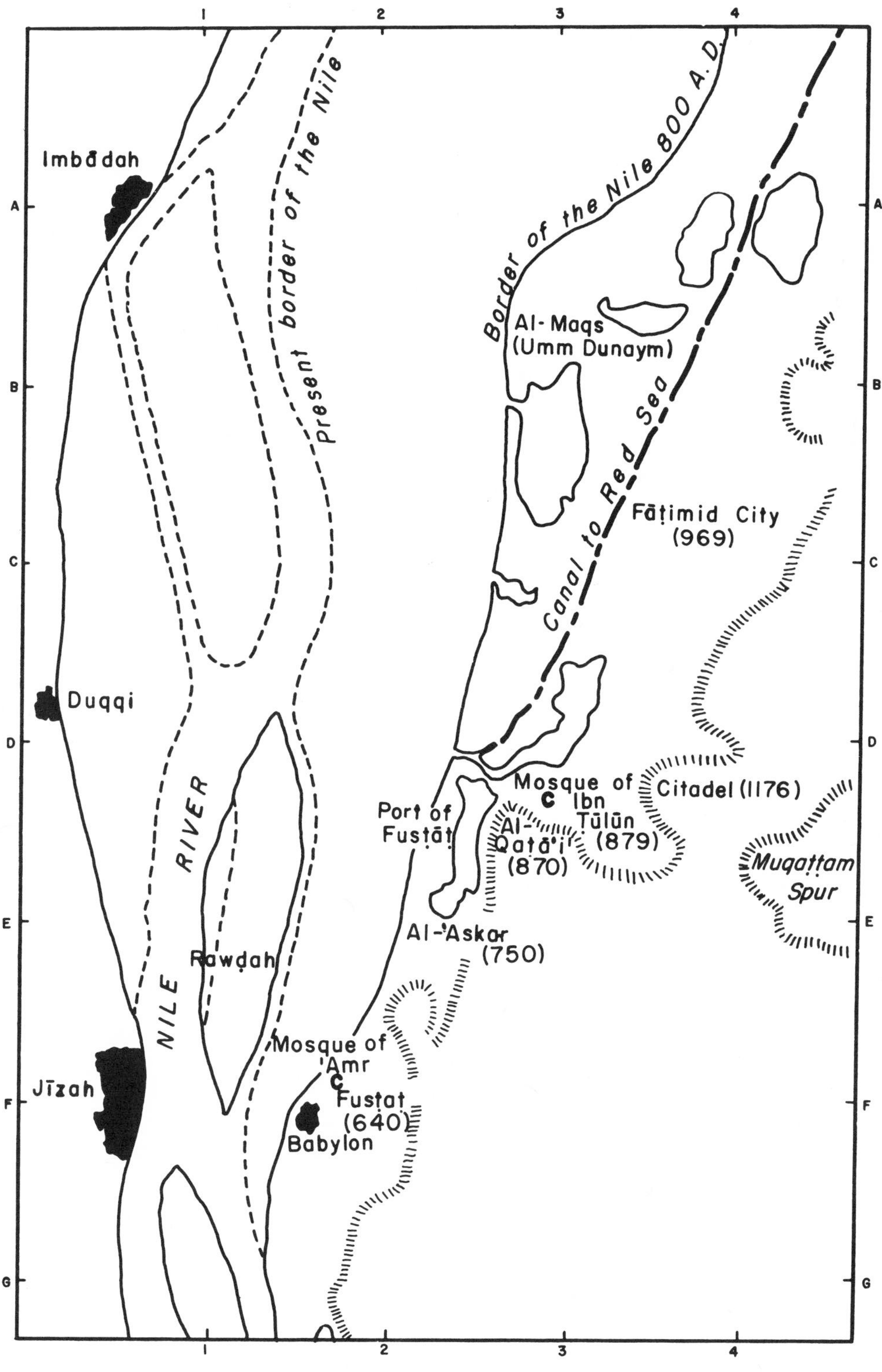

19. MEDIEVAL FUSTAT (CAIRO)

Based on Abu Lughod

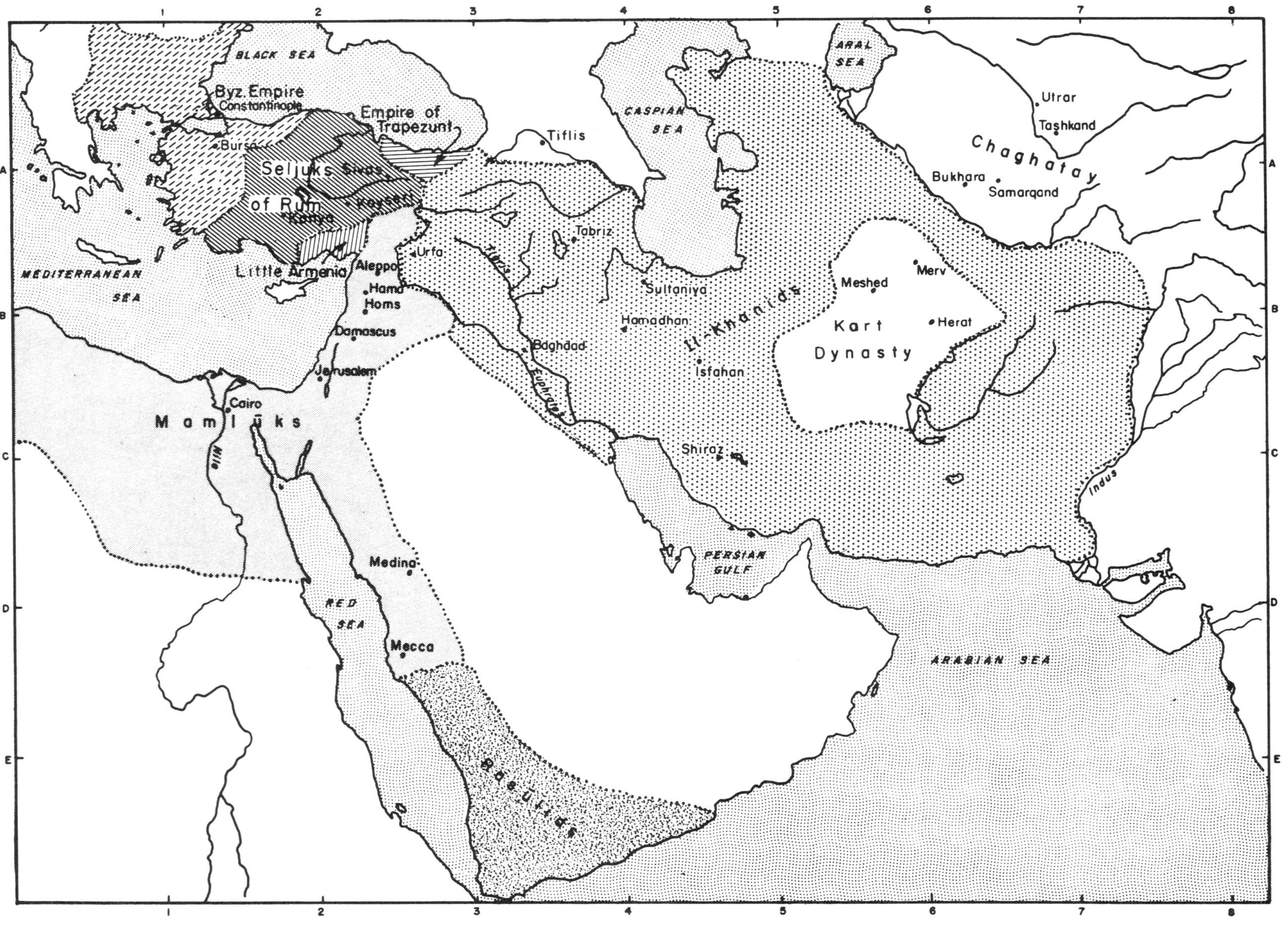

20. EGYPT AND SOUTHWEST ASIA, EARLY 14th CENTURY

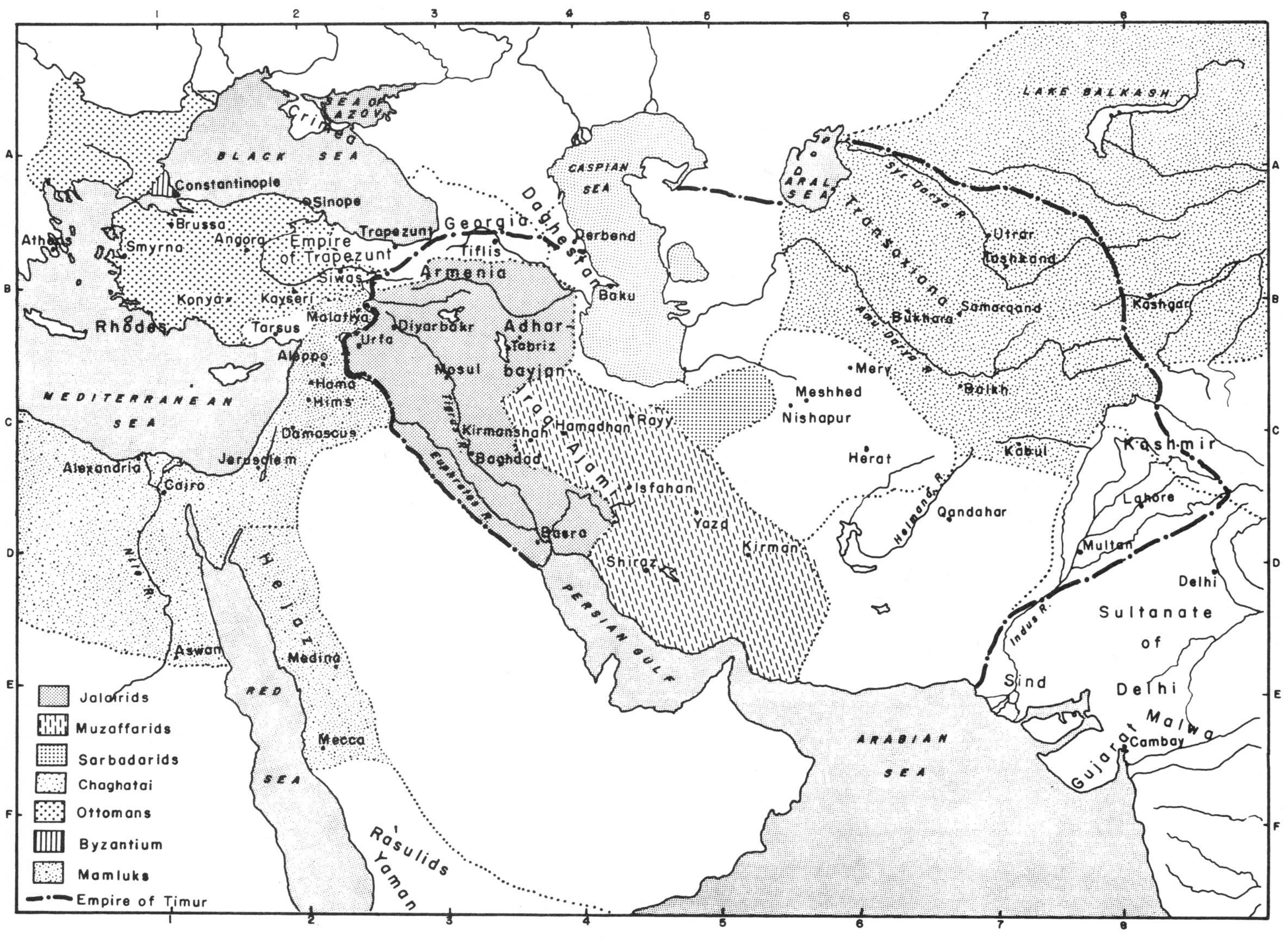

21. EGYPT AND SOUTHWEST ASIA, LATE 14th CENTURY

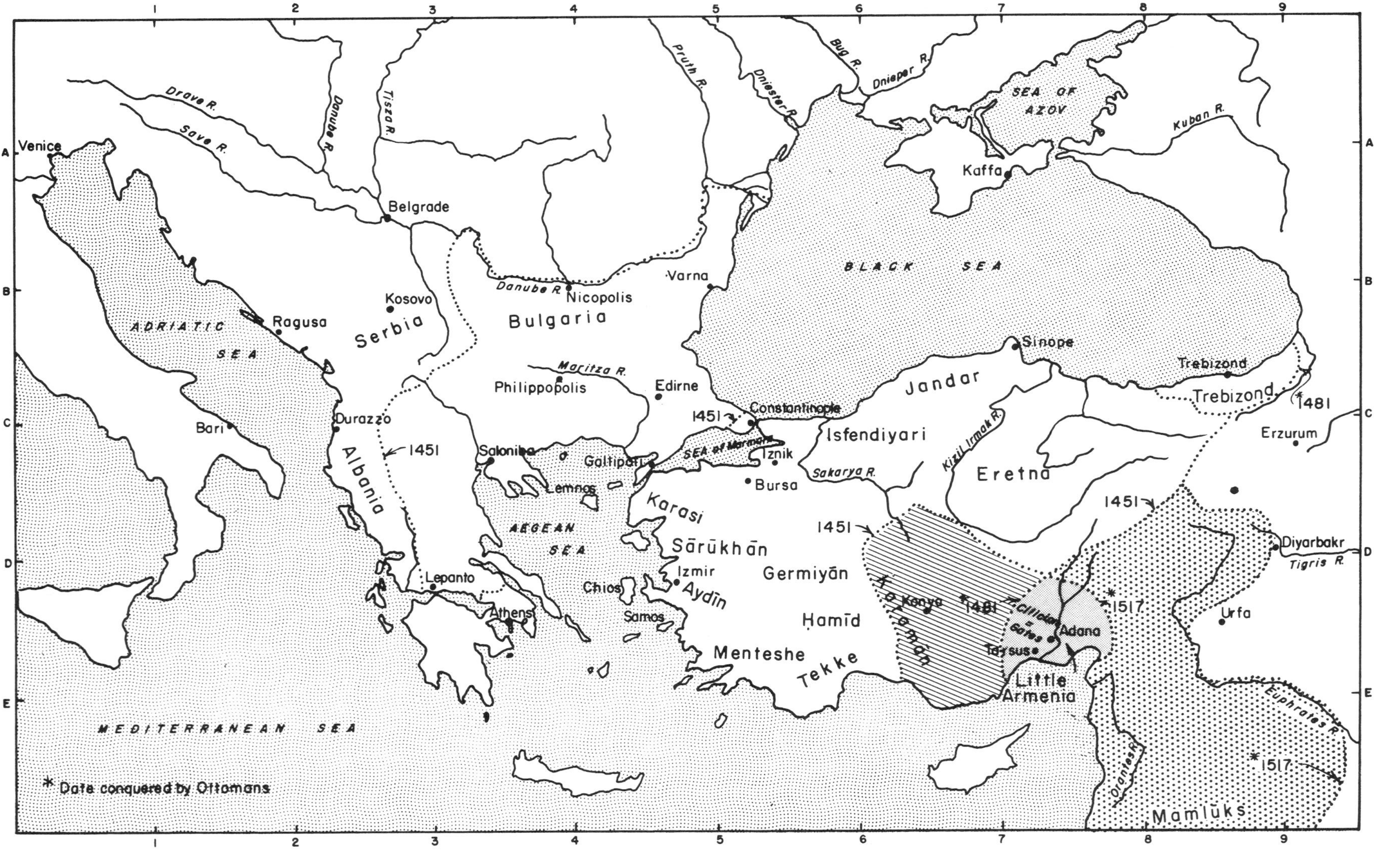

22. OTTOMAN CONQUESTS TO 1451

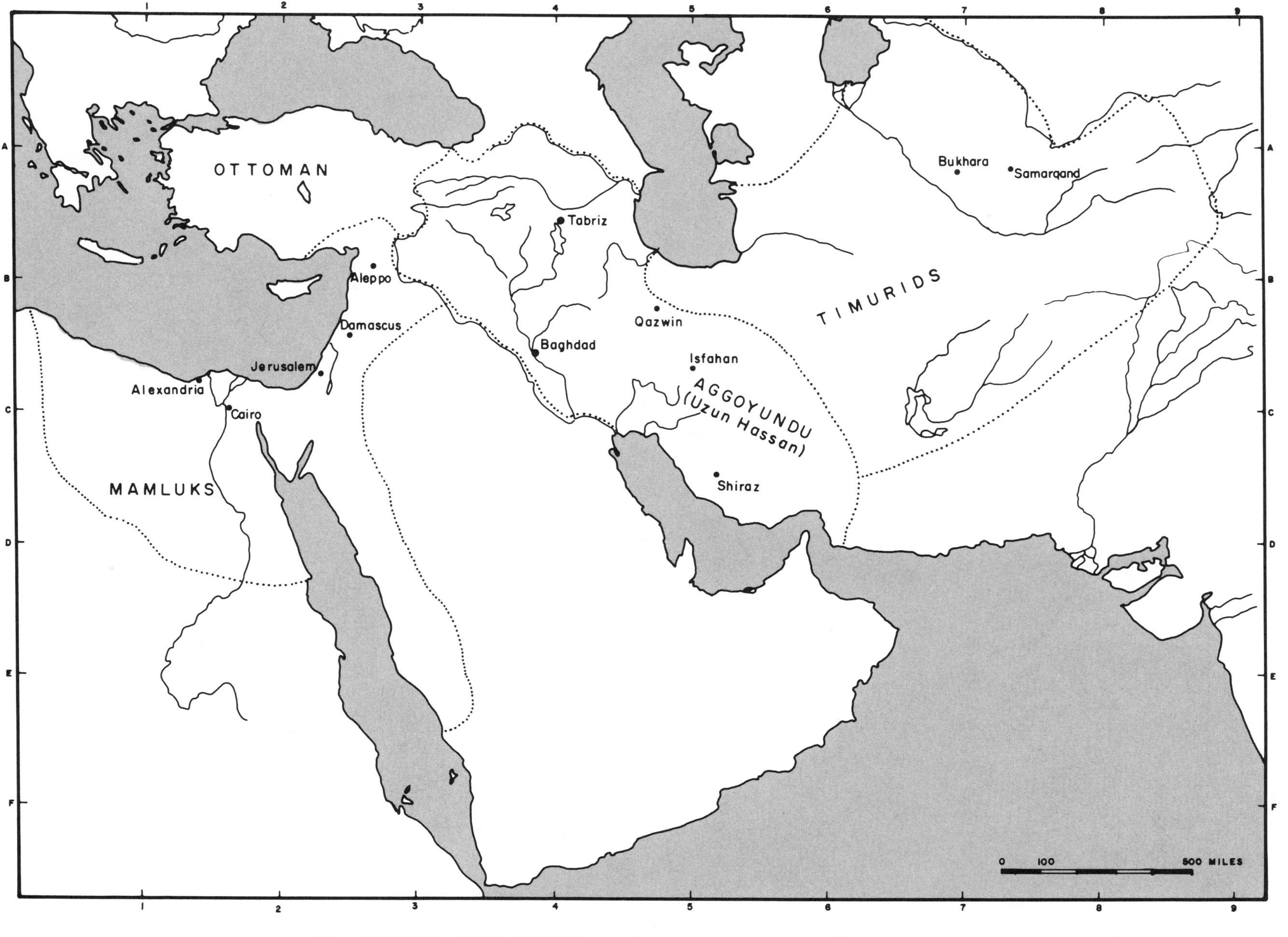

23. EGYPT AND SOUTHWEST ASIA, LATE 15th CENTURY

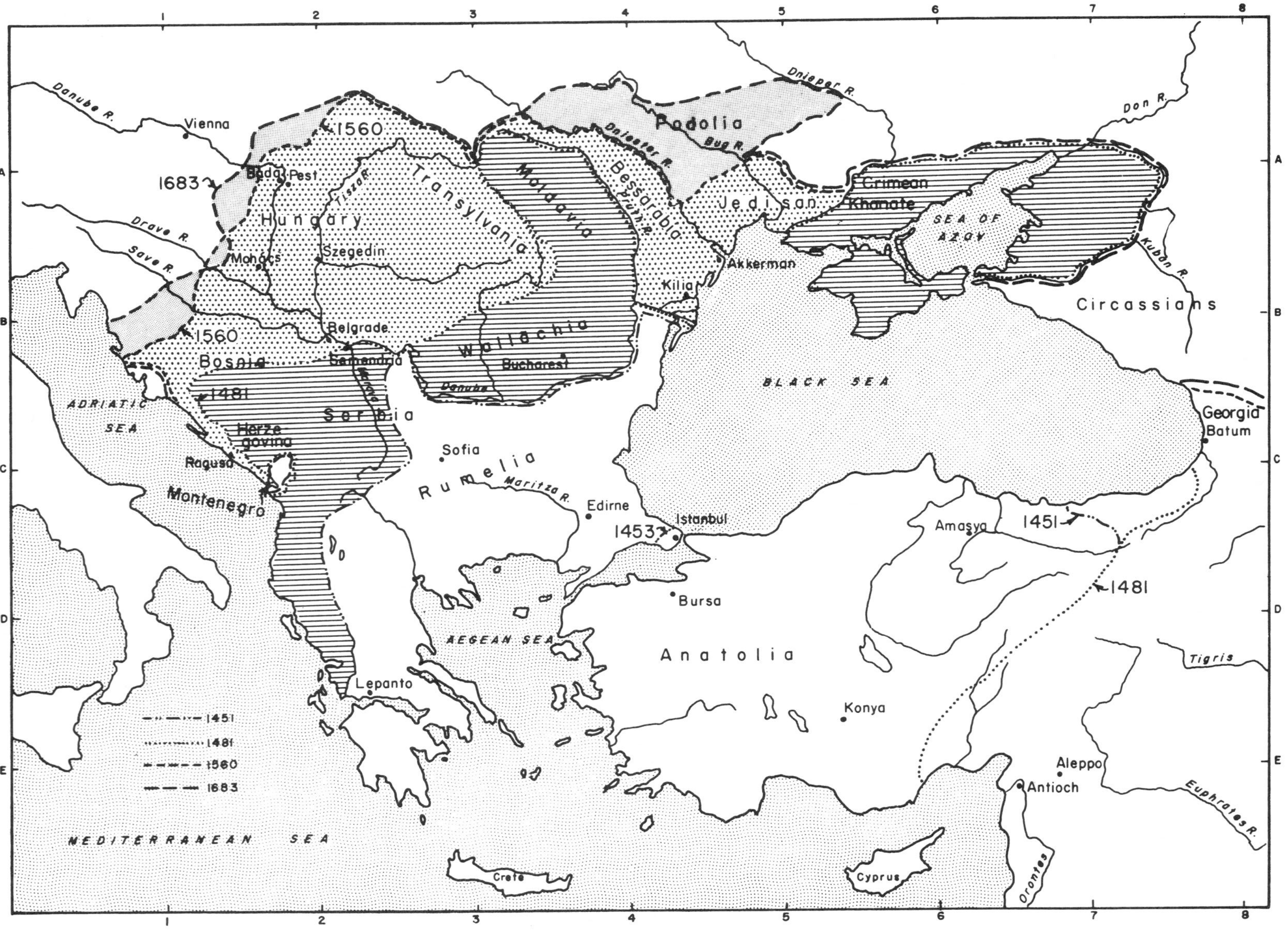

24. OTTOMAN EMPIRE IN EUROPE AND ANATOLIA, 1451-1683

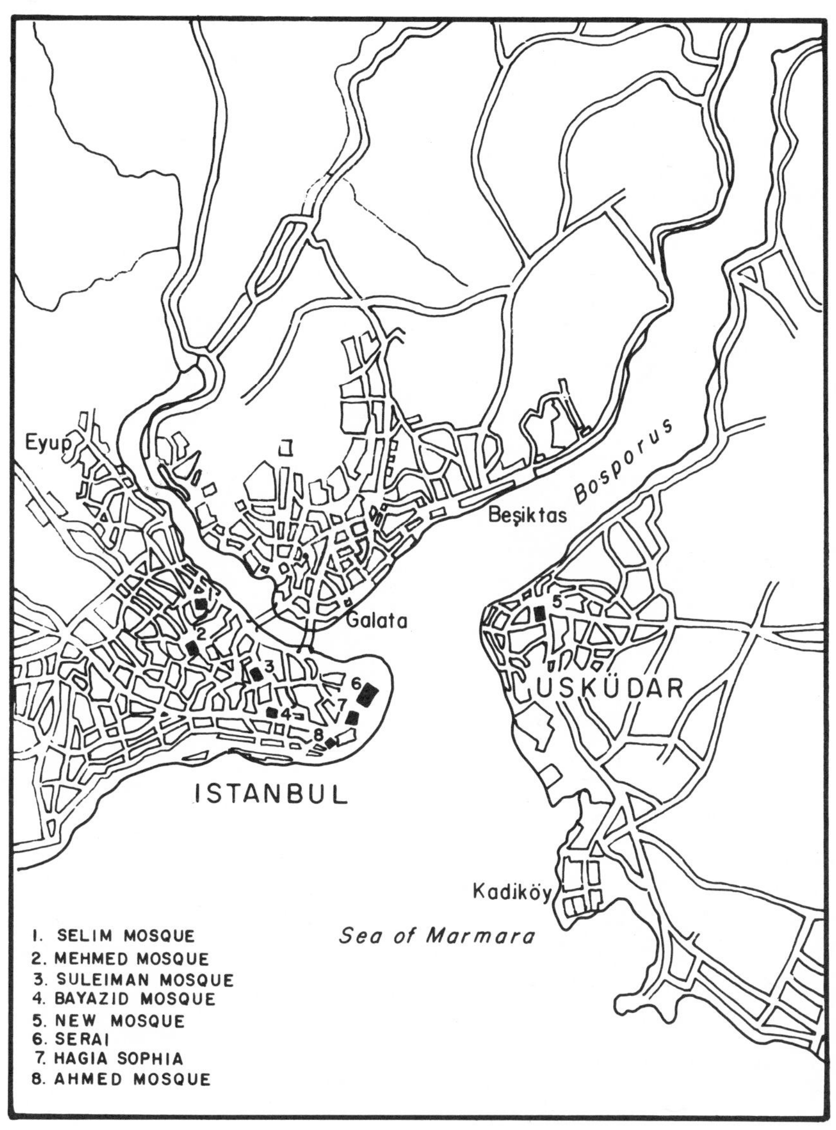
Eyup
Beşiktas
Bosporus
Galata
USKÜDAR
ISTANBUL
Kadiköy
Sea of Marmara
1. SELIM MOSQUE
2. MEHMED MOSQUE
3. SULEIMAN MOSQUE
4. BAYAZID MOSQUE
5. NEW MOSQUE
6. SERAI
7. HAGIA SOPHIA
8. AHMED MOSQUE

25. ISTANBUL

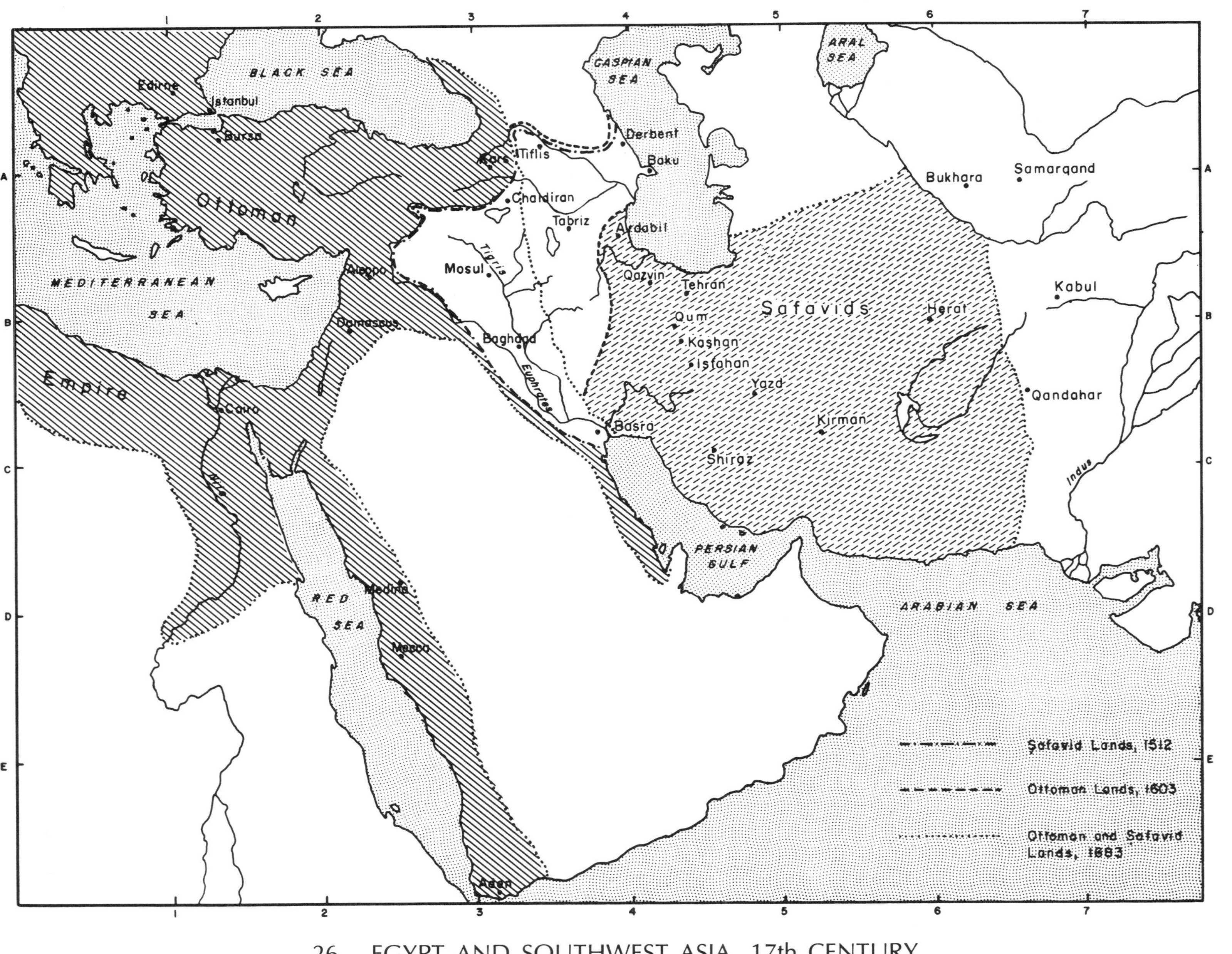

26. EGYPT AND SOUTHWEST ASIA, 17th CENTURY

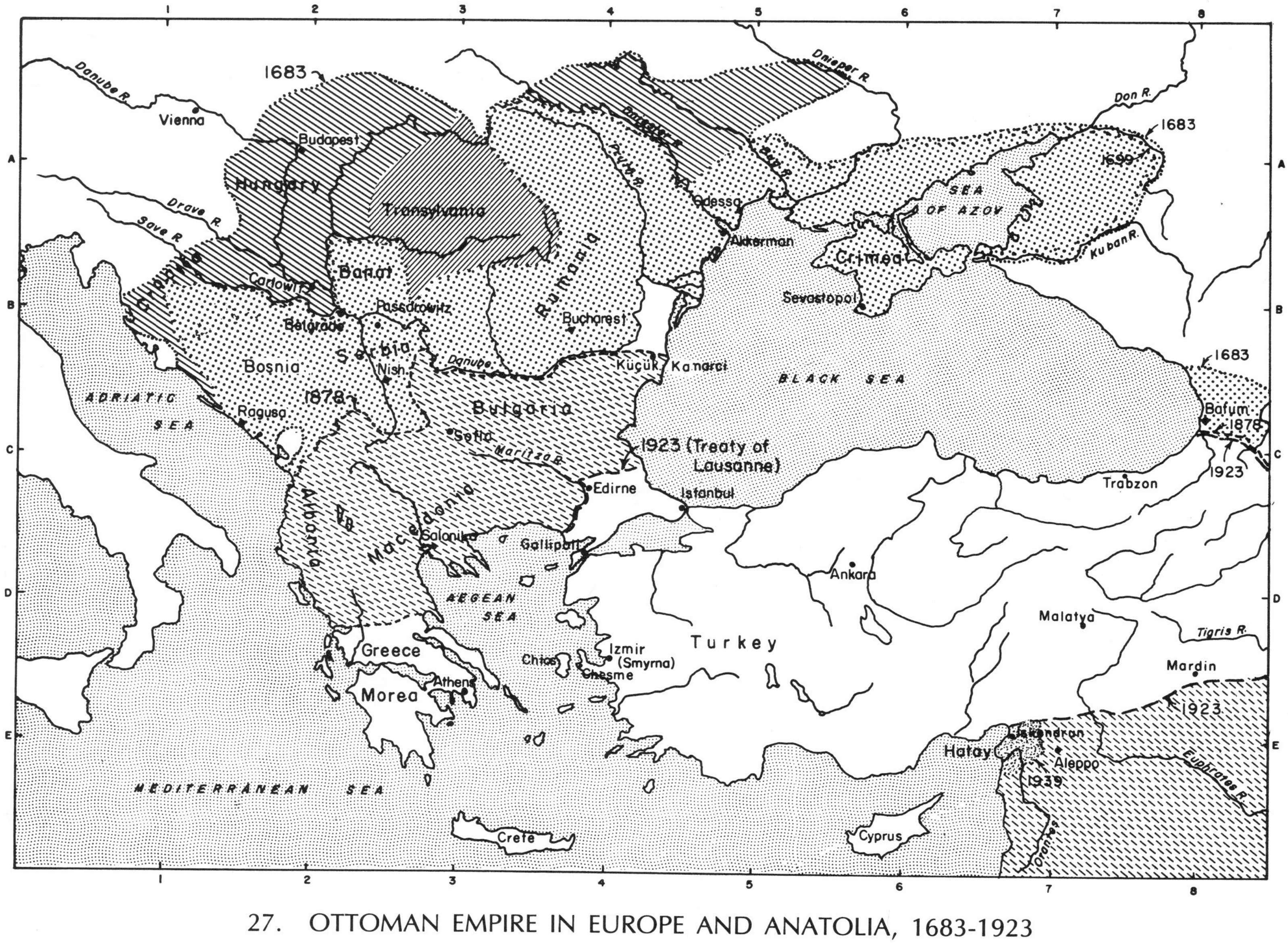

27. OTTOMAN EMPIRE IN EUROPE AND ANATOLIA, 1683-1923

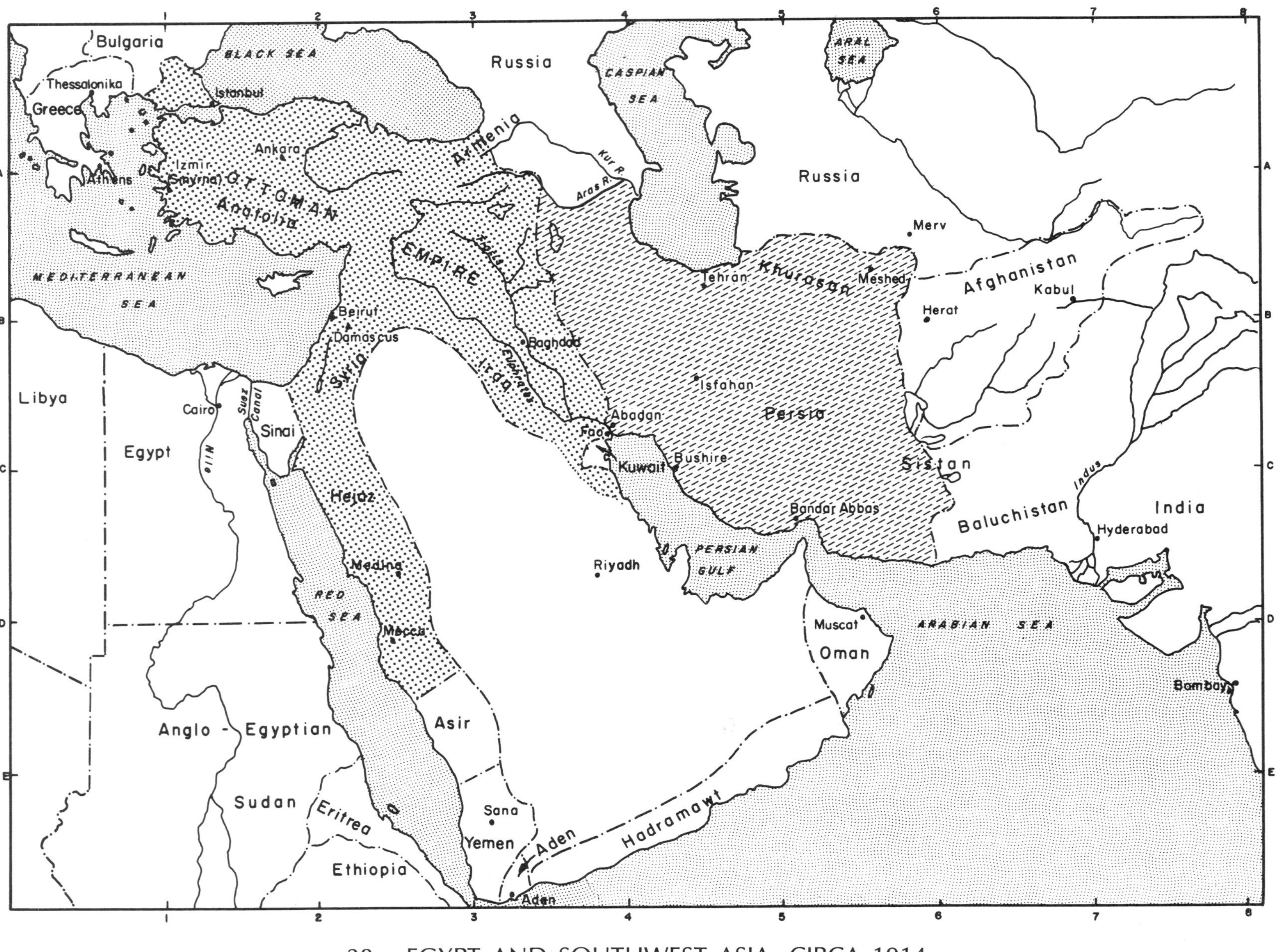

28. EGYPT AND SOUTHWEST ASIA, CIRCA 1914

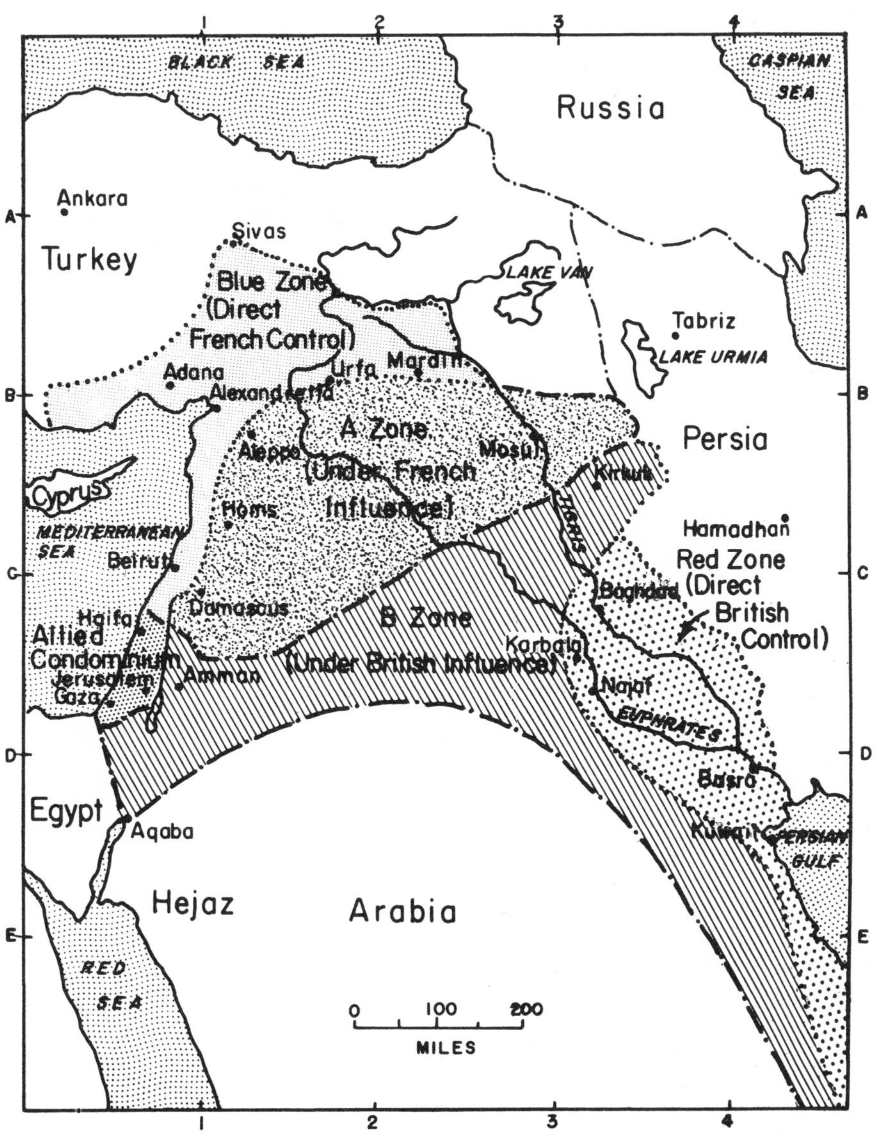

29. THE SYKES-PICOT AGREEMENT, 1916

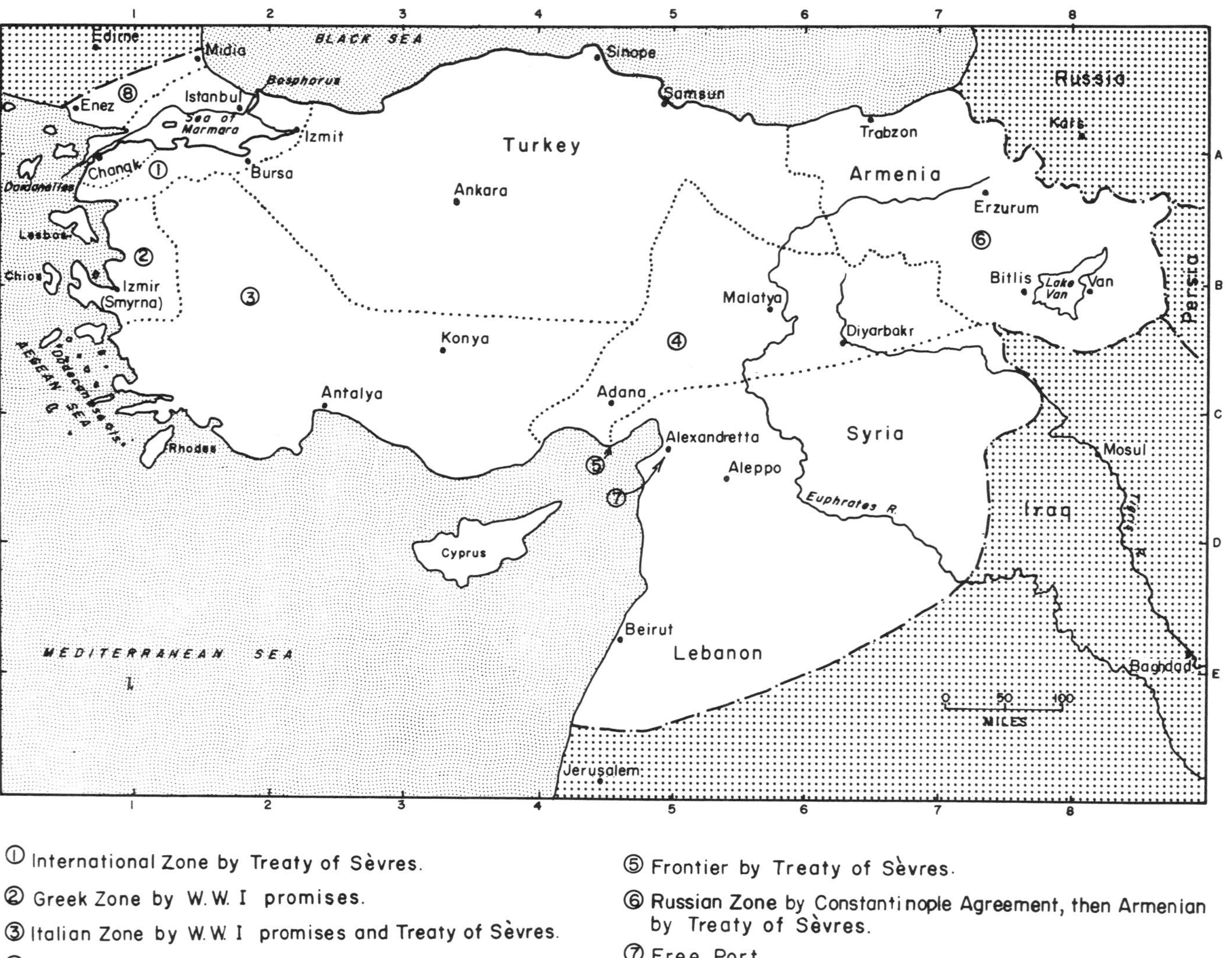

① International Zone by Treaty of Sèvres.
② Greek Zone by W. W. I promises.
③ Italian Zone by W. W. I promises and Treaty of Sèvres.
④ French Zone by W. W. I promises and Treaty of Sèvres.
⑤ Frontier by Treaty of Sèvres.
⑥ Russian Zone by Constantinople Agreement, then Armenian by Treaty of Sèvres.
⑦ Free Port.
⑧ Russian Zone by Constantinople Agreement.

30. ALLIED PLANS FOR TURKEY, 1915-1920

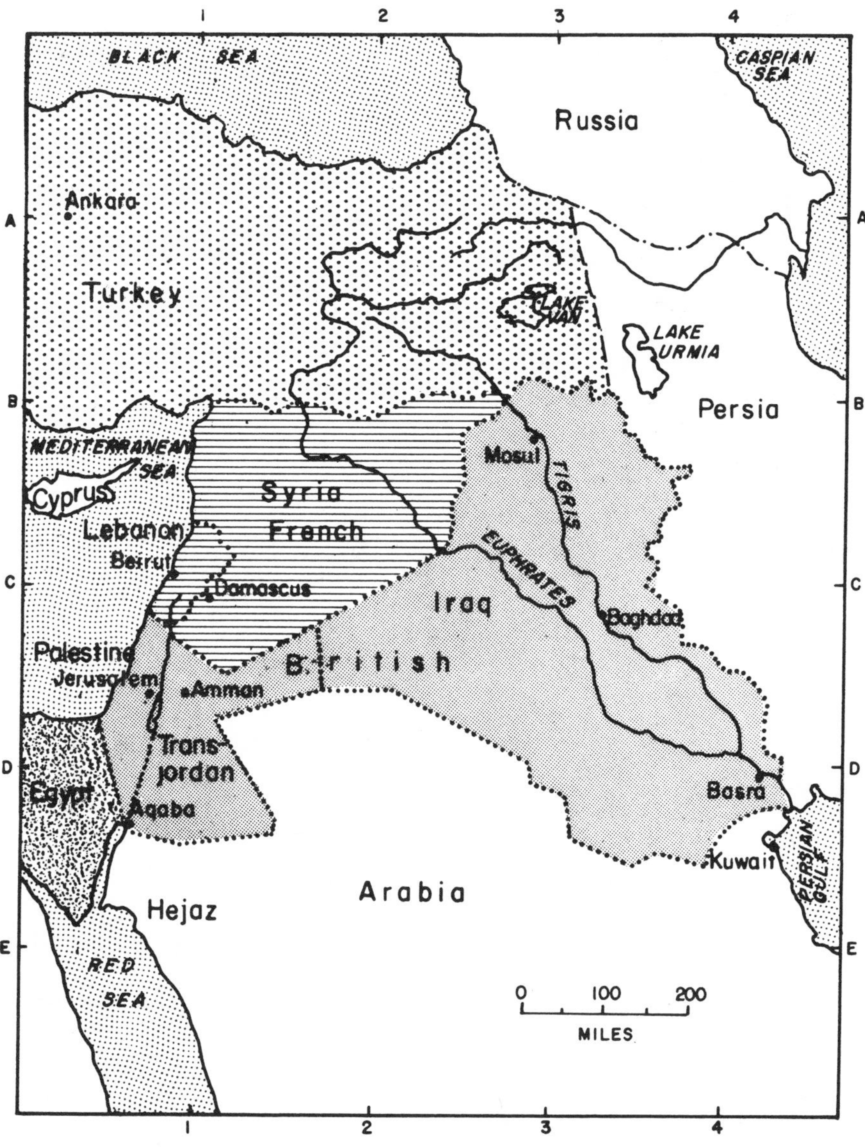

31. THE SAN REMO AGREEMENT

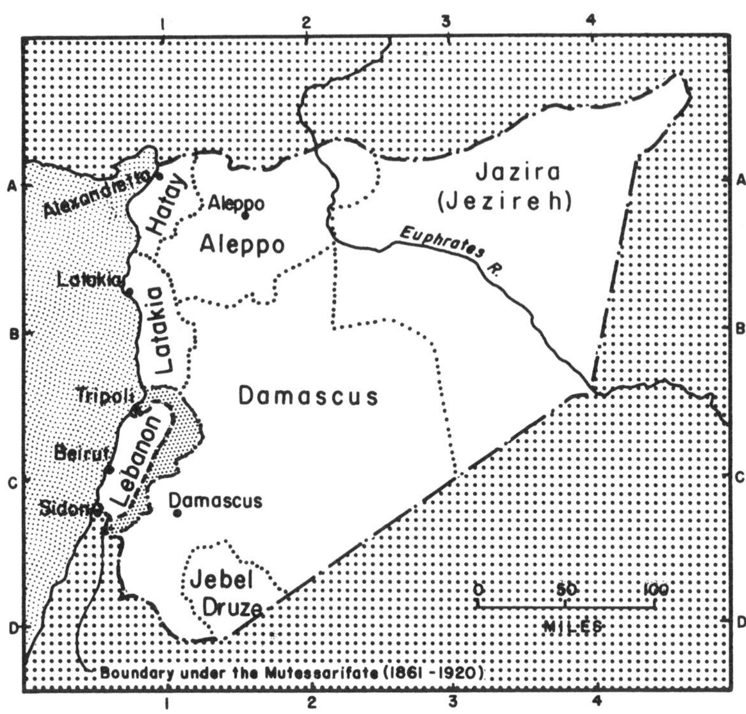

32. SYRIAN AND LEBANESE PROVINCES DURING FRENCH MANDATE

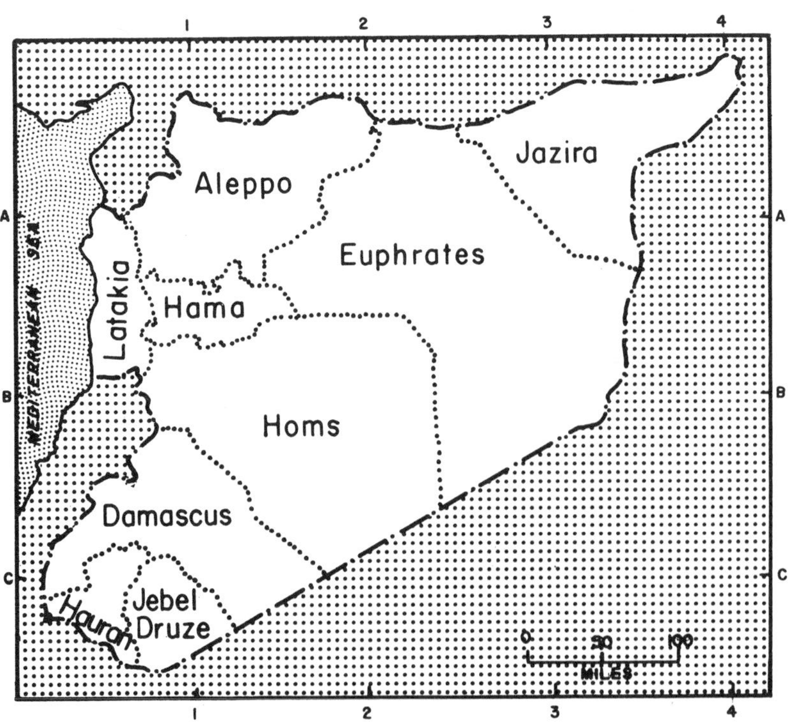

33. SYRIAN ADMINISTRATIVE PROVINCES, POST WWII

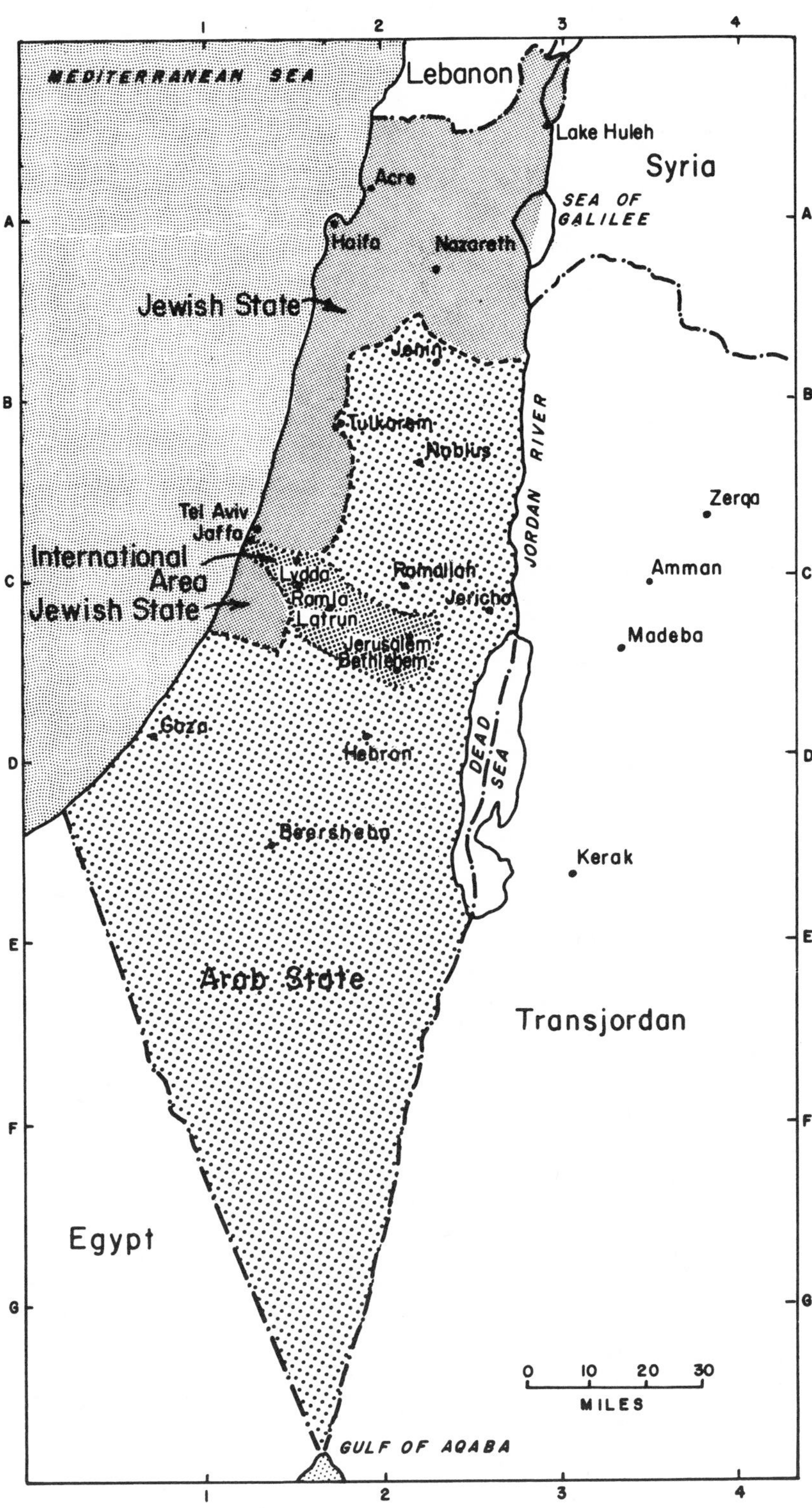

34. THE PEEL COMMISSION PARTITION PLAN, 1937

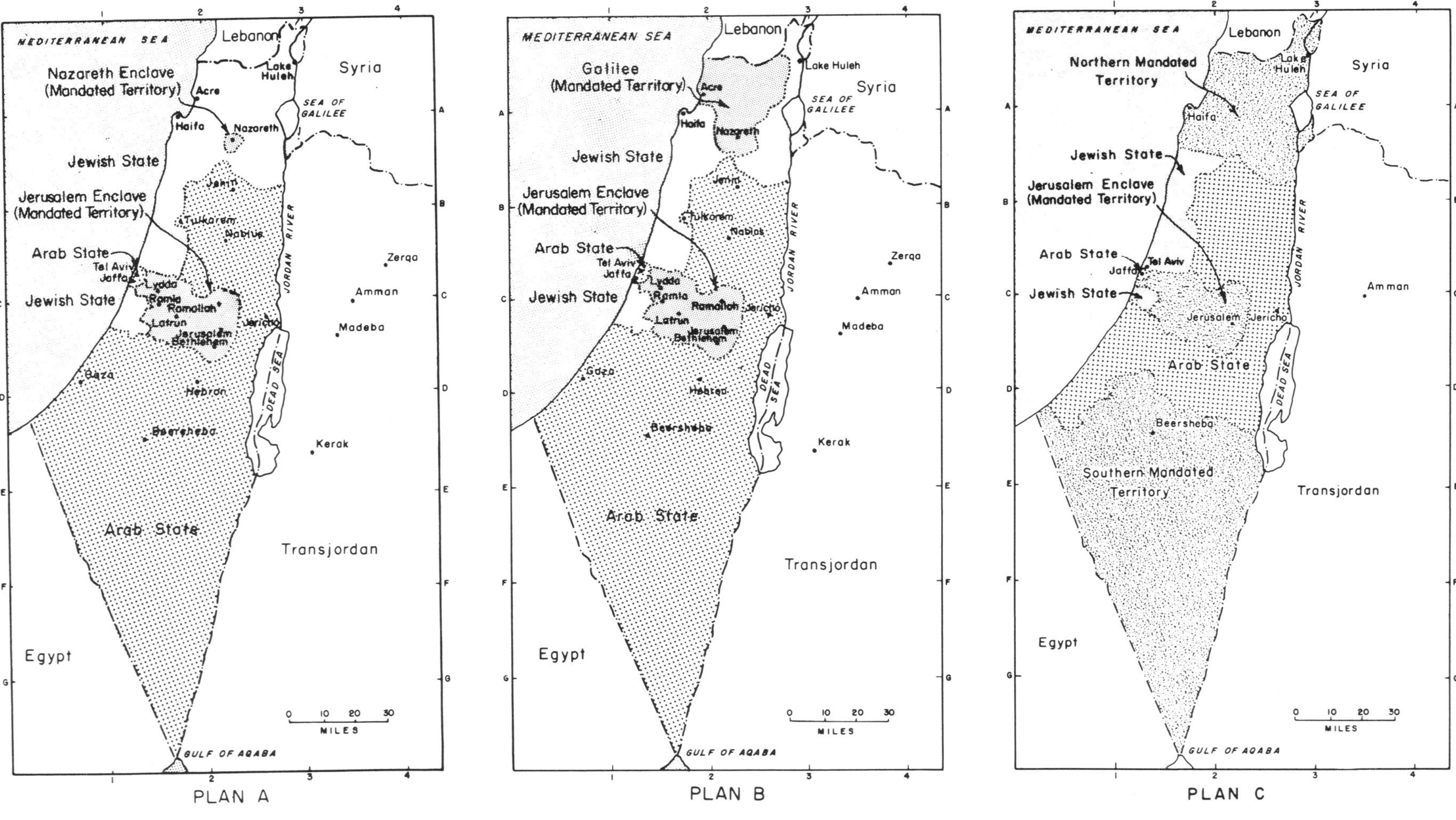

35. WOODHEAD COMMISSION PARTITION, 1939

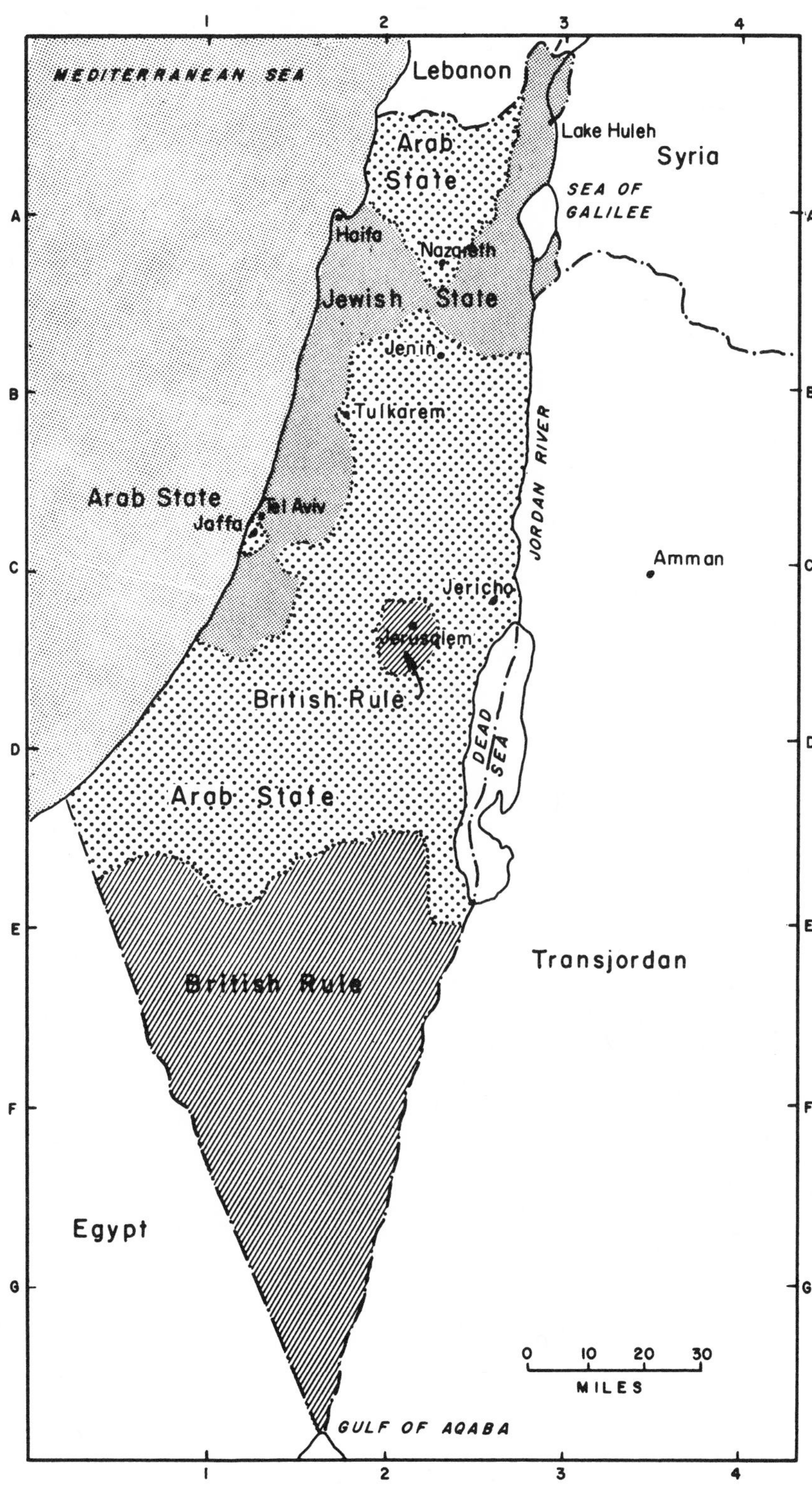

36. MORRISON-GRADY PARTITION PLAN, 1946

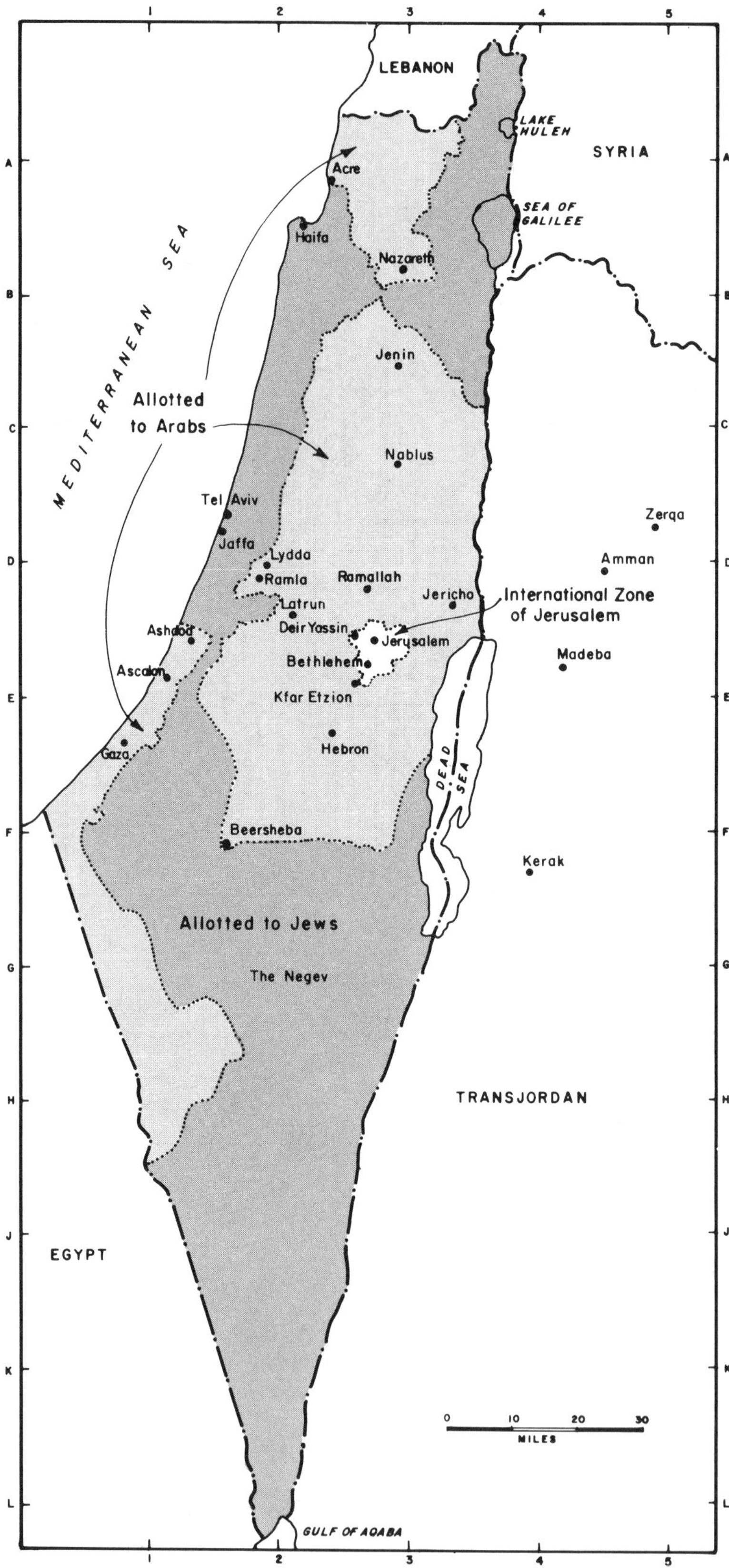

37. U.N. PARTITION PLAN, NOVEMBER 29, 1967

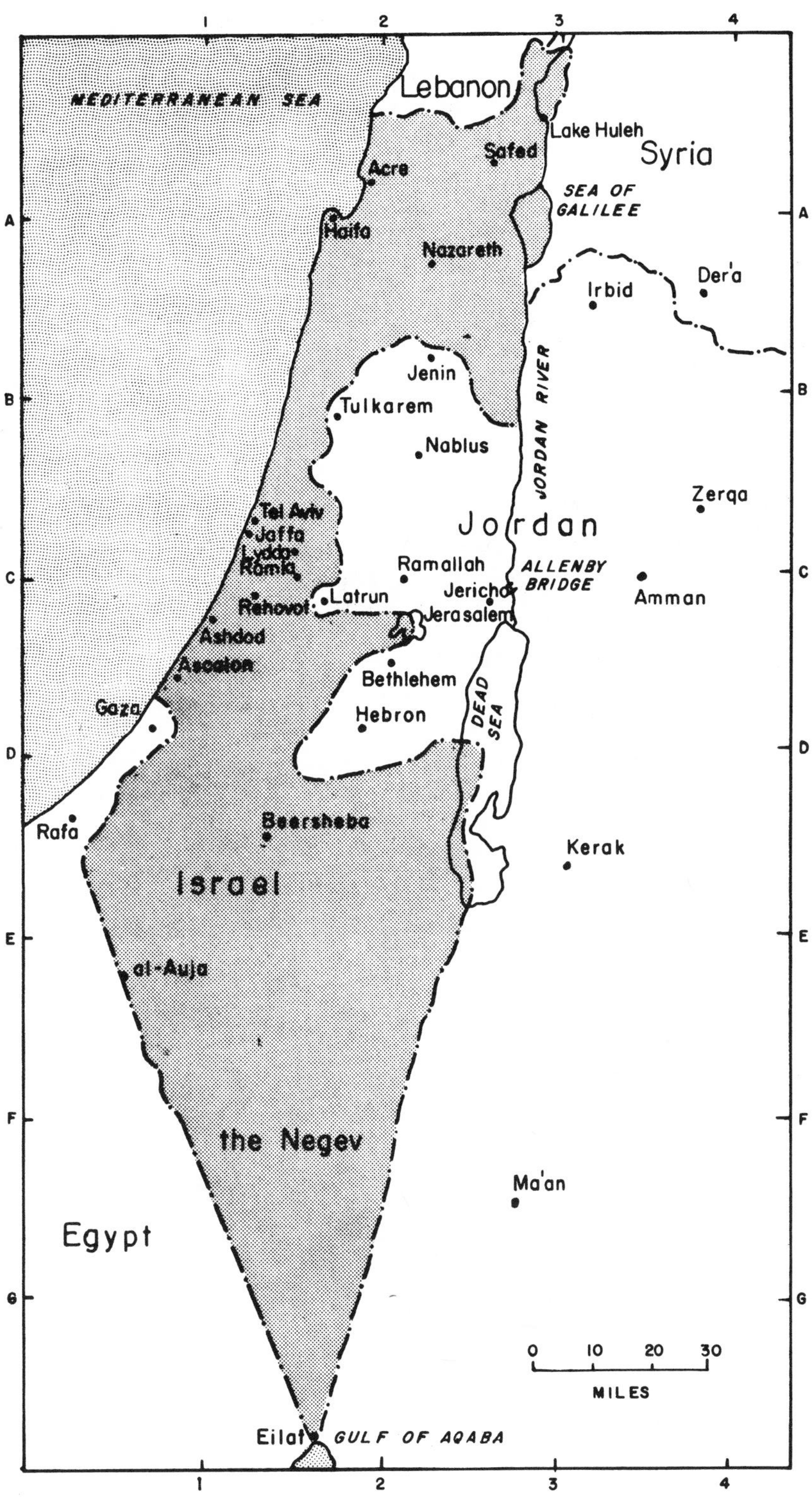

38. THE ISRAELI-ARAB ARMISTICE LINES, 1949

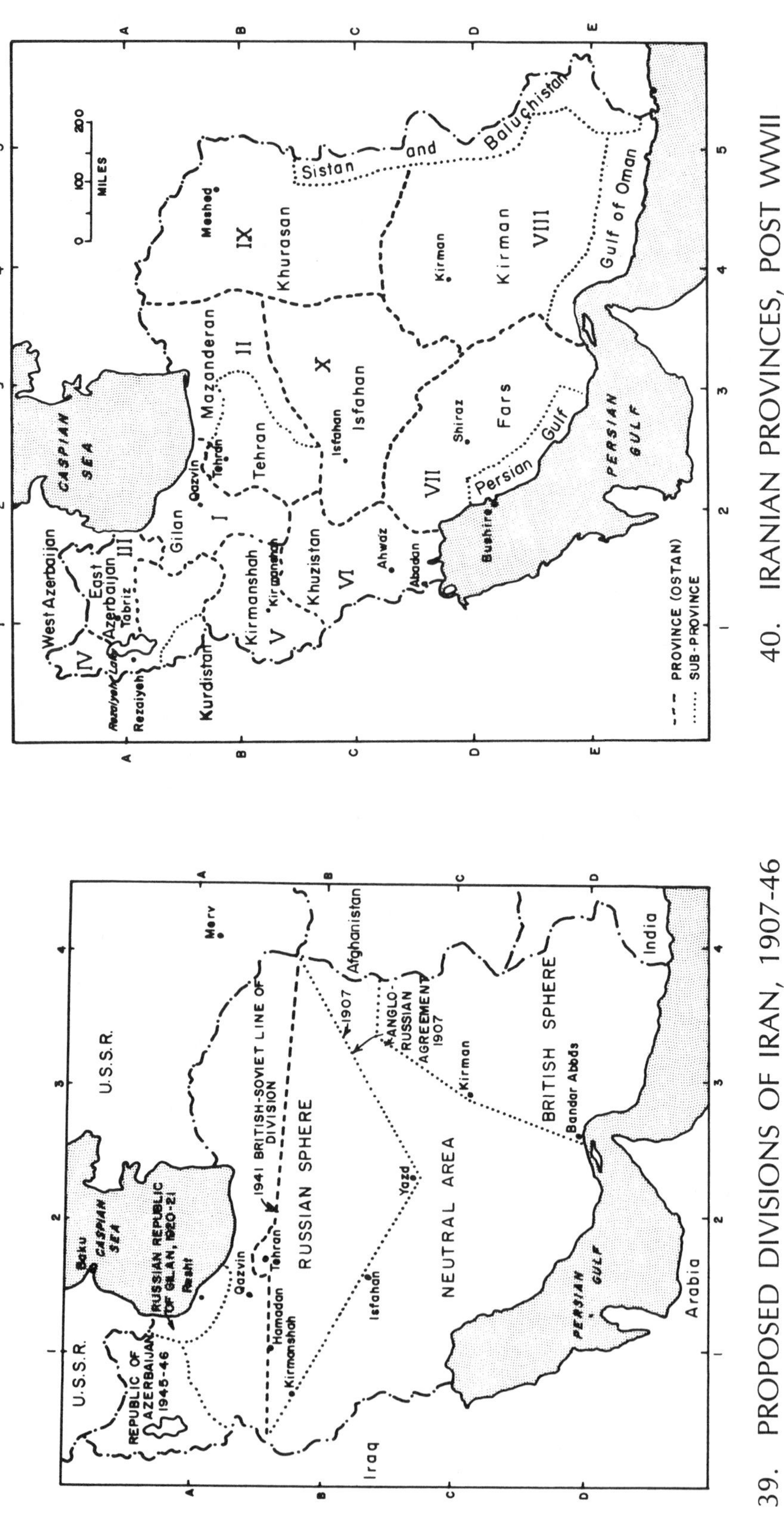

39. PROPOSED DIVISIONS OF IRAN, 1907-46

40. IRANIAN PROVINCES, POST WWII

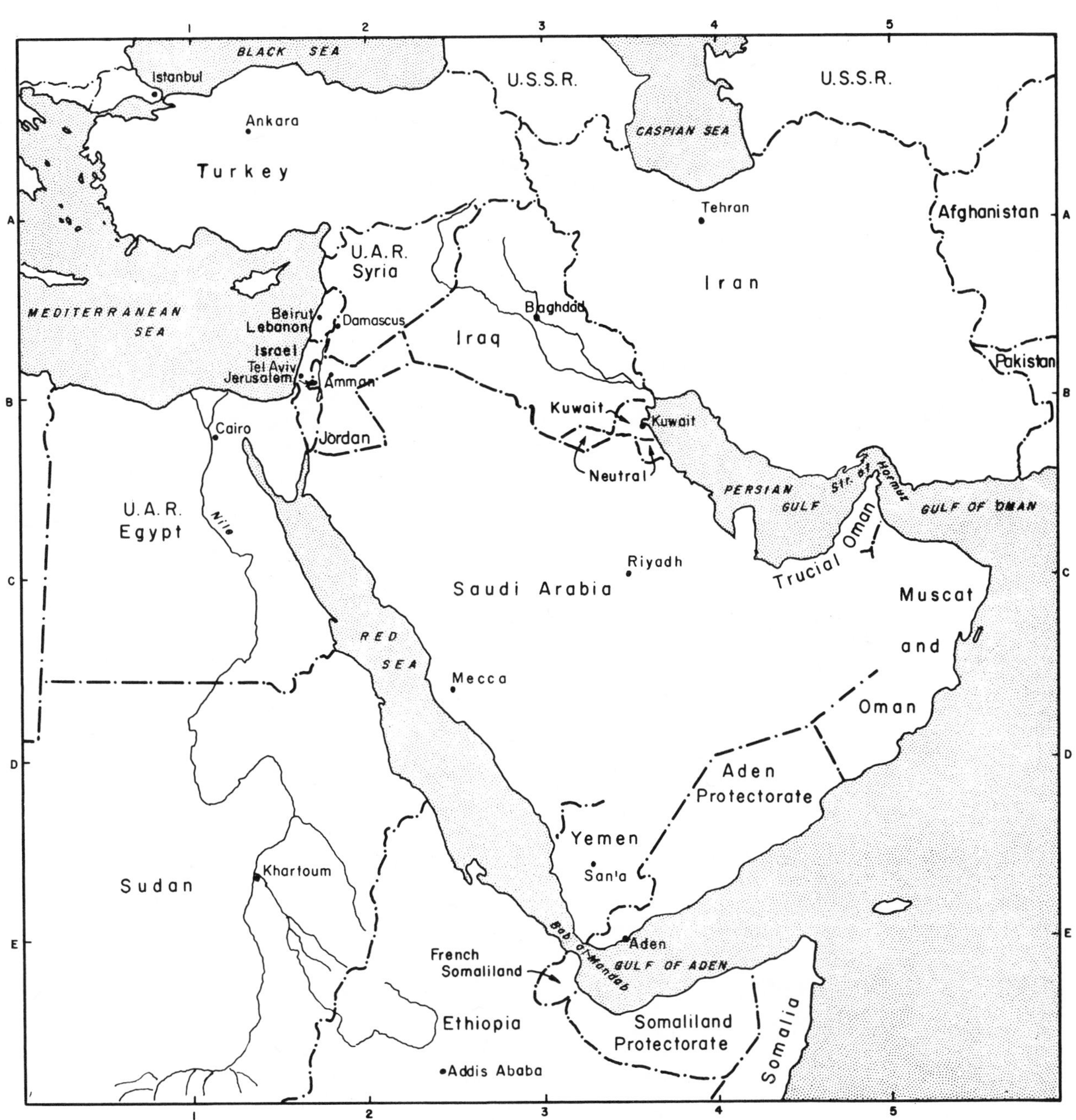

41. EGYPT AND SOUTHWEST ASIA, 1960

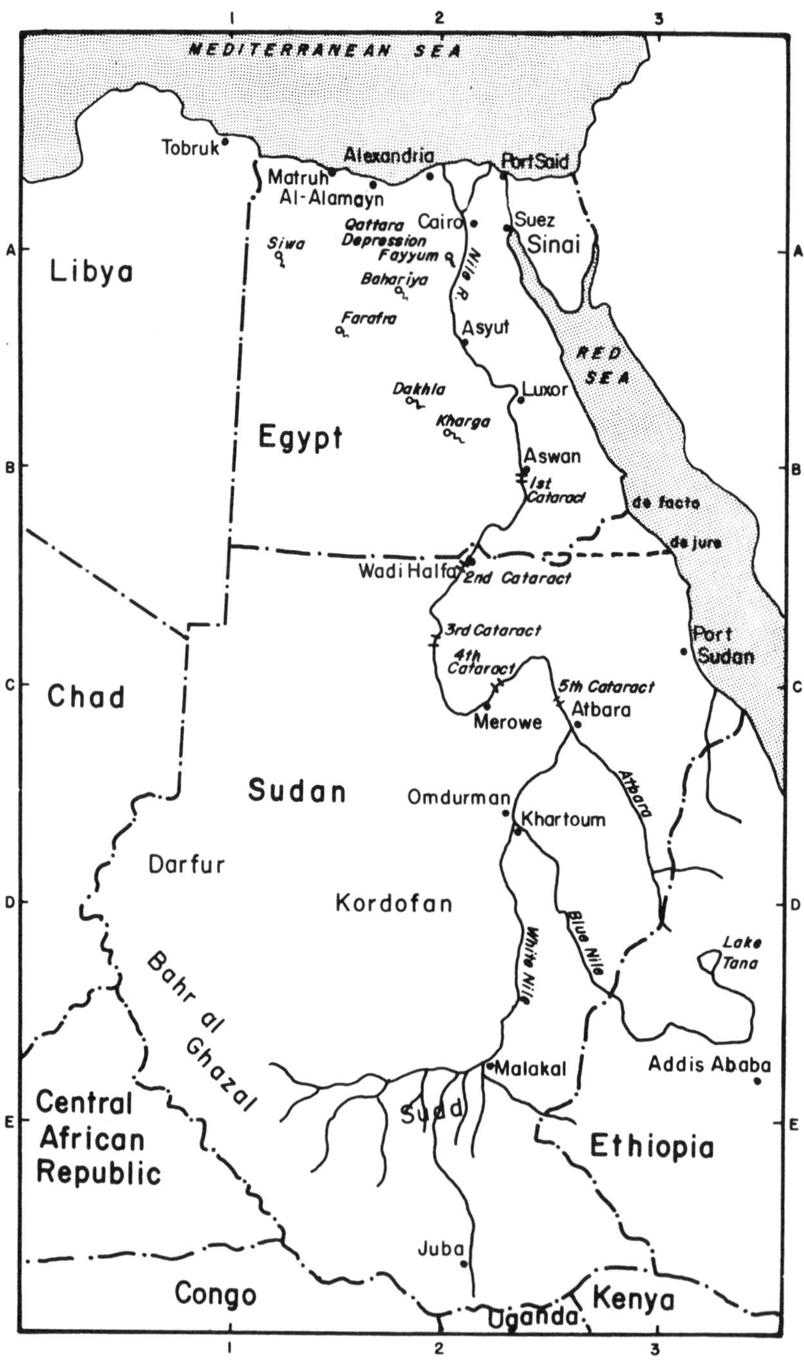

42. EGYPT AND SUDAN

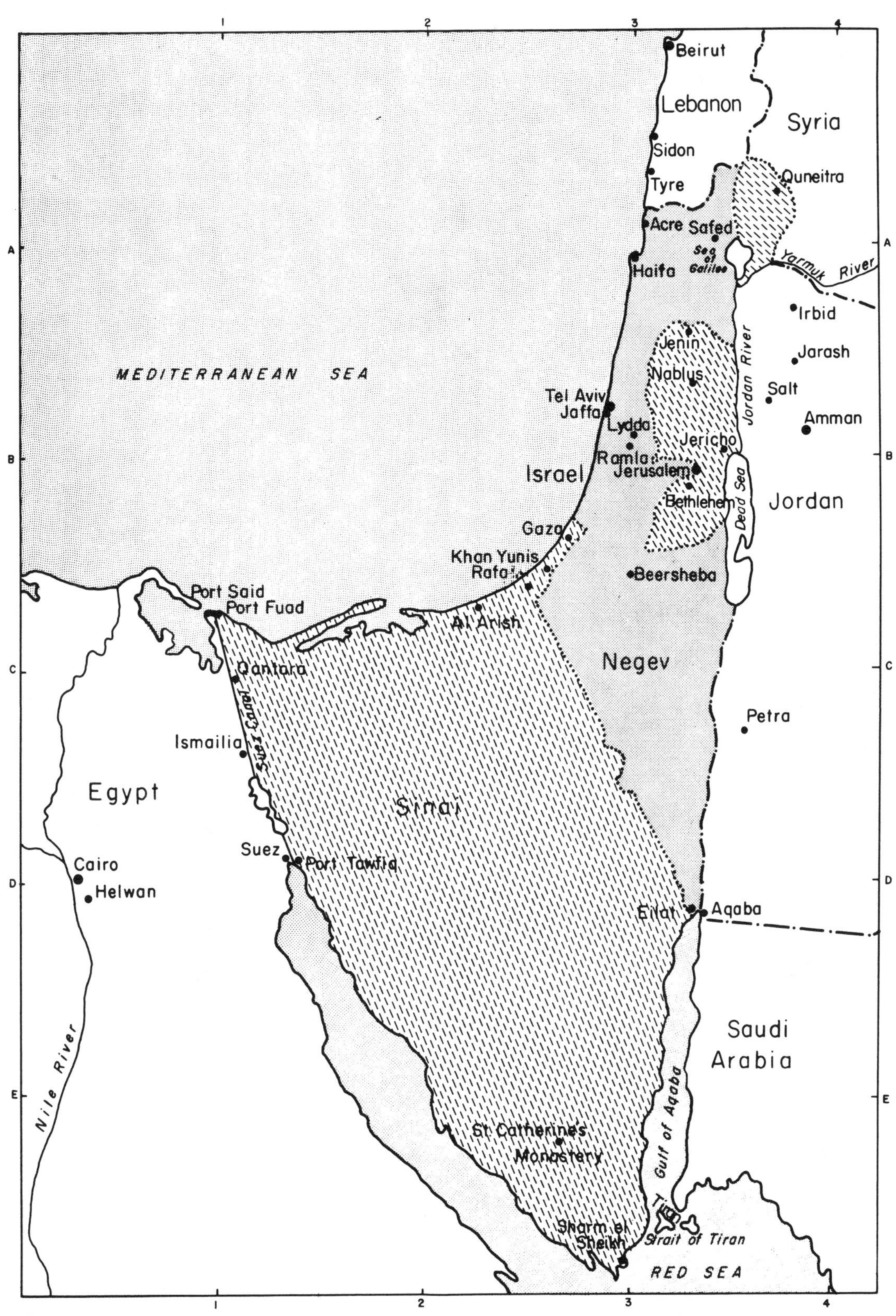

43. ISRAEL AND OCCUPIED LANDS, 1967

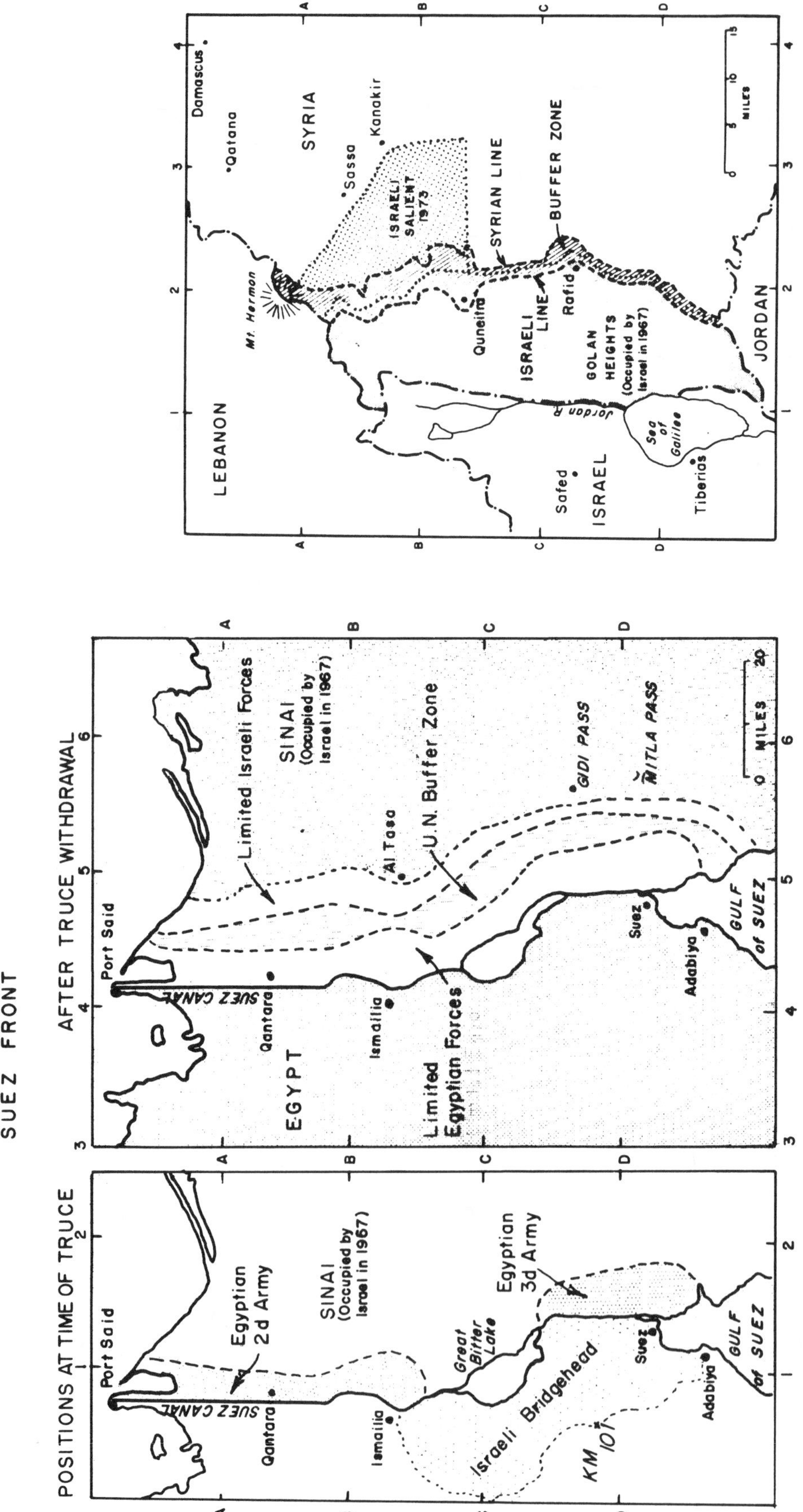

44. ARAB-ISRAELI DISPUTE, 1973-74

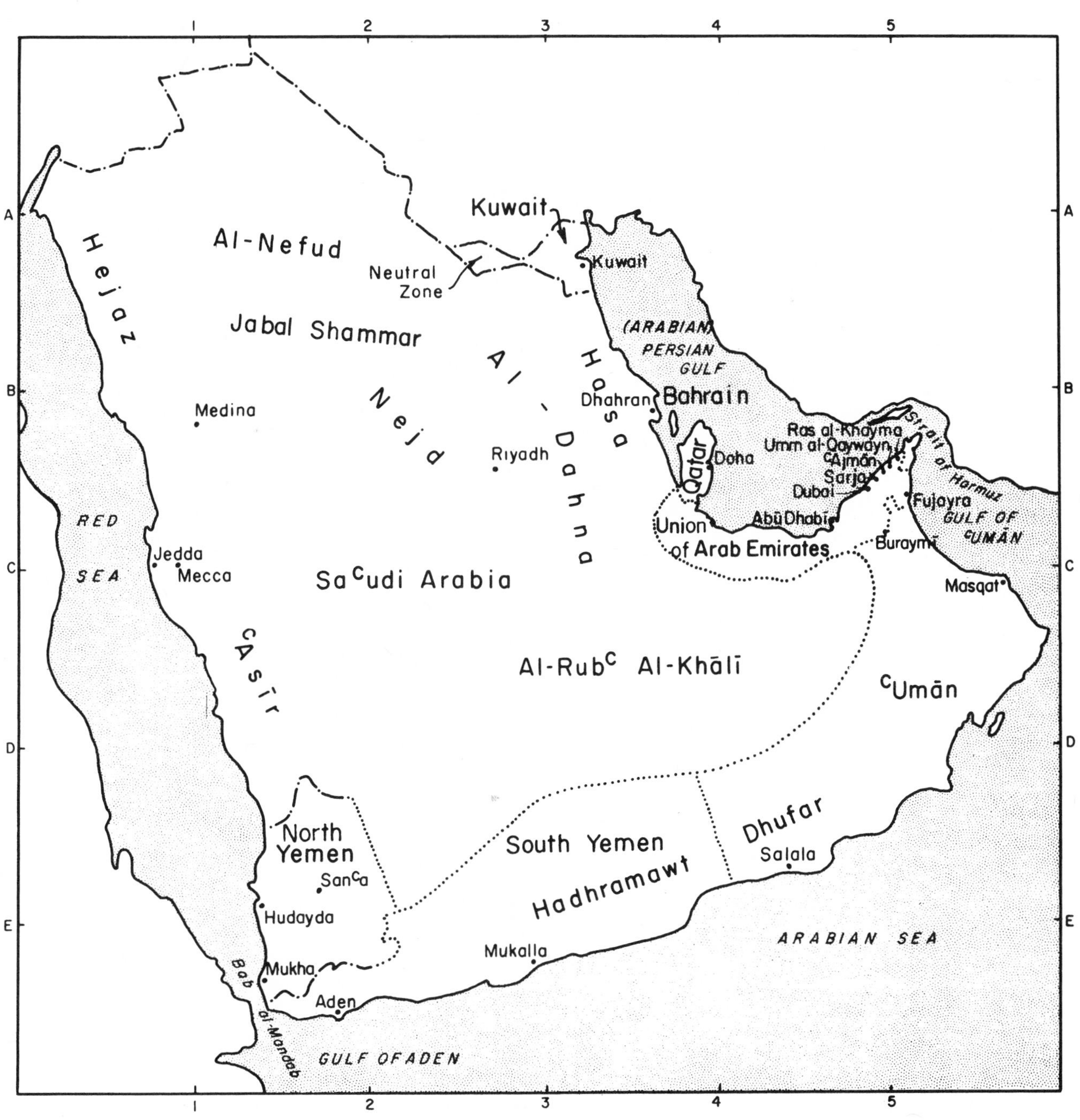

45. ARABIAN PENINSULA, 1974

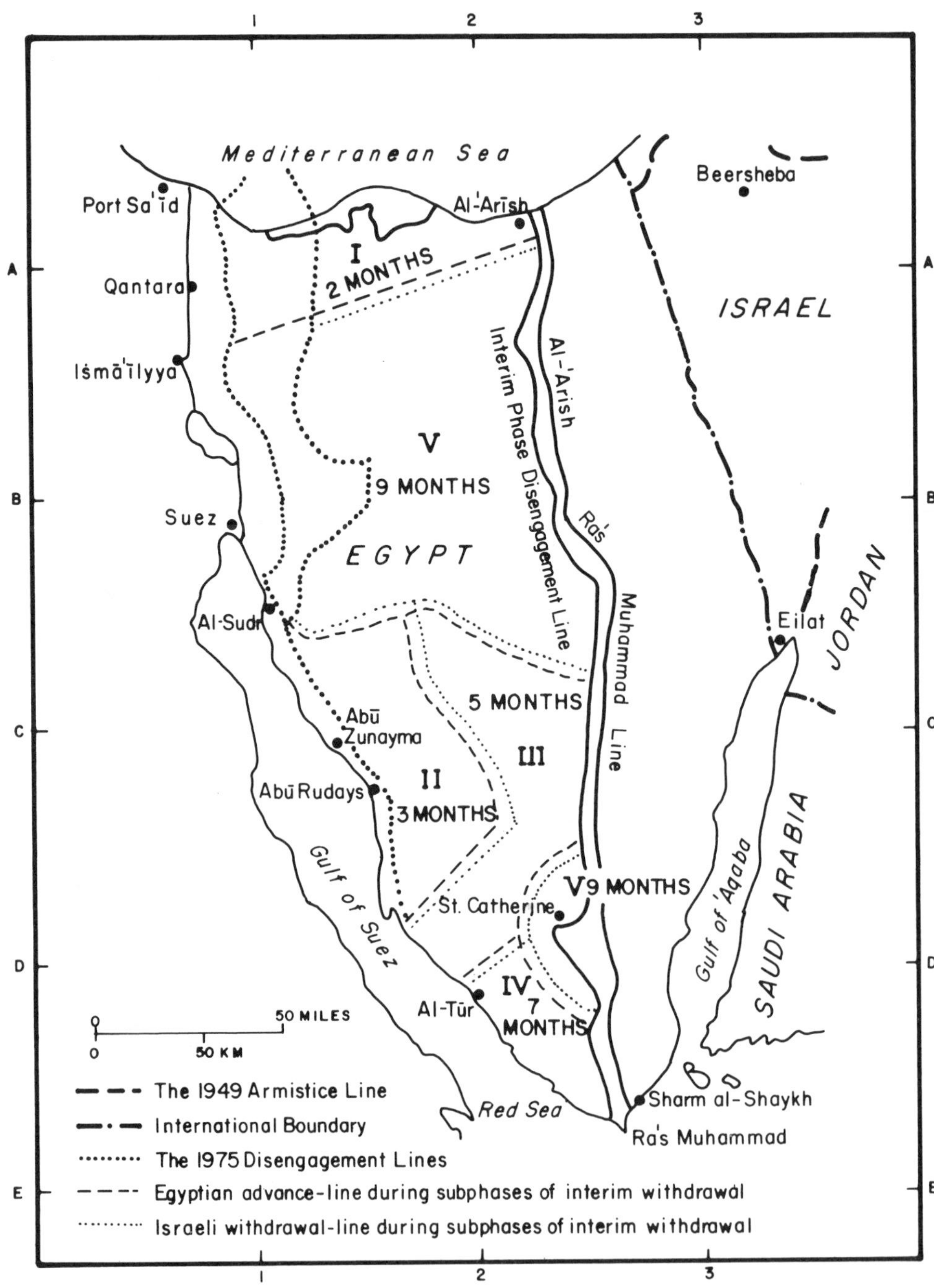

46. EGYPTIAN-ISRAELI DISENGAGEMENT AGREEMENT, 1975

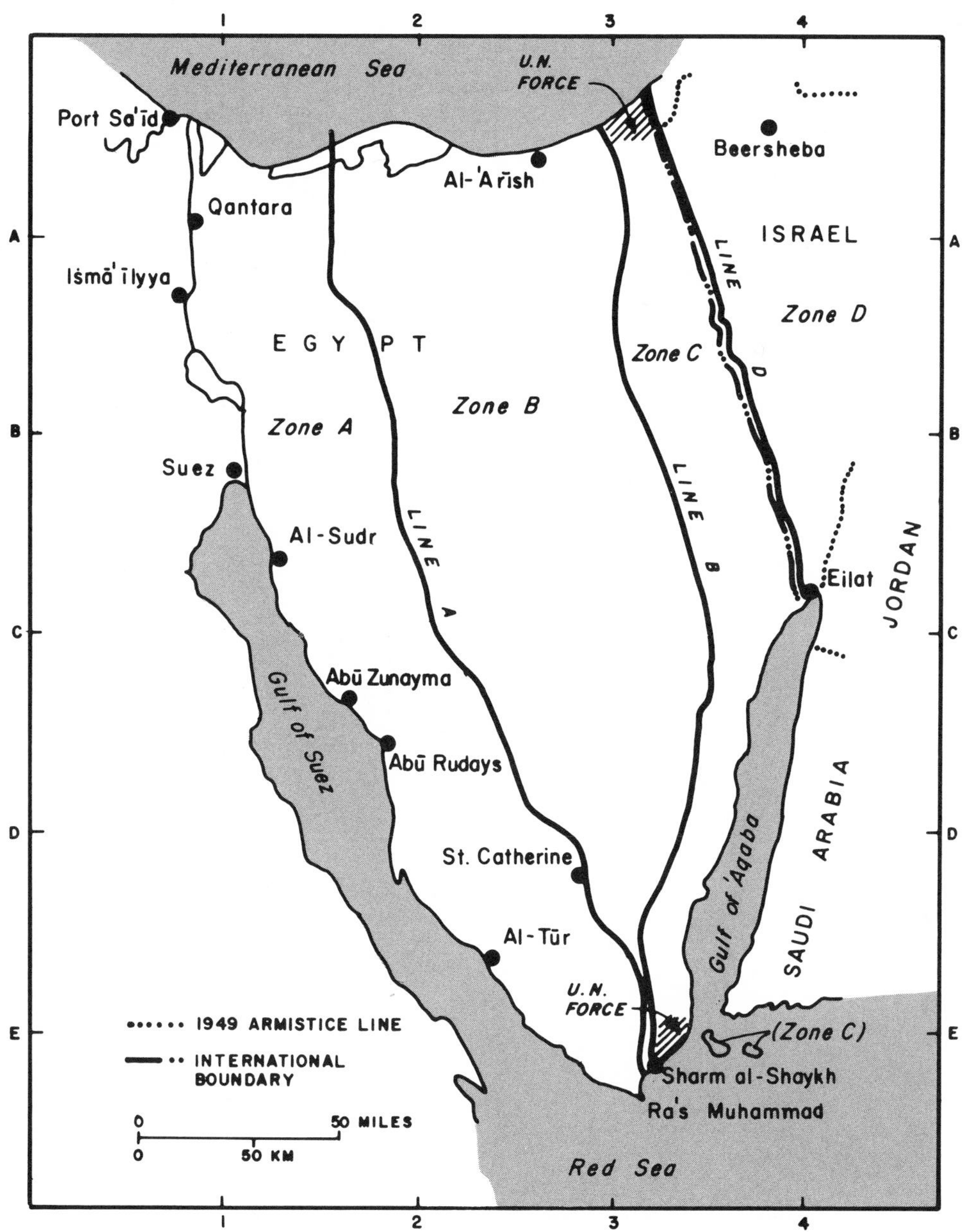

47. EGYPTIAN-ISRAELI PEACE AGREEMENT

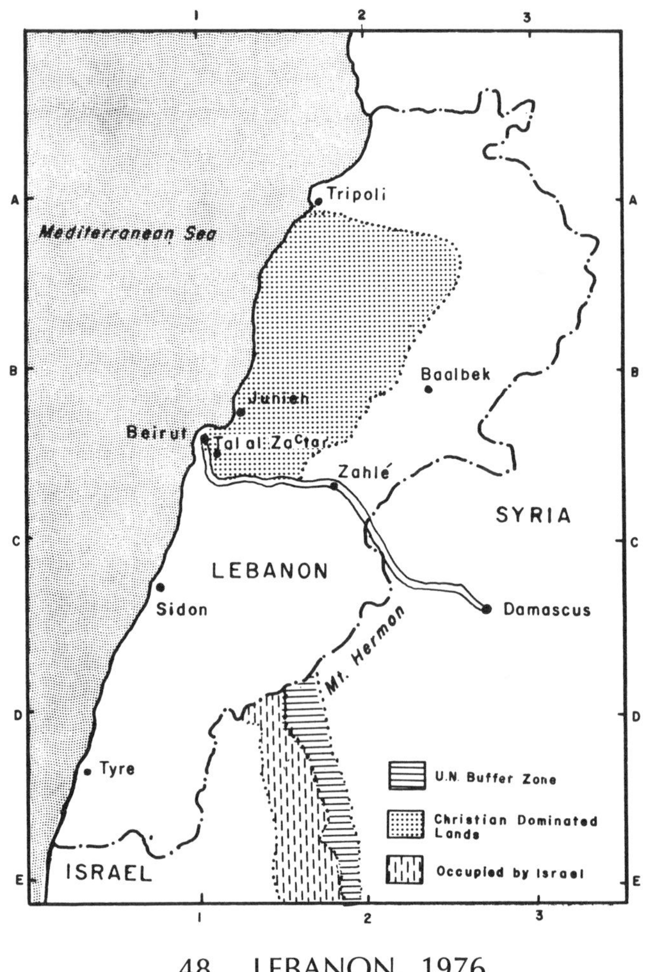

48. LEBANON, 1976

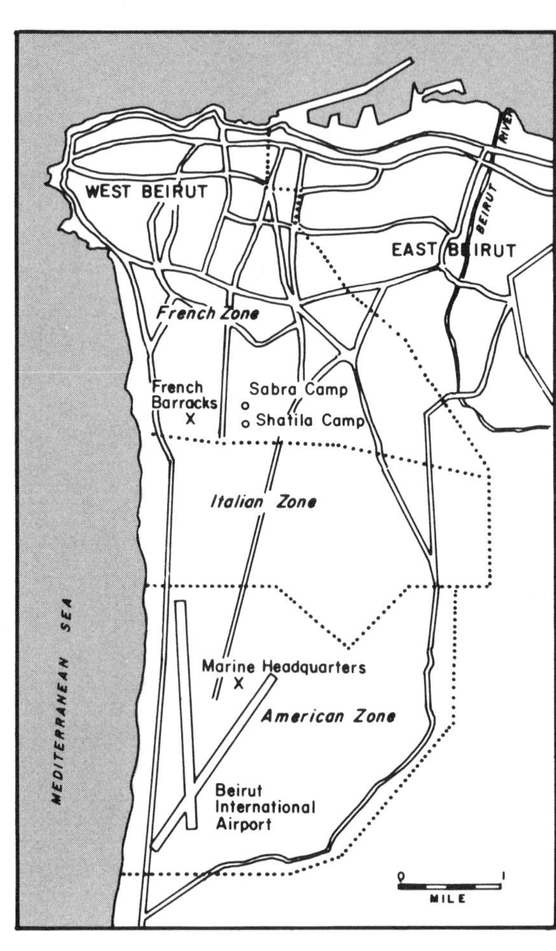

49. BEIRUT, 1983

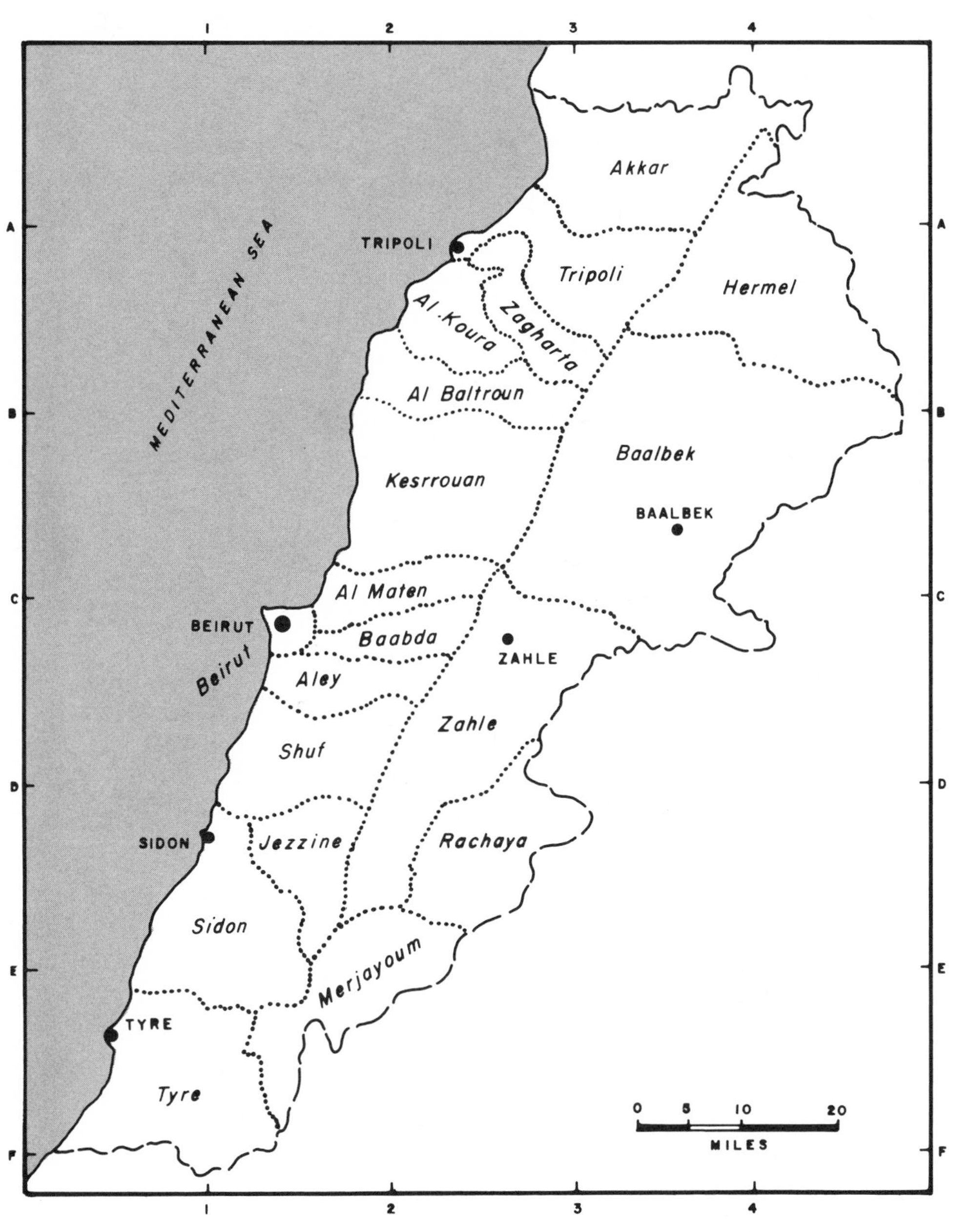

50. PROVINCES OF LEBANON

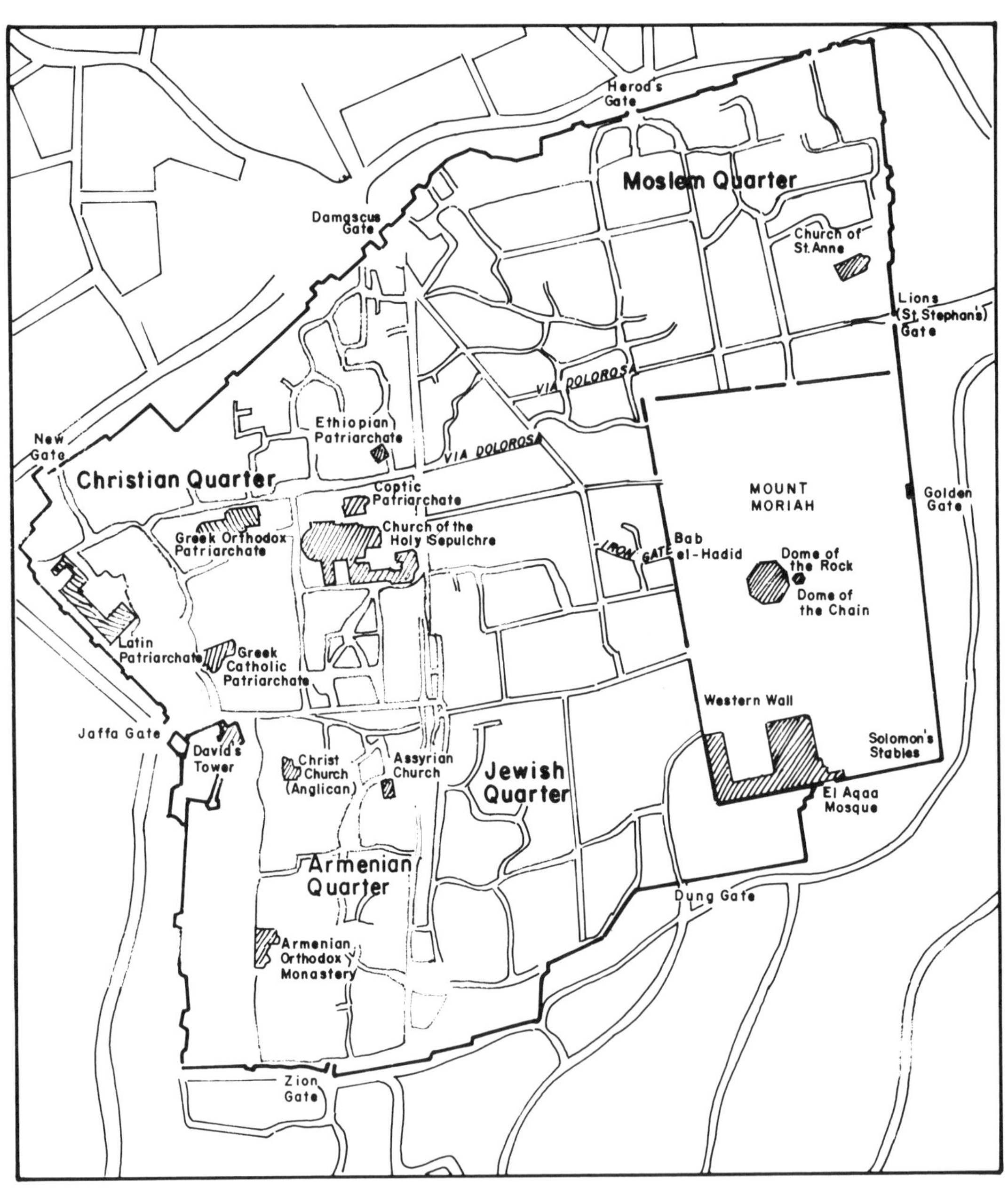

51. JERUSALEM

IX. Gazetteer

Data for this Gazetteer were gathered from a number of sources, the most important of which are listed below. While there was an agreement on the longitudinal and latitudinal co-ordinates for each of the cities, there was no agreement on the estimated populations. Thus, population figures should be used with great caution and should be treated as reflecting a general level or order of magnitude. For those cities where population figures were not available, a "*" has been placed after their names.

- *1981 Commercial Atlas and Marketing Guide* (Chicago: Rand McNally & Co., 1981).
- *The Times Atlas of the World* (Boston: Houghton Mifflin Co., 1967).
- John Paxton, ed. *The Statesman's Year-Book, 1982-1983* (New York: St. Martin's Press, 1982).
- *Webster's New Geographical Dictionary* (Springfield, MA: G & C Merriam Co., 1980).
- *Middle East and North Africa, 1982-1983.* 29th ed. (London: Europa Publications, Ltd., 1982).
- *Rand McNally's World Atlas, Census* (Chicago: Rand McNally & Co., 1981).

City	Population / Coordinates
Abadan, Iran [Ābādān]:	Pop.: 296,081 (1976) 31° 06' N; 52° 40' E
Abu Dhabi, UAE [Abū Zaby]:	50,000 (1968) 24° 28' N; 54° 25' E
Acre, Israel [^{c}Akkol]:	37,900 (1979) 32° 55' N; 35° 04' E
Adana, Turkey:	574,515 (1980) 37° 00' N; 35° 19' E
Aden, PDRY [South Yemen]:	264,326 (1973) 12° 47' N; 45° 03' E
Ahwaz, Iran [Ahvaz]:	329,006 (1976) 31° 17' N; 48° 43' E
Aleppo, Syria [Halab]:	639,326 (1970) 36° 14' N; 37° 10' E
Alexandretta, Turkey [Iskenderun]:	72,297 (1970) 36° 37' N; 36° 08' E
Alexandria, Egypt [al-Iskandariyah]:	2,317,705 (1976) 31° 13' N; 29° 55' E
Amman, Jordan [^{c}Ammān]:	648,587 (1979) 31° 57' N; 35° 56' E
Ankara, Turkey:	1,877,755 (1980) 39° 55' N; 32° 50' E
Antalya, Turkey:	Pop.: 173,501 (1980) 36° 53' N; 30° 42' E
Antioch, Turkey [Antakya, Anṭākiyah]:	66,520 (1970) 36° 12' N; 36° 10' E
Aqaba, Jordan [al-^{c}Aqabah]:	26,986 (1979) 30° 08' N; 43° 40' E
Ardebil, Iran [Ardabil]:	147,404 (1976) 38° 15' N; 48° 18' E
al-Arish, Egypt [al-^{c}Arīsh]:	40,388 (1966) 31° 08' N; 33° 48' E
Ascalon, Israel [Ashqelon, al-^{c}Ashqalān]:	40,338 (1976) 31° 40' N; 34° 35' E
Aswan, Egypt [Aswān]:	144,654 (1976) 24° 05' N; 32° 56' E
Asyut, Egypt [Asyūt]:	213,751 (1976) 27° 14' N; 31° 07' E

City	Population / Coordinates
Baalbek, Lebanon [Ba^{c}labakk]:	16,000 (1970) 34° 00' N; 35° 55' E
Baghdad, Iraq:	1,300,000 (1970) 32° 20' N; 44° 26' E

---

* = Population figure not available.

City	Pop.	Coordinates
Bandar Abbas, Iran [Bandar ᶜAbbās]:	Pop.: 89,103 (1976)	27° 12' N; 56° 15' E
Baniyas, Syria [Bānyās]:	*	35° 12' N; 35° 57' E
Basra, Iraq [al-Baṣrah]:	370,900 (1970)	30° 30' N; 47° 50' E
Beersheba, Israel [Be'er Sheva]:	109,600 (1981)	31° 15' N; 34° 77' E
Beirut, Lebanon [Bayrut]:	800,000 (1972)	33° 52' N; 35° 31' E
Bursa, Turkey:	445,113 (1980)	40° 12' N; 29° 04' E
Bushire, Iran [Bushehr, Bushehir]:	*	28° 59' N; 50° 51' E
Cairo, Egypt [al-Qāhirah]:	8,539,000 (1979)	30° 03' N; 31° 15' E
Damascus, Syria [Dimashq]:	836,668 (1970)	33° 30' N; 35° 31' E
Damietta, Egypt [Dumyāt]:	86,327 (1966)	31° 26' N; 31° 48' E
Dhahran, Saudi Arabia [al-Ẓahrān]:	22,500 (1965)	26° 18' N; 50° 05' E
Diyarbakir, Turkey [Diyarbakr]:	235,617 (1980)	37° 55' N; 40° 14' E
Doha, Qatar [al-Dawhah]:	80,000 (1980)	25° 15' N; 51° 36' E
Dubai, UAE [Dubayy]:	60,000 (1968)	25° 14' N; 55° 17' E
Edirne, Turkey:	53,806 (1970)	41° 40' N; 26° 34' E
Eilat, Israel [Elat, Elath]:	12,800 (1972)	29° 33' N; 34° 57' E
Erzurum, Turkey [Erzerum]:	190,241 (1980)	39° 57' N; 41° 17' E
Gallipoli, Turkey [Gelibolu]:	14,716 (1970)	40° 25' N; 26° 41' E
Gaza, Gaza Strip [Ghazzah]:	118,272 (1967)	31° 30' N; 34° 28' E
Haifa, Israel:	230,000 (1981)	32° 49' N; 34° 59' E
Hama, Syria [Hamāh]:	137,421 (1970)	35° 09' N; 36° 44' E
Hamadān, Iran:	155,846 (1976)	34° 46' N; 48° 35' E
Hebron, West Bank [al-Khalīl]:	38,348 (1973)	31° 32' N; 35° 06' E
Helwan, Egypt [Ḥulwān]:	*	29° 51' N; 31° 20' E
Hilla, Iraq [al-Hillah]:	Pop.: 128,000 (1970)	32° 30' N; 44° 24' E
Hodeida, Yemen [al-Hudaydah]:	126,386 (1980)	14° 50' N; 42° 38' E
Homs, Syria [Ḥimṣ]:	215,423 (1970)	34° 44' N; 36° 43' E
Irbid, Jordan:	113,000 (1973)	32° 33' N; 35° 51' E
Isfahan, Iran [Esfahan]:	671,825 (1976)	32° 41' N; 51° 41' E
Ismailia, Egypt [al-Ismāᶜīliyah]:	145,930 (1976)	30° 36' N; 32° 15' E
Istanbul, Turkey:	2,772,708 (1980)	41° 02' N; 28° 57' E
Izmir, Turkey [Smyrna]:	757,854 (1980)	38° 25' N; 27° 10' E
Izmit, Turkey [Ismid, Nicomedia]:	164,675 (1979)	40° 27' N; 29° 43' E
Jaffa, Israel [Yaffo][with Tel Aviv population]:	334,900 (1981)	32° 05' N; 34° 46' E
Jedda, Saudi Arabia [Jiddah]:	561,104 (1974)	21° 30' N; 39° 10' E
Jericho, West Bank [Arīḥā]:	*	31° 51' N; 35° 27' E
Jerusalem, Israel [Yerushalayim, al-Quds]:	407,100 (1981)	31° 47' N; 35° 13' E
Karbalā', Iraq:	107,500 (1970)	32° 37' N; 44° 03' E
Kāshān, Iran:	84,545 (1976)	33° 59' N; 51° 35' E
Kermān, Iran:	140,309 (1976)	30° 18' N; 57° 05' E
Kermānshāh, Iran:	290,861 (1976)	34° 19' N; 47° 04' E
Khartoum, Sudan [al-Khurtūm]:	333,921 (1973)	15° 33' N; 32° 31' E
Kirkūk, Iraq:	207,900 (1970)	35° 26' N; 44° 26' E
Konya, Turkey:	329,139 (1980)	37° 51' N; 32° 31' E
Kufa, Iraq [al-Kūfah]:	30,862 (1966)	32° 02' N; 44° 25' E
Kuwait, Kuwait [al-Kuwait, Kuwayt]:	80,008 (1970)	29° 20' N; 48° 00' E
Latakia, Syria [al-Lādhiqiyah]:	125,716 (1970)	35° 31' N; 35° 47' E
Luxor, Egypt [al-Uqsur, al-Qusur]:	77,578 (1966)	25° 41' N; 32° 24' E

Ma'an, Jordan: Pop.: 9,500 (1973)
30° 11' N; 35° 45' E

Malatya, Turkey: 179,074 (1980)
38° 22' N; 38° 18' E

Mansura, Egypt [al-Manṣūrah]: 259,387 (1976)
31° 03' N; 31° 23' E

Mardin, Turkey: 33,740 (1980)
37° 19'N; 40° 43' E

Mecca, Saudi Arabia [Makkah]: 366,807 (1974)
21° 26' N; 39° 49' E

Medina, Saudi Arabia [al-Madīnah]: 198,186 (1974)
24° 31' N; 39° 35' E

Meshed, Iran [Mashhad]: 670,180 (1976)
36° 16' N; 59° 34' E

al-Minya, Egypt: 146,423 (1966)
28° 06' N; 30° 45' E

Mosul, Iraq [al-Mawṣīl]: 293,100 (1970)
36° 21' N; 43° 08' E

Muscat, Oman [Masqat]: 50,000 (1981)
23° 37' N; 58° 38' E

Nablus, West Bank [Nābulus]: 44,223 (1978)
32° 13' N; 35° 16' E

al-Najaf, Iraq: 179,200 (1970)
31° 59' N; 44° 19' E

Najrān, Saudi Arabia: 47,501 (1974)
17° 31' N; 44° 19' E

Nazareth, Israel [Nazerat]: 33,300 (1972)
32° 42' N; 35° 18' E

Omdurman, Sudan [Umm Durmān]: 299,401 (1973)
15° 37' N; 30° 29' E

Port Fuad, Egypt [Būr Fuʿād]: *
31° 16' N; 32° 19' E

Port Said, Egypt [Būr Saʿīd]: 282,977 (1966)
31° 17' N; 32° 18' E

Port Sudan, Sudan [Būr Sūdān]: 132,631 (1973)
19° 38' N; 37° 07' E

Port Taufiq, Egypt: *
29° 57' N; 32° 34' E

---

al-Qanṭara, Egypt: 22,477 (1966)
30° 52' N; 32° 20' E

Qazvīn, Iran [Kazvin]: 138,527 (1976)
36° 16' N; 50° 00' E

Qom, Iran [Qum]: 246,831 (1976)
34° 39' N; 50° 57' E

Quneitra, Syria [al-Qunayṭiraḥ, Kuneitra]: *
33° 08' N; 35° 49' E

Qusair, Egypt [al-Qusayr]: 5,525 (1966)
26° 04' N; 34° 15' E

Rafah, Gaza Strip [Rafiah]: Pop.: 49,800 (1968)
31° 18' N; 34° 15' E

Ramallah, West Bank [Rām Allāh]: *
31° 55' N; 35° 12' E

Resht, Iran [Rasht]: 187,203 (1976)
37° 18' N; 49° 38' E

Riyadh, Saudi Arabia [al-Riyādh]: 666,840 (1974)
24° 39' N; 46° 46' E

Rosetta, Egypt [Rashīd]: 36,711 (1966)
31° 25' N; 30° 25' E

Safed, Israel [Zefat]: 13,600 (1972)
32° 57' N; 35° 27' E

Sāmarrā', Iraq: 24,746 (1970)
34° 13' N; 43° 52' E

Samsun, Turkey: 198,749 (1980)
41° 17' N; 36° 22' E

Sanʿā', Yemen: 227,817 (1980)
15° 24' N; 44° 14' E

Sharm al-Shaykh, Egypt [Sharm el-Sheikh]: *
27° 51' N; 34° 16' E

Shīrāz, Iran: 416,408 (1976)
29° 38' N; 52° 34' E

Sidon, Lebanon [Ṣaydā']: 34,500 (1970)
33° 32' N; 35° 22' E

Sinop, Turkey: 15,096 (1970)
42° 02' N; 35° 09' E

Sivas, Turkey: 172,864 (1980)
39° 44' N; 37° 01' E

Suez, Egypt [al-Suways]: 193,965 (1967)
29° 59' N; 32° 33' E

Taʿizz, Yemen: 81,000 (1975)
13° 35' N; 44° 02' E

Tabrīz, Iran: 598,576 (1976)
38° 05' N; 46° 18' E

Tabūk, Saudi Arabia [Tabouk]: 74,825 (1974)
28° 22' N; 36° 32' E

Taif, Saudi Arabia [Taʿif]: 204,857 (1974)
21° 15' N; 40° 21' E

Ṭanṭā, Egypt: 283,240 (1976)
30° 48' N; 31° 00' E

Tehrān, Iran: 4,496,159 (1976)
35° 40' N; 51° 26' E

Tel Aviv, Israel [with Jaffa population]: 334,900 (1981)
32° 05' N; 34° 46' E

Tiberias, Israel [Teverya, Ṭabariyah]: 23,900 (1970)
32° 48' N; 35° 32' E

Trabzon, Turkey [Trebezond]: 80,795 (1970)
41° 00' N; 39° 43' E

Tripoli, Lebanon [Ṭarābulus]: 150,000 (1972)
34° 27' N; 35° 50' E

Tyre, Lebanon [Ṣūr]:	Pop.: 12,500 (1970) 33° 16' N; 35° 12' E
Urfa, Turkey:	100,654 (1970) 37° 08' N; 38° 45' E
Yazd, Iran:	671,825 (1976) 31° 55' N; 54° 22' E
Zagazig, Egypt [al-Zagāzīg]:	202,575 (1976) 30° 35' N; 31° 30' E
Zahle, Lebanon [Zaḥlah]:	29,500 (1970) 35° 50' N; 35° 55' E

X. Glossary

^{c}abd — 1. Ordinary word for "slave": *ghulām*, *kul* and *mamlūk*.
2. When used with one of the names of Allāh, it means "servant"; e.g., ^{c}Abd al-Raḥmān.

abū — The *kunya* part of a name when used in a construct: "The father of ..."

adab — Until ^{c}Abbāsid period, it meant necessary, general culture for gentlemen; later associated with more narrowly defined, specific knowledge needed for a given office or social function. *Belles-lettres*.

ādāt — Customary taxes, authorized by secular law: *kanun*.

adhān — The call to prayer in Arabic by the *muezzin*.

āghā, ağa — Most common usage is as an Ottoman title, usually translated as "chief/senior/master" and used for medium-level and some high-level officials of the Janissary Corps, a sultan's palace service, and local officials. "Sir/gentleman" in Persian. Also applied to eunuchs in the Ottoman palaces.

ahl — "Family/intimates/people/household" or, alone, "wife." Often used in conjunction with other words, as follows:

ahl al-bayt — "The people of the house." Usually means the leading family of an Arabian tribe and, by extension, the Prophet's house.

ahl al-dhimma
ahl al-kitāb — "People of the indefinitely renewed contract"; "People of the Book." Christians and Jews who have a revealed Holy Book and have entered into special relationship with a Muslim community. They are permitted religious freedom in return for payment of the *jizya*.

ahl al-Sunna — "The people of the Sunna" [Sunnī].

akhbār — The term preferred by Shī^{c}ites for *ḥadīth*.

akhbārīs — The minority Ithnā ^{c}Asharī Shī^{c}ite legal tradition, which emphasizes reliance on only the *Qur'ān* and *ḥadīth*.

akīncı — Raider.

aqçe, akçe — An Ottoman silver coin of varying weight, fineness and value; known in the West as *aspre* or *asper*.

Alawite — Name given by French and used by Westerners for an extreme Shī^{c}ite group, the Nuṣayrīs, found in modern Syria, who played a critical role in post-1945 Syrian politics. *^{c}Alawī* is used by Sunnīs, probably in a pejorative sense.

^{c}ālim [pl. ^{c}ulamā'] — One learned in the Islamic sciences. Also, a scientist, in modern usage.

aliya — Wave of or period of Jewish immigration to Palestine and Israel, beginning in 1882.

Allāh — God.

^{c}āmil — "Agent," who could hold various posts, including that of Provincial Governor; but by 4th/10th century, it usually meant a finance officer, especially in control of the *kharāj*.

amīr, emīr — Originally a military commander. Under the ^{c}Abbāsids, the title was held by governors and some military commanders. Later used for commander, ruler or prince.

Amīr al-Mu'minīn — "Commander of the Believers." Title adopted by Caliph ^{c}Umar b. al-Khaṭṭāb and succeeding caliphs.

Amīr al-Umarā' — "Commander of the Commanders." Title granted to powerful military leaders in Baghdad from 324/936.

amṣār [sing. miṣr] — Fortified military camps established by Muslims, such as Fusṭāṭ, al-Baṣra and al-Kūfa.

al-Anṣār — "The helpers." Term used to designate the Medinans who supported Muḥammad.

^{c}ārif — "One who knows." Used by *ṣūfīs* to contrast their knowledge with that of an *^{c}ālim*.

^{c}aql — Legal, systematic reasoning — a source of *sharī^{c}ah* for Shī^{c}ites.

^{c}aṣabīya — Term made famous by historian, Ibn Khaldūn; implies group solidarity, an *esprit de corps*.

Ashkenazim — "Western" Jews—those of European or American origin—primarily those from Eastern Europe and Yiddish-speaking, in contrast to Sephardic Jews [Sephardim].

assassin — Westernized form of *ḥashshāshīn*, one who might have used *ḥashish*. Applied to medieval Nizārī Shī^{c}ites of Persia and Syria who used assassination as a weapon.

Assyrian — See Nestorian.

atabeğ, atabey — "Father Prince." A Seljuk term for an advisor and guardian to a Seljuk prince. Some *atabeğs* established their own bases of power and dynastic rule, such as the Zangids.

awqaf — See *waqf*.

a^{c}yān — "Notable persons." Originally most important inhabitants of an area; but by 17th century A.D., under Ottomans, it meant local notables with virtual control over their districts; often officially recognized by the Sublime Porte.

^{c}Ayatallāh — A Shī^{c}ite clergyman who has reached the 3rd level of Shī^{c}ite higher education, is recognized as a *mujtahid*, and is over 40.

Bāb-i Ālī — See Sublime Porte.

Badawi — See Bedouin.

Bahā'īs — Adherents of a religion founded in 19th-century Persia by Bahā' Allāh and disseminated to Middle East, Europe and the U.S.

bairām — Ottoman term used to refer to the two Muslim festivals: ^{c}Īd al-Fiṭr and ^{c}Īd al-Aḍḥā (see Calendar, p. 9).

banū — Refers to a family/tribe/people when followed by the name of that group's eponymous ancestor.

barīd — "Postal service," specifically the medieval postal and intelligence service.

bast — The sanctuary from secular authority provided by mosques, residences of *^{c}ulamā'*, and other places.

Ba^{c}th — "Renaissance/Resurrection." A major Arab Socialist political party founded in Syria, having at various times controlled the governments of Syria and Iran.

bāṭinī — Devotee of esoteric interpretation of sacred texts, particularly associated with Ismā^{c}īlīs. The sect appears as *Bāṭinīya* or *Batinites*.

bayt al-māl — Generally refers to a Muslim state treasury, with the *jizya* and *kharāj* as main sources of revenue.

Bedouin — From *badw*. Refers to pastoral nomads whose language and culture are Arabic.

beğ, bey — Turkish title usually translated as "lord," but also as "chief/master/mister." Found among Turkish peoples or in areas they ruled.

beylerbey — "Bey of Beys." Ottoman title for governor of a province. Title was superseded by *wālī*.

bid^{c}a — "Innovation." A belief or practice not found in the *sunna* and which the traditionalists consider unacceptable.

---

caliph, khalīfa — "Successor." Title implied continuation by its holder of Muḥammad's leadership over the Muslim community, but without direct, divine revelation.

celali [jelali] — Brigands, military retainers.

Cid — A medieval Spanish form of *sayyid*.

Copt, Qibṭ — A Monophysite Egyptian Christian.

---

dā^{c}ī — "He who summons." Refers to propagandists or missionaries for particular dissenting sects, such as the original ^{c}Abbāsid movement and the Ismā^{c}īlīs.

Dār al-Ḥarb — "The Abode of War." Territories not under Muslim political control where *jihāds* take place.

Dār al-Islām — "The Abode of Islam." Territories in which the *sharī^{c}a* prevails.

dawla — The state or dynasty. Also used as the 2nd part of a *laqab*.

defter, daftar — A register or account book used by administrative officials.

defterdār, daftardār — Keeper of the *defter* (account book); also head of the treasury.

derebey — "Valley lord." Local Anatolian rulers who, in the 18th century A.D., were virtually independent of the central Ottoman government.

dervish, dervis/darwīsh — A member of a Muslim mystical order: a *ṣūfī*.

devshirme, devşirme — Term for Ottoman system of collecting subject Christian boys for training, conversion and eventual use in palace, Janissary Corps, other government branches.

dhikr — A practice to foster remembering God, usually repeating particular phrases.

dhimmī — See *ahl al-dhimma*.

Dhū-l-Ḥijja — 12th month of Muslim year, in which every Muslim is to make a pilgrimage to Mecca if physically and financially able: *ḥajj*.

Diaspora — Dispersion of Jews from Palestine after Second Temple destroyed in 70 A.D. All Jews outside Israel comprise the Diaspora.

dihqān — Arabized form of Persian term for "head of a village." Historically referred to lower Sassanian feudal nobility and descendants under Muslim rule.

dīn — "Religion." Also found as part of a compound *laqab*.

dīnār — Muslim gold coin of varying weight, fineness and value.

dirham — Muslim silver coin of varying weight, fineness and value.

dīwān, divan — 1. Collection of poetry or prose; 2. A register; or 3. A government department.

dragoman — Translator/interpreter. A Europeanized form of the Arabic *turjamān*.

Druze — Religious group found chiefly in Greater Syria, whose faith derives from Fāṭimid Ismā^{c}īlī doctrines and identifies al-Ḥākim as the final Imām.

---

effendi — Ottoman title of a learned man, a member of a religious or bureaucratic institution and, later, to numerous military officials and members of an Ottoman family.

Derived from a Byzantine term for land.

emīr, amīr — See *amīr*.

---

fals [pl. fulūs] — A copper coin.

falsafa — Philosophy, including natural and moral sciences.

faqīh [pl. fuqahā'] — Specialist in *sharīᶜa*, particularly its derivative details; that is, a jurist.

al-Fatah, Fatḥ — Palestinian *fidā'īyīn* group founded by Yāsir ᶜArafāt, which has undertaken operations since 1965.

Fātiḥa — The opening *sūra* of the *Qur'ān*, often used in prayer.

fatwā, fetvā — Opinion on a legal question, issued by a *muftī*.

fallāḥ/fellah [plural: fallāḥin] — "Peasant." Used most often when speaking of Egyptian agricultural population, but applies to any Arab country.

fidā'ī — One who sacrifices himself, especially for his country.

fidā'īyīn, fedayeen — Religious and political organizations in which members risk their lives to achieve their goals. Term is associated with such religious groups as the Assassins; in modern times with various Palestinian organizations.

fiqh — "Jurisprudence," the science of *sharīᶜa*.

firmān, ferman — An Ottoman or Persian imperial rescript or diploma.

fitna — "Rebellion/civil strife," which breaks up the unity of a community.

funduq — "Inn/warehouse/hostel" for foreign merchants, especially Europeans.

---

gazel — A lyric poem of 4-15 couplets, with the 1st couplet rhyming and the 2nd hemistich rhyming with the hemistich of the 1st couplet.

ghaybah — "Occulation." Refers to the withdrawal of the Shīᶜite Imāms.

ghaybat-i kubra — "Greater Occulation." The period marked by the absence of human intermediaries between the Imām and the faithful, starting with the death of the last *vakil* in 940 and still continuing.

ghāzī — One who takes part in raids against infidels. It later became a title of honor. Muṣṭafā Kemal Atatürk was called *ghāzī*.

ghulām — "Male slave," particularly a military or palace slave.

ḥadīth — "Tradition." Relates to words or actions of Prophet Muḥammad or his companions. One of four principal sources of the *sharīᶜa* in Sunnī tradition.

ḥāfiẓ — One who has learned the *Qur'ān* by heart.

Haganah — "Defense." Military arm of the Jewish Agency, which became nucleus for the modern Israeli army.

ḥājib — "Chamberlain." Actual power of an individual with this title varied among medieval Islamic states. In Islamic Spain this office-holder ranked above the *wazīr*.

ḥajj — Formal pilgrimage to Mecca and its environs during particular period in Dhū-l-Ḥijja. Obligatory once in the lifetime of every adult Muslim who is physically and financially able to do so.

ḥājj — Title held by one who has made the "Greater Pilgrimage."

ḥākīm — An arbitrator or judge.

han — See *khān*.

Ḥanafī — Follower of Sunnī *madhhab* or school of law named after Abū Ḥanīfa.

Ḥanbalī — Follower of Sunnī *madhhab* or school of law named after Aḥmad Ibn Ḥanbal.

ḥanīf — A pre-Islamic Arab monotheist.

ḥarām — "Forbidden," particularly an act prohibited by *sharī^{c}a*.

ḥaram — "Sanctuary." Associated with particular areas in Mecca and Medina, as well as Jerusalem and Hebron.

ḥarīm/harem — Primarily restricted areas of a Muslim's house, particularly the women's quarters.

ḥashīshīya — Name given to Syrian followers of Nizārī Ismā^{c}īlī Movement.

hijra, hegira — "Emigration/departure" of Muḥammad, when he went from Mecca to Medina in 622 A.D. Name is now applied to Muslim calendar that begins in 622 A.D.

ḥisba — 1. Functions of one supervising business and public morality, the *muḥtasib*.
2. Duty of every Muslim to fulfill obligations in *sharī^{c}a*.

Histadrut — General Federation of Labor, founded in Palestine in 1920 by Jewish workers. Involved in traditional trade union activities, cooperative economic ventures, and social/cultural/welfare services.

---

^{c}Īd al-Aḍḥā — "Sacrificial Feast." Celebrated on 10th of Dhū-l-Ḥijja. Also called al-^{c}Īd al-Kabīr and Büyük Bayram [the Major Festival].

^{c}Īd al-Fiṭr — Festival on 1st of Shawwāl, marking end of month of fasting: Ramaḍān. Also called al-^{c}Īd al-Ṣaghīr and Küçük Bayram [the Minor Festival].

idhān — The call to prayer.

ijāza — Certificate given on completion of a critical text reading, which conveys to recipient (in personal attendance) the authority to expound the text to others.

ijmā^c — Consensus of a scholarly community of believers on a religious regulation. One of the main sources of the *sharī^{c}a*.

ijtihād — Use of individual reasoning to determine a specific Islamic rule. Term has shifted meaning over time, varying from very general to extremely restricted applications of personal reasoning.

Ikhwān al-Muslimīn — "The Muslim Brethren." Politico-religious movement, founded by Ḥasan al-Bannā' in Egypt in 1926. Stresses fundamentals of Islām as a guide for all activities. Has played important role in modern Egyptian politics and recently gained popularity in other Middle East nations.

^{c}ilm — "Knowledge," particularly religious or scientific.

iltizām — Ottoman system of tax farming, where *iltizām*-holder (the *multazim*) paid fixed fee to government for right to collect local taxes, usually from peasants, but also applied to urban taxes. It was prevalent in Arab provinces.

Imām — 1. "Prayer Leader" of whole community of believers; as such, was a title of caliphs.
2. For Ismā^{c}īlī and Ithnā ^{c}Asharī Shī^{c}ī, the Imām, is the necessary, divinely guided, infallible, sinless political/religious leader.

iqṭā^c — Medieval administrative grant, whereby land revenues but not ownership were turned over to a *muqta^c* in return for service, usually military. This tax-farming system has often been mistranslated as "fief."

^{c}irḍ — "Honor," particularly of a family/lineage. Usually related to virtue of a family's female members.

^{c}irfān — "Gnosis." Mystically attained knowledge.

Irgun — Irgun Zvai Leumi (national military organization). Founded in 1937 by Palestinian Jews as a military organization, whose goal was to establish a Jewish state by any means, but not necessarily under Jewish Agency control. Nucleus of Herut Party in State of Israel.

Islām — Submission to Allāh and accepting Muḥammad as His prophet. To be a Muslim.

ism — Given name of a Muslim; for example, Muḥammad.

Ismā^{c}īlī, Ismailites — Member of Shī^{c}ite sect who believes an infallible Imamate passed from ^{c}Alī to his descendants through a seventh Imām (Ismā^{c}īl) and to his descendants. Fāṭimids and Assassins were Ismā^{c}īlīs. Also called Seveners.

isnād — "Chain of transmitters," particularly applied to chain of those who passed on the *ḥadīths* until they were collected. Used to verify validity.

istiḥsān — Act of reaching a personal opinion on a legal question without the strict use of analogy.

istiṣlāh — Act of reaching a legal decision by taking the public welfare into account.

Ithnā ^{c}Asharī — Member of Shī^{c}ite sect who believes there were 12 successive Imāms descended from ^{c}Alī, the last of whom disappeared but will one day return. Usually translated as the Twelvers or Imāmīs.

īwān — "Vaulted hall/recessed-like room," usually enclosed on 3 sides with the 4th opening onto a courtyard.

Jāhilīya — "Days of Ignorance." The period of Arab history before Islām.

jāmi^{c} — Usually the major or Friday mosque in a city.

Janissary — "New troops." A corruption of the Turkish *yeni cheri*. Refers to the Ottoman infantry recruited through the *devshirme*.

jazīra — "Island/peninsula." May refer to Arabian Peninsula, the land in northern Iraq and Syria between the Tigris and Euphrates Rivers, or a province in modern Syria.

jihād — Striving in Allāh's path, commonly translated as a Holy War, whose goal is either the expansion or defense of Islām.

jinn, genie — Creatures created from smokeless flame who can appear in different forms and carry out all types of activities. A *jinn*, unlike angels, is subject to judgment like men.

jizya — "Poll/head tax" leveled on *dhimmis* living in Muslim lands.

jund — "Military troop/military settlement"—later a "district/province," especially in Syria.

Ka^{c}ba — Name of sacred, cube-shaped building in Mecca. Contains the Black Stone (meteorite) which, along with the building, is regarded as holy. Muslims pray toward the Ka^{c}ba. It serves as a unifying focus among Muslims.

kadi — See *qāḍī*.

kāfir — Applies to an unbeliever or infidel.

kalām — "Debate" (literally); scholastic theology.

kānūn — See *qānūn*.

kānūnnāme — Collection of *kanuns*.

kapi kular — High Ottoman officials who were theoretically "slaves of the Porte."

Kapudan Pāshā — The admiral of the Ottoman fleet.

kātib — A secretary.

kazi ^{c}asker/ qāḍī ^{c}askar — Chief military judge. Important under Mamlūks and Ottomans.

khamsīn — Arabic for 50; term for hot desert winds.

khān — Title implies authority; used in post-Mongol Iran for rulers and local governors, but eventually a polite title for males.

khān — Large building for travelers and/or merchandise.

kharāj — The specific meaning has varied but, as a general rule for the pre-Ottoman period, it referrs to the land tax as opposed to *jizya*.

Khārijī, Kharijites — Minor Muslim sect, usually in political opposition to a Sunnī or Shī^c^ite ruler. They believed that equality of all believers applied to those qualified for caliph's office, as well as all other offices. Sect appears as Kharijites.

khaṭīb — The one who gives the *khuṭba*.

khātūm — Mongol title for empresses and other court women; came to be applied to women generally.

Khedive — Ancient Persian title acquired in 1866 for a high price by Ismā^c^īl, Governor of Egypt. Held by his family members until 1914, when they took title of *Sulṭān*.

al-Khulafā', al-Rāshidūn — "The Rightly Guided" caliphs. Term refers to the first 4 caliphs: Abū Bakr, ^c^Umar, ^c^Uthmān and ^c^Alī (632-661 A.D.).

khums — A 5th of all profit earned in trade; a charitable tax.

khuṭba — "Sermon"; given at the Friday noon prayer by a *khaṭīb*. Sermon used to disseminate political information and to give religious instruction. A symbol of political sovereignty of a ruler was to mention that ruler's name in the *khuṭba*.

kibbutz [pl. kibbutzim] — Collective, communal, agricultural settlements established in Palestine and Israel by Jews.

kibla — See *qibla*.

al-Kitāb — "The Book"; i.e., the *Qur'ān* [Koran].

Knesset — Israeli Parliament.

Koran — See *Qur'ān*.

Kuds — See *al-Quds*.

Kūfic — A variety of forms of Arabic script, with an emphasis on straight, vertical and horizontal strokes. One of the earliest scripts.

kul [kullar] — "Man of the Sulṭān." Often translated as "slave."

kunya — Patronymic part of a Muslim name: Abū [father of]. May refer to an actual son or be an honorific title, an attribute or a characteristic. Also Umm [mother of].

Kurd — Person identified with a linguistic (Kurdish) cultural group whose traditional home has been northern Iraq, S.E. Turkey and N.W. Iran. Most Kurds have been engaged in nomadic occupations and are Sunnī Muslims.

---

laqab — Honorific part of a Muslim name, many times as a compound ending in al-Din or al-Dawla, such as Ṣalāḥ al-Dīn [Saladin]. Now means "family name."

levend [pl. levendāt] — "Robber/adventurer/irregular fighter/sailor/one uprooted from the soil."

---

madhhab — Refers to the accepted Sunnī legal school or rite, which today number four: Ḥanafī, Ḥanbalī, Mālikī and Shāfi^c^ī.

Madīna, Medina — Specifically Madīnat al-Rasūl [City of the Prophet]. Refers to pre-Islamic, western Arabian oasis community at Yathrib, after Muḥammad moved his new politico-religious community there (622 A.D.).

madrasa, medrese — Muslim school, originally a Sunnī school for teaching *sharī^c^a*. Term later applied to most secondary schools that taught the Islamic sciences.

Maghrib — "West." Term came to mean the general area of Libya, Tunisia, Algeria and Morocco. Al-Maghrib is the Arabic name of Morocco.

mahdī — "The Guided One." Usually refers to one who is divinely guided, a Messiah.

majlis — An "assembly" and, today, a "parliament."

malik — "King." Title held by modern monarchs, but relatively rare in earlier times.

Mālikī — Follower of the Sunnī *madhhab*; named after Mālik Ibn Anas.

Mamlūk — "One possessed." Technically meant "a slave," but came to refer to a white male (usually Turkish) who was a member of an elite cavalry corps. They were manumitted after being trained/instructed in Islām. The height of their power was when they controlled Egypt from 1260 to 1517 A.D.

Mapai — Major Israeli political party, labor and socialist, which has dominated Israeli governments until 1977. Now Ha-ᶜAvoda [Labor] Party.

maqṣūra — Enclosed portion of a mosque where a monarch could pray, separated from the rest of the congregation.

marjaᶜ-i taqlīd — A *mujtahid* whose practices and pronouncements furnish a binding example on those unable to exert independent judgment in matters relating to the religious law.

Maronite — Christian sect, primarily found in Lebanon, that has been in communion with Roman Catholicism since 17th century. Lebanese president is always a Maronite.

mashhad — Tomb of a *shahīd* [martyr].

masjid — A mosque.

mawlā [pl. mawālī] — "Client." Relationship by which a non-kin person could be brought into a tribe; one system used to bring non-Arabs into the early Muslim system. Also used to refer to a religious leader: *mawlānā* [our lord], or as a form of address to a ruler, in the sense of "my lord."

Mawlid al-Nabī — Muḥammad's birthday, celebrated on Rabīᶜ I, 12.

medrese — See *madrasa*.

Melchite, Melkite — A sect that broke from Greek Orthodox and is in communion with Roman Catholicism [Greek Catholic].

miḥna — "Court of inquiry/trial," particularly associated with Muᶜtazilite position of some of the early ᶜAbbāsid caliphs.

miḥrāb — "Niche" in the *qibla* wall of a mosque. It signifies the direction of prayer.

millet, milla — An internally autonomous religious community in Ottoman Empire. The 3 major *millets* were: Armenian Orthodox, Greek Orthodox and Jewish. Modern research shows Muslims were considered a *millet*.

manāra/minaret/mi'dhara — The tower of a mosque from which the *muezzin* gives the call to prayer.

minbar — The pulpit in a mosque from which the *khuṭba* is given.

mīrī — "Government" or "publicly owned property."

miṣr [pl. amṣār] — "Garrison center." Term used for Fusṭāṭ and, generally, for Egypt.

Monophysite — Member of an Eastern church, who believes Christ has a single nature.

mudīr — "Director" or "administrator."

mu'adhdhin — The one who calls the faithful to prayer 5 times daily: *adhān*.

muezzin — See *mu'adhdhin*.

muftī — Person trained in the *sharīᶜa*, who gives a non-binding legal opinion [*fatwā*] in response to questions submitted to him.

Muhājirūn — Meccan emigrants who joined Muḥammad in Medina.

Muḥarram — First month of Muslim year. On the 10th of the month, Shī^{c}ites mourn the martyrdom of Ḥusayn, ^{c}Alī's son, at Karbala in 61/680.

muḥtasib — "Market inspector," who was also in charge of enforcing public morality. See also *ḥisba*.

mujtahid — Person who exercised personal interpretation of the *sharī^{c}a* to form a legal opinion. Shī^{c}ites permit their *^{c}ulamā'* this role; while, for most periods, it was denied to most Sunnī *^{c}ulamā'*. See also *ijtihād*.

mukhtār — "Head of a village" in Greater Syria.

mulk — "Private property."

mullā, mollā — Member of the *^{c}ulamā'*, but particularly applied to Shī^{c}ite *^{c}ulamā'* of Iran. The title is earned when one has reached the 2nd level of Shī^{c}ite education and has mastered one book of *fiqh*.

mültezim, multazim — The holder of an *iltizam*.

Munāfiqūn — Medinan group who rejected Muḥammad's message; translated as "hypocrites."

muqarnas — An architectural, decorative element, which are also called "stalactite" or "honeycomb" vaults.

murshid — A "spiritual guide" on the *ṣūfī* path.

Muslim — "One who submits." The official name for those who accept Islām.

Mu^{c}tazilī — A member of a particular school of Islamic rational thought, strongly influenced by Hellenism. The sect is called Mutazilite.

---

nabī — "A prophet," while al-Nabī or al-Nabī al-Ummī refers to Muḥammad.

nā'ib — A "deputy" or "delegate."

nasab — The part of a Muslim name that refers to his/her lineage; i.e., *ibn* or *bint* [son/daughter] of an immediate or distant ancestor.

Naskh — General name for cursive Arabic scripts. Refers to a specific form, which is small and highly legible. One of earliest scripts.

naṣrānī [pl. naṣārā] — A Christian.

Nasta^{c}liq — This script, invented in 14th century, is extremely popular in areas influenced by Persian. It has short verticals, sloping horizontals, and has been described as "hanging."

Nestorian — Christian sect which holds that Crist has two separate natures: a divine and a human one. Members were found in Iraq/Iran/Syria.

nisba — The adjectival part of a Muslim name, which can denote family origin, profession, etc.

Nuṣayrī — Follower of an extreme Shī^{c}ite group in Syria, who believes ^{c}Alī is the incarnation of the Deity. See Alawite.

Osmanlı — An Ottoman; i.e., one who was a Muslim, knew Ottoman ways; and, originally, in theory, a "slave of the Sulṭān."

---

padishāh — A Persian title for rulers, used by Ottoman emperors.

Pahlavi — 1. Name of a former dynasty ruling Iran until 1979.
2. Name of pre-Islamic form of Middle Persian.

Pāsdārān [plural] — A general Persian name for "guards," applied since 1979 to the Revolutionary Guards of the Islamic Republic of Iran.

pāshā, paşa — Turkish title of very high rank, normally military, under the Ottomans. Held by Ottoman officials into the 20th century.

pīr — A title for the head of a *ṣūfī* order. Also means "elder" or "veteran."

Porte — See Sublime Porte.

---

qāḍī — Muslim judge learned in the *sharīᶜa*, whose decisions were legally binding.

qānūn — Laws issued by Ottoman *sulṭān*s, based on their right of *ᶜurf* [custom], as opposed to laws based on the *sharīᶜa*.

qānūmnāme — A collection of *qānūn*s.

qibla — "The direction of prayer." Also refers to the wall of any mosque facing the Kaᶜba in Mecca which has a *miḥrāb*.

qirā'a — Certificate that verifies that a student has read the text aloud before the holder of the *ijāza*. Recitation of the *Qur'ān*.

qiyās — Process of juridical reasoning by analogy that is accepted by Sunnī *madhhab*s as one of the sources of the *sharīᶜa*.

al-Quds — "The Holy Place," in particular the Muslim name for Jerusalem.

al-Qur'ān, Koran — The Muslim Holy Book. Considered divine, contains God's revelations as given in Arabic to Muḥammad, and is the basis for the Islamic way of life.

Quraysh — Name of the major Meccan clan [6th-7th centuries] into which Muḥammad was born. Medieval Muslim political theorists believed that a caliph, to be legitimate, had to be descended from the Quraysh through the male line.

---

ra'īs, reis — "Chief/leader/president/etc." of a modern state. Sometimes used as part of a compound name. Also "sea captain" or "Ottoman naval commander."

raᶜīya/rayah/reaya — "A flock." In the Ottoman Empire it initially meant all non-Osmanlı, but eventually came to refer only to non-Muslim taxpayers.

rakᶜah — One cycle of the prayer ritual, including bowing and prostration.

Ramaḍān — Ninth month of Muslim year, when Muslims are to fast from dawn to sunset.

rasūl — "Messenger," but also used to refer to prophets as "messengers of God."

ra'y — "Personal opinion." Muslim juridical term implying personal speculation.

razzia, ghazwa — A Bedouin raid.

ribāṭ — A *ṣūfī* hospice; originally a fortified military hospice.

Ridda — "Apostasy." In particular, refers to breaking away from Islām by a number of tribes, just before and immediately following the death of Muḥammad.

risāla [pl. rasā'il] — A treatise.

Rūm — First the Byzantine (Roman) Empire, then Anatolia, particularly under Seljuk rule.

Rumeli — Ottoman territories in Europe.

Sabra — 1. A Jew born in Palestine or Israel since the late 19th century A.D.
2. Cactus fruit with prickly exterior and sweet interior.

Ṣadr Aᶜẓam — Ottoman title for the Grand Wazīr.

ṣaḥn — The courtyard of a mosque.

ṣalāt — Prayer 5 times a day. One of the so-called 5 pillars of Islām: *shahādah/zakāt/ṣawm/hajj*.

samāᶜ — Certificate stating that a student has attended a reading presided over by one holding an *ijāza*.

sancak, sanjak — Ottoman military or administrative district. The number of *sanjak*s varied in different periods.

sāqiya — Water wheel used for raising water into an irrigation canal/ditch.

saray/serail/ seraglio — "Palace." Later, the "seat of government." For Europeans, the women's quarters of a palace: *ḥarīm*.

sardār — "Military commander." Title was held even by Englishmen when they were Commanders-in-Chief of the Egyptian army.

ṣawm — "Fasting/abstinence." Al-Ṣawm is the legal, prescribed fast during the month of Ramaḍān.

sayyid — "Master/lord/etc.," but became an honorific title for Muḥammad's descendants. Used today for "mister."

Sephardim — Jews whose ancestors came from Spain, knew the Spanish Jewish rites and, possibly, spoke Ladino. Term has sometimes been applied to Mediterranean, Middle Eastern or "Oriental" Jews.

shādūf — Means of raising irrigation water with a counterweight in Egypt.

Shāfi^{c}ī — Follower of the Sunnī *madhhab*, named after Shāfi^{c}ī

shāh — "King." Title used by a number of Persian dynasties.

shahādah — Bearing witness to Muslim creed by stating: "There is no God but Allāh, and Muḥammad is His Messenger." One of the 5 duties of a Muslim: *ḥajj/salāt/ṣawm/zakāt*.

shahīd — A "martyr," a particularly important concept for Shī^{c}ites.

sharī^{c}a — Islamic law based on the *Qur'ān*, *ḥadīth*, *qiyās* and *ijmā^{c}*.

sharīf — A title meaning "highborn/noble." Came to be applied to the descendants of ^{c}Alī's son, Ḥasan.

shaykh/ṣeyh/ sheikh — Literally "old man." Used as a title of respect to refer variously to: head of a tribe/leader of a village/head of a *ṣūfī* order/head of a Muslim guild.

Shaykh al-Islām, ṣeyhülislām — Title of leading religious figure, aside from the caliph in a Muslim state. Under the Mamlūks he was a *qāḍī* while, eventually, the Ottomans appointed the *muftī* of Istanbul to the office.

shayṭān — The devil, Satan.

Shī^{c}a — That group of Muslims, who split from Islamic community over caliphate issue, believe the caliphate is hereditary and should have gone to ^{c}Alī and his descendants. Have further divided into many groups, including the Ithnā ^{c}Asharī and Ismā^{c}īlīs. Became dominant political force in Iran in 16th C.

Shī^{c}ī, — Follower of the Shī^{c}a; the sect is called Shī^{c}ite.

shurṭa — Police.

silsilāh — For a *ṣūfī* order, the chain of transmitters of their knowledge.

sipāhī — Cavalryman in the Ottoman Empire, usually holding a *timar*.

sīra — "Biography," but particularly associated with the biography of Muḥammad.

Sublime Porte — European translation of *Bāb-ī ^{c}Alī* [high gate]. Term stood for the Ottoman Grand Wazīr office and, eventually, Ottoman government.

Ṣūfī — Generic term for Muslim "mystic." Derived from Arabic for "wool," referring to a person wearing a wool robe and living an ascetic life. Later meant a member of a *ṭarīqa* or *ṣūfī* order.

sulṭān — Title that came to mean "supreme secular power." Primarily associated with rulers of Turkish origin.

sunna — Customary procedure for living that came to mean "the way and customs of Muḥammad and his companions."

Sunnī — "One who follows the way of Muḥammad," particularly those who accept one of the 4 *madhhab*s, as opposed to Shī^{c}ī sects. Sometimes mistranslated as "orthodox." The majority sect among Muslims.

sūq Marketplace.

sūra A chapter in the *Qur'ān*.

tafsīr Qur'ānic exergesis.

takbīr The phrase *Allāhu akbar* [God is great].

Tanzimat "Reordering/reorganization." Term used to describe period of modernization and Westernization in the Ottoman Empire (mid-19th century).

taqīya Act by which a person disavows his true beliefs when such avowal would threaten his well-being. Practiced by Ismā^{c}īlīs and other Shī^{c}ī sects at various times.

taqlīd "Imitation," in the sense of blind acceptance and following of the *sharī^{c}a*, as expounded in the various *madhhab*s.

ta'rīkh "Era/dating." It became the general name for "history/a chronicle/annals."

ṭarīqa Term applied to *ṣūfī* orders, as well as the path followed by them to reach gnosis.

ta^{c}zīya The commemoration in dramatic performances of the martyrdom of the Imāms, particularly that of Imām Ḥusayn at Karbala.

tekke Building in which *ṣūfī* members of an order live and perform rituals.

Thuluth A large, cursive script. The verticals have a leftward slant, while the horizontals have a deep curve.

timar Ottoman grant of income from a tax source, usually land, in return for services—in particular, for the Ottoman cavalry: *sipāhī*s.

timarcı, timariot The holder of a *timar*.

ṭirāz State factories that produce fine cloth. Term became associated with the inscribed bands on the cloths, and even inscribed bands on buildings.

Tūdeh A Leftist; then meant the Communist Party of Iran.

tugh Ottoman badge of rank (crest or pennant of horse tails) attached to a flagstaff.

tughra Official signature of Ottoman *sulṭān*s.

turjamān "Translator/interpreter." See *dragoman*.

turkman, turkoman A Turkic-speaking nomad.

^{c}ulamā', ulema [s. ^{c}ālim] Refers to those learned in Islām. Sometimes translated as the "Muslim clergy."

^{c}umda "Head/chief" of a village, particularly used in Egypt.

'umma The "community" of Islamic faithful. Also used in modern sense of a "nation" or "people."

^{c}urf "Custom/customary practice," having a limited/restricted role as a *sharī^{c}a* source, but used extensively by Ottomans. See *qānūn*.

usūl al-fiqh Four sources or "roots of law": *Qur'ān*, *ḥadīth*, *ijmā^c* and *qiyās*.

ūsulīs The dominant Ithnā ^{c}Asharī Shī^{c}ite legal tradition, which emphasizes the use of reason within the confines of religion.

vali, wālī "Governor," particularly of a *vilayet*.

vilayet, wilāya An Ottoman administrative unit of varying size and number.

wādī A "valley/river/dry river bed."

wafd "Delegation." Name of the major Egyptian political party founded by Sa^{c}d Zaghlūl.

wakil, vakil "Representative/deputy."

waqf Prior endowment, whereby revenues from a particular source are permanently allocated for purposes of public benefit, such as the building of a mosque.

wazīr/vezir/vizier Advisor to a ruler who, under the early ᶜAbbāsids and other dynasties, was the equivalent of a Prime Minister.

wuḍū Ritual ablutions.

yishuv Name for the Jewish community in Palestine before 1948.

yörük, yürük Nomads in Turkey. Turkish nomads in the Balkans.

zakāt Obligatory alms tax on all Muslims.

zeamet, ziᶜamet Ottoman *timar*, with an annual revenue between 20,000 and 100,000 *aqçe*.

zimmī See *ahl al-dhimmī*.

Historical Atlas Index

** Diacritical marks have been omitted.

Index

**Diacritical marks have been omitted.